The Dogs of Our Lives

Heartwarming Reminiscences of Canine Companions

Compiled by
Louise Goodyear Murray

A Citadel Press Book
Published by Carol Publishing Group

Carol Publishing Group Edition, 1997

A Citadel Press Book
Published by Carol Publishing Group
Citadel Press is a registered trademark
of Carol Communications, Inc.

Editorial, sales and distribution, rights and permissions
inquiries should be addressed to Carol Publishing Group,
120 Enterprise Avenue, Secaucus, N.J. 07094

In Canada: Canadian Manda Group, One Atlantic Avenue,
Suite 105, Toronto, Ontario M6K 3E7

Carol Publishing Group books may be purchased in bulk at special
discounts for sales promotion, fund-raising, or educational purposes.
Special editions can be created to specifications. For details, contact:
Special Sales Department, Carol Publishing Group, 120 Enterprise
Avenue, Secaucus, N.J. 07094.

Manufactured in the United States of America
10 9 8 7 6 5 4 3 2 1

The Library of Congress has cataloged the Birch Lane Press edition as
follows:

Murray, Louise Goodyear.
    The dogs of our lives : heartwarming reminiscences of
canine companions / compiled by Louise Goodyear Murray.
        p.   cm.
    "A Birch Lane Press book"
    ISBN 1-55972-289-4 (hardcover) ISBN 0-8065-1859-6 (paperback)
    1. Dogs—Anecdotes.   2. Celebrities—Anecdotes.   I. Title.
SF426.2.M87   1995   94-25241
636.7'0887—dc20   CIP

To my mother and father

Mary Clare Archibald Goodyear
1910 – 1984

Emil S. Goodyear, M.D.
1904 – 1992

PERMISSIONS

"Farley" from Lynn Johnston's "For Better or Worse." Reprinted by permission of the author.

"Raison D'etre" by Joe Camp. Reprinted from *Underdog*. Copyright © 1993 with permission from Longstreet Press.

"Feeney and the Top Ten" by Dick Dougherty. Reprinted courtesy of *Democrat and Chronicle*, Rochester, New York, 1994.

"Avoiding the Empty Nest" by Marilyn G. Furman. Reprinted courtesy *Dog Fancy*, 1990.

"The Doggie Dictionary" by Peg Kehret. Reprinted by permission of Meriwether Publishing, Ltd.

"Barry" by Norman Vincent Peale from "Try, Believe & Pray Intensley," published in *Plus: The Magazine of Positive Thinking*, June 1990. Reprinted by permission of the author.

"The Soul of a Dog" from Daniel Pinkwater's *Fish Whistle*. Copyright © 1989 by Daniel Pinkwater. Pages 128-33. Reprinted with permission of Addison-Wesley Publishing Co., Reading, Mass.

"Cathy" cartoon reprinted with permission of Cathy Guisewite.

"Scamp, Address Unknown" by Louise Goodyear Murray. Reprinted courtesy of the Rochester *Democrat and Chronicle*.

"Arnold Comes Home" from Daniel Pinkwater's *Fish Whistle*. Copyright © 1989 by Daniel Pinkwater. Pages 128–33. Reprinted with permission of Addison-Wesley Publishing Co., Reading, Mass.

"Gentle Giants of Orchard Glen" by Schuyler Forbes Baldwin. Reprinted by permission of Joan Hahn.

"Almost Nothing Hurts More Than the Loss of Your Dog" by William F. Buckley Jr. Reprinted by permission of the author.

"Man, Bytes, Dog" by James Gorman. Reprinted by special permission. Copyright © 1984 James Gorman. Originally in *The New Yorker*. All rights reserved.

"To Walk a Dog" from *Here at Eagle Pond*. Copyright © 1990 by Donald Hall. Reprinted by permission. All rights reserved.

"A Day Gone to the Dogs" by Maxine Kumin. Copyright © 1990 by Maxine

COMPILER'S NOTE

*The sole purpose for this book is to raise money
to assist Lollypop Farm Animal Shelter of The Humane Society
of Rochester & Monroe County, New York in their care,
shelter and placement activities. To the best of my knowledge,
all contributions are original unless otherwise stated.*

—*Louise Goodyear Murray*

*I know Lollypop Farm well; we got a very fine dog
from there when we lived in Rochester.*

—*John Jakes*
best-selling author of historical novels
including *The Kent Family Chronicles*
and *The North and South Trilogy*

for the joy of them all! Anne Branagan

Contents

PART II: *Second-Hand Dogs*

PART III: *Dogs and the Company They Keep*

PART IV: *Early Childhood Education*

PART VII: *Very Truly Yours*

Good luck with your collection of Canine conflabbery

FARLEY ADDS HIS STAMP OF APPROVAL!

Lynn Johnston FOR BETTER or FOR WORSE!

Ontario, Canada, resident Lynn Johnston is the writer and artist of the popular cartoon "For Better or Worse!" which has featured Farley for fourteen years. Before Farley's heroic death, *The Dogs of Our Lives* received one of Farley's last wishes.

In Appreciation

I received many writing donations—more than I ever anticipated. Unfortunately space constraints limited the number of writings that could be published.

In tribute to some of the writers whose pieces could not be included, their dogs' names are printed here.

For their support and interest, I thank them.

Shasta	Daisy	Olivier	Buffy	Molly
Rikki	Cassie	Rocky	Stripes	Blackie
Mr. Bone	Marley	Prince	Pood	Amorak
Bridgette Marie	Pow-Wow	Grover	Meeter	Cookie
Duke	Scamp	Buster	Connors	Pat
Sammy	Dooley	Spot	Gruff	Barbara Ann
Foxy	Butch	Peaches	Brandy	Chester
Rusty	Angel	Howie	Penguin	Future
Keisha	Chris	Vincent	Poopsy	Spotty
Whiskers	Scruffy	Cindy	Sophie	Amos
Hashbrown	Boots	Ernie	Jena	Huckleberry
Sam	Jefferson	Cody	Cinders	Kelly
Ben	Rosco	Pluto	Sandy	Alix
Lucky	Grover	Maggie	Abby	Chocolate
Pierre	Bandit	George	Alfe	Stonewall
Barnaby	Lucy	Pookie	Fugi	Dutchess
Beau	Hobo	Gabbie	Spencer	Casey
Gigi	Vito	Alfred	Homer	Mookie
Dino	Cyrus	Trooper	Tippy	Jolly
Midas	Lady	Tess	Geta	Maggie O!Brian
Max	Snoopy			

Acknowledgments

During the process of putting this book together, dozens of people and dogs became new friends and new household names. Without them, *The Dogs of Our Lives* would not be. I am grateful for their input.

Special thanks to Carolyn Coit Dancy for introducing me to computer technology and accompanying me on a journey from typewriter to computer.

To Andy Kendrot for his computer expertise and his indispensable assistance.

To attorneys Paul V. Nunes and Andrew M. Greenstein of the Rochester law firm Underberg & Kessler for their valuable counsel.

For the rescue services provided by the staff of my husband's accounting firm, I extend my thanks. With their assistance, faxes were sent, computer glitches resolved, and overnight mail dispatched.

I am especially grateful to my caring and talented friend Barbara Noble of Ponce Press, California, who served as my on-call cheerleader and consultant. She professionally shepherded *The Dogs of Our Lives*.

I also wish to acknowledge the libraries of Monroe County and Fairport Central School District for their many services.

Special thanks to my editor Kevin McDonough for his enthusiasm and for his sense of fairness and foresight.

And finally my husband Jim and our sons Bill and Bob. Their belief in *The Dogs of Our Lives* is what kept the process moving.

Introduction

You are his pal. That is enough for him.

—Jerome K. Jerome

For over twenty thousand years, dogs have been at our side. Without a doubt, their friendship has passed the test of time. Regardless of our education or employment, religion or heritage, fame or fortune, dogs agreeably share our room and board. Lucky for us to have such all-weather friends. They enrich our lives with love, joy, service, devotion, and companionship.

Dogs are treasured members of my family tree and have always been a major part of my life. With our family today is Kaycee, a former Rochester street dog and animal shelter resident. An eclectic dog, he shares his name with a small town in the state of Wyoming where, at the time of his adoption, our younger son had temporary summer work. A Western name with a hint of Irish for an all-American, later labeled a Portuguese water dog, seems fitting.

Being a thoughtful dog, Kaycee is pleased to be credited as a partial catalyst for this book's being. His former home, an animal shelter maintained by the Humane Society of Rochester and Monroe County, played a major part. Kaycee assisted behind the scenes. He listened to each tale. He tolerated my noisy printer. And as my appointed representative for all dogs, his constant presence kept me mindful of my ultimate goal.

Several events prompted the idea for *The Dogs of Our Lives*. One involved two old family dogs, Patches, a sweet dog we selected, and Scamp, a wandering minstrel who entered our household and my heart.

Another came from the gratifying response I received subsequent to a newspaper article I wrote on Scamp and her impact on our family. Phone calls and letters indicated that we dog lovers are in the best company.

The contagious element of dog storytelling sessions prodded the idea loose. Not surprising, dog tales are abundant among those who share the companionship of dogs.

A writing workshop supplied magic and impetus to set the idea in motion—to compile a book of original dog tales donated by a variety of contemporary personalities and to donate my profits to the Humane Society of Rochester and Monroe County's Lollypop Farm.

The Humane Society of Rochester and Monroe County was formed over a hundred years ago to stop the abuse and cruel treatment of beasts of burden on the tow path of New York's Erie Canal. Today it supports and protects many animals. Lollypop Farm, under Humane Society auspices, shelters abandoned, neglected, unwanted, surplus dogs and other pets. Through careful screening, these animals are placed in new homes with responsible owners.

Building *The Dogs of Our Lives* meant reaching dog enthusiasts. "Donate a Dog Tale" flyers, mailings, news releases, and word of mouth brought overwhelming and reassuring response. There were offers for assistance, wishes for success, inquiries from media, and presentation requests. Kind letters of regret were often accompanied by enthusiastic words of support.

The first donated dog tale came promptly from writer Robert Newton Peck, dispelling any reservations I had about the project. I marvel still at the responses that followed. For certain, dog lovers are among the most enthusiastic and appreciative people.

New Year's Eve day, musician Lou Gramm called to confirm information for his story. Then Steve Allen's poem arrived, followed by Congresswoman Susan Molinari's submission. On a follow-up phone call, even her dog could be heard barking approval. As well known and not-so well known added their tales, the collection grew. *The Dogs of Our Lives* began to take on shape and meaning.

Now, after months of gathering, compiling, keyboarding, editing, consulting, writing, researching, and waiting, *The Dogs of Our Lives* is ready for all to enjoy.

Within its pages, you'll find that each story and storyteller is unique. Only the remarkable relationship shared by dogs and their people remains a common feature. That relationship inspires writings of joy, humor, compassion, mystery, and marvel. Some writers come close to defining the bonding chemistry. Some reminisce. Several retell ancient stories. Others embellish their tales with eyes twinkling. Humorous anecdotes are recorded. Profound musings are scribed.

On behalf of the Humane Society of Rochester and Monroe County's Lollypop Farm, I offer my appreciation to those who believed in this project, to those who gave support by listening, suggesting, confirming, and encouraging, and to those who generously donated dog tales to *The Dogs of Our Lives*.

—Louise Goodyear Murray, 1995

PART I

Dear Dogs and Gentle People

"Dear Dogs and Gentle People" is our salutation—the underlying theme.

Steve Allen's poem "Missing Our Dogs" takes the lead. Allen has embraced many dogs who have left their imprint on his heart.

In Chris Van Etten's "Rufus," we hear clean-cut words of a young boy who expresses the agonizing emptiness left by his departed childhood dog.

The flow of love between dogs and their people moves in two directions in "Barry" by Norman Vincent Peale. Love compels and sustains a remarkable dog to overcome insurmountable obstacles.

Joe Camp lets us peek behind the scenes at the infamous movie star Benji and the impact he has on one quiet admirer.

Smiles and tears are packed into Daniel Pinkwater's "The Soul of a Dog." Laugh with Lou Gramm as the actions of his "'Deer' Mister Bear" justify Gramm's faith in his dog.

"Dear Dogs and Gentle People" presents writings by young and old, the well known and the not-so well known. Read their poems, tributes, and testimonies. Listen to the medley of voices and glimpse into the marvelous mystery of enduring partnerships.

Dogs

Anonymous

There is a language known only to you
and
of course dogs.

A peculiar sort of dialect
of glances
motions
and sounds.

What strange creatures we think they are
yet
you have recorded their conversations in detail
and placed their orders at mealtime.

Nicky

Nita B. Allen

One summer day, when I was ten, my dad left work to come home for lunch. When the car pulled up in front of the house, we saw the reason for his unexpected midday trip home. Out of the car came a big dog, all black except for a white chest and some white on his feet. He was beautiful.

As it happened, the dog that lived next door to my cousins was a big black Lab named Nicky, and so, from that time on this dog was also called Nicky.

We had never had a dog before and there are no words, now or ever, to tell you how much we all loved Nicky. His heritage was dubious, but we didn't care. Nicky was ours, all ours. My dad said the dog had walked into his plant that morning and had proceeded to follow him. Nicky adopted my dad and got my mom and three kids in the bargain. Nicky was not a young dog, but you would never have known it. If I remember correctly, the veterinarian said he was about ten when we inherited him.

His special resting place was behind our couch, the back side of which bore a black smudge where he rubbed before lying down. He also liked to go upstairs to see Grandma. One time, he was resting upstairs in the dining room, and not knowing he was there, she tripped over him and fell. We were never sure who felt worse over the fall, Nicky or Grandma.

Nicky hated thunder. I've heard it said that a dog's hearing is more acute than a human's and thus a loud noise can be more scary. At any rate, whenever it was thundering, wherever Nicky was, he dashed for the couch and there he'd stay.

He used to do the same thing on the Fourth of July. My dad always displayed massive fireworks on the Fourth. Our relatives would come over at night to watch, as did all the neighbors. Everyone would be there—except Nicky. At the first sound of the fireworks Nicky was behind the couch and no amount of coaxing could budge him.

Nicky dearly loved to ride in cars, so one day my cousin Dorothy and Grandma took him downtown with them shopping. While they were gone a thunderstorm came up, and when they returned to the car, Nicky was gone! They had left the window open some for him to get air, apparently just wide enough for a getaway because he was gone.

Our Nicky was gone. Grandma could hardly tell us when she came home. We were all heartbroken.

Then the telephone rang. Did we own a big black dog named Nicky? the caller asked. Boy did we ever. A lady had him. Walking home, she had seen our big black dog trying to get out of the rain and into a shoemaker's shop. The shoemaker kept pushing him out. Taking pity, she brought him to her house, where she had gotten Nicky's name and our telephone number from his collar where my dad had written it.

Would we like to come get Nicky? she went on. Would we . . . would we!!! Boy, you bet we would . . . and did.

Another time, we couldn't find Nicky anywhere. We didn't think anyone had let him out, but he was nowhere to be found in the house. Then, when I looked out my bedroom window, I saw him. He was lying in the backyard in the snow. This was very peculiar. We called and called to him but he wouldn't move. We knew something was wrong.

We called my dad at work. "Daddy, you just have to come home. Something's wrong with Nicky. He's lying in the snow and he won't get up or move at all."

We had all heard that dogs go off to die so as not to bother their masters and we were terrified. Nicky just couldn't die . . . he just couldn't!

My dad always could be counted on in an emergency. He raced home, gathered Nicky up in his arms and away to the veterinarian he went. We waited and waited. Would our Nicky be all right . . . Oh please, God!

Some time later my dad returned, with Nicky, and Nicky was all right. He had eaten pork bones and they had splintered, cutting his intestines. Nicky knew he was sick and he knew the snow made him feel better. So that's where he was, lying in the snow. Perhaps he had a fever, I don't know. I do know that the veterinarian made him better and that we never gave him pork bones again.

The years passed and our Nicky was always there at our side. He waited while we played baseball at night. He greeted us when we came home from school. During dinner he could always be found under the table waiting to see who was going to slip him something next. He never waited long, for we all did.

During the summer months Nicky lay on the front porch and surveyed his world. If he wandered off, it only took a whistle from my dad and he would come running. The few times he dashed across the street in front of cars, our hearts stopped. But so did the cars. It was as if they were afraid of hitting this big dog for the damage he would do to their cars.

Nicky and the resident cat next door were not the best of pals but always tolerated each other. However, one more door down lived a very small lady dog. This little lady had a habit of periodically emitting an odor Nicky couldn't resist. Once he was determined to spread his seed for all to see. He lay at her door step for one week and wouldn't eat. I was very distressed. Mr. Russlander, the female dog's owner, was very distressed. "Please, Nita, won't you come and get your dog? This has been going on for a week now!"

I did and Nicky didn't and that sums it up pretty well.

And then one day Nicky was sick. Very sick. Daddy took him to the veterinarian. He told us the kindest thing we could do for Nicky was to put him to sleep. Dear God, no, not our Nicky. Ted, my younger brother, was away at National Guard camp. We couldn't put Nicky down with Teddy away, we just couldn't . . . it wasn't fair.

But each day Nicky got worse. Soon he just lay, not moving.

He tried to get water for he seemed to have a terrible thirst. But he could barely lift his head to drink and if he got any water, he promptly vomited.

My heart was breaking. The decision seemed to be mine. I asked Mom to call the S.P.C.A. They would come and get Nicky and put him down humanely. Although Teddy was due home in three days, I couldn't endure it any more.

Nicky was put down. We all cried.

When Teddy came home, it was my job to tell him. Please, God, give me the right words, let Ted understand.

I told him and he sobbed. My big brother, still in his soldier's uniform, lay his head down and sobbed.

All this was long ago, but time does not make some things better, only easier to bear. I know wherever he is, he is still doing what he did for us. Nick asked nothing and gave everything. We shall always remember our dear and gentle dog.

I can hug him still, smell him still, hear him still, feel him still and I love him still . . . our Nicky.

Nita B. Allen is a published writer and an art instructor for adults at Rochester Institute of Technology (R.I.T.) in Rochester, New York. She enjoys traveling and camping.

A dog is the only thing on this earth that loves you more than he loves himself.

—Josh Billings (1818–1865)
American humorist

Missing Our Dogs

Steve Allen

Old men miss many dogs.
They only live a dozen years, if that,
And by the time you're sixty, there are several
The names of which evoke remembering smiles.
You see them in your mind, heads cocked and seated.
You see them by your bed, or in the rain,
Or sleeping by the fire by nights
And always dying.

You are young but they are old. They go,
The German shepherd and the poodle,
The bassett hound and mutt.
They are remembered like departed children
Though they gave vastly more than ever they took,
And finally you're seeing dogs that look like them.
They pass you in the street but never turn
Although it seems they should, their faces so familiar.
Old men miss many dogs.

Steve Allen is a nationally known television humorist,
entertainer, author and song writer.

Dogs remembered by Steve Allen include Snoopy, shown here in a quest for a tennis ball, and Snowball, shown resigned to the inconvenience of a bath.

9

Raison d'Etre

Joe Camp

It was a fine fall morning in Paris, crisp and clear, and Benji was quite full of himself, cavorting near the fountain, playing with the children who had inexplicably materialized out of nowhere at the first whiff of a movie star. Their faces radiated and they took turns gently stroking his head. Those Benji chose to favor with a big sloppy lick exploded with laughter, and one young girl ran to her mother, screeching in French that she would never wash her face again.

A younger boy, perhaps eight, stood alone, apart from the crowd, a conspicuous shyness depriving him of the fun. I slid away from the camera, walked over and took the boy's hand and lead him through a jungle of groping arms to what I imagine was his first kiss from an international superstar. He beamed up at me and for that moment, in his eyes, I was King of France, maybe the world. For this was no ordinary canine, this was the embodiment of all the emotions he had felt while snuggled in a dark corner of a theatre somewhere in Paris, living Benji's desperate struggles as if they were his very own.

How well I understood, for I had been there so many times. Always dreaming beyond the emotion of the moment to the day when I might stir such magical feelings in others. So, the smile I returned was genuine. For this was the best reward of all. The very best.

The talented team of Joe Camp and Benji entertains families worldwide. Photo credit: Bob Mader.

Joe Camp, founder and president of Mulberry Square Productions, is the writer, producer and director of *Benji*. Mr. Camp is a native of Texas.

In life the firmest friend, the first to welcome, foremost to defend.

—adapted from Lord Byron (1788–1824)
British poet

Feeney and the Top Ten

Dick Dougherty

Every year my friend Feeney watches for the American Kennel Club's designation of Top Dog honors and every year he has the same complaint:

"How could they list ten so-called top breeds and not include a single one of mine?" he wants to know.

Politics, I tell him. Plain old snob politics.

I can think of no other explanation. Feeney's family tree surely contains at least a hundred pure breeds, some of which can actually be identified, so no one can argue that he does not have a pedigree.

It's just that, as a native of Peaks Island, Maine, his otherwise pristine lineage has been enhanced by romances with generations of *Summah Dogs*. (Purists would say "contaminated." I prefer "enhanced," and I feel the same way about people.)

Whenever we go to Peaks, we'll find ourselves exclaiming: "Look, there's Feeney's tail! There's Feeney's this! There's Feeney's that! Look the way that dog is rolling in that dead fish; who does that remind you of?"

Whenever someone looks at Feeney and asks what breed he is, we go down the list: "Well, he's got a lot of Newfie in him, some English setter maybe, that tail and the paws are collie, sort of; you name it.

"But most of his pedigree is simply the breed known as Dog."

This year's AKC Top Ten includes Labrador retriever, rottweiler, German shepherd, cocker spaniel, golden retriever, poodle, beagle, dachshund, dalmatian and Shetland sheepdog.

All very distinguished breeds, I'm sure. Mix them up and you'd have one hell of a dog. In fact, we've had dogs that have contained all those breeds in different combinations, but as far as we know, none of them had the papers to prove it. We never asked.

The thing that has distinguished all our dogs is that the one in residence at any given time sooner or later becomes "the best dog we ever had."

Right now that's Feeney, a skillfully blended genetic masterpiece containing the best of an estimated one hundred or so breeds, any of them indistinguishable.

So here's looking at you, Feen. Kennel Club or no Kennel Club you're the lifetime best-in-show Top One Hundred purebred at our house.

Dick Dougherty is a columnist for the Gannett Rochester Newspapers.

A heart-beat
At my feet.

—Edith Wharton (1862–1937)
American author

My Pet Hound

Louise M. Fatum

She was not pretty, her eyes had grown dim,
She walked with a waddle, her form was thin.
The usual whistle her master gave,
Was answered slowly, painfully brave.
To fetch the ball was really a chore,
And climbing stairs was done no more.
But when at her master's feet she sat,
Her eyes adored him, she was his pet.
No longer they hunted or ran as before,
Her master had reached the seventy score.
And sitting or dreaming together was fun,
For master and pet could no longer run.
But let doorbell ring and strange voice sound,
She could still bark and growl, the lovable hound.
Protect you and love you until I die.
That was old hound's motto. And I did cry
As we laid her to rest I somehow know,
I will meet her when it's my time to go.

Floridian Louise M. Fatum, midway through her tenth decade,
is an active community volunteer. She enjoys writing and has recently
completed a novel.

Avoiding the Empty Nest

Marilyn G. Furman

There is, without a doubt, some grand design in this universe that has set about to ensure that my husband and I do not suffer from the empty-nest syndrome. Having launched our third and last daughter into her freshman year at college, we find ourselves the proud parents of the son we never had when we were young enough to handle him.

Our ten-month-old black Labrador retriever puppy named Popper is everything I always thought a two-year-old boy would be: affectionate, lovable, playful, bright, stubborn, messy, rough, tough and altogether incredible. At this tender age he already has distinct likes and dislikes. He definitely has an aversion to clean kitchen floors. His favorite pastime is to drink water from his bowl, carry it gingerly in his jowls, dribble it randomly over the floor and deftly place his dirty paws in each little puddle.

The landscaping and lawn are obviously not to Popper's liking, so he has systematically trimmed the euonymus and the cotoneaster, dug holes around the lamp post, and removed every Johnny-jump-up and zinnia from the edge of the front porch.

Operating from purely altruistic and unselfish motives, knowing full well that we are getting on in years, and being convinced that exercise is essential for our health and well-being, he manages to get us out for long walks in some of the worst (and best) of our upstate New York weather.

When it is too hot and humid for him, he sees that we get our exercise indoors by playing tug-of-war, wrestling or throwing a ball for him to fetch.

However, Popper has developed a new twist to this game of fetch. When we are reading, listening to music or just relaxing in our lower level room (where he is not allowed), he coyly drops or pushes his ball, bone or rope toy down the stairs, barks his command for "human, go fetch," and waits for one of us to respond. We are well trained, and I think he's rather proud of us.

He's certainly not college material, but he does show a strong interest in reading. He attempts to climb up on our laps every morning as we try to read the paper. Granted, it might be the food we're eating that interests him the most, but I'll give him the benefit of the doubt.

He seems more attached to my apron strings than anyone else raised in this house. When he feels neglected, he lodges himself in the corner where the stove meets the kitchen sink (the location where I spend at least three-quarters of my life) and whines, paws and tugs at my apron strings until I acknowledge his presence with words of love and approval, or perhaps just body contact.

Like all good Labs, he loves water and is a true conservationist. Rather than let the water that sprays from the poor connection between the two segments of our garden hose go to waste, he uses it as his personal shower. Unfortunately, in his delight, he manages to create a mud hole and a major mess on our lawn.

But most of all, Popper is that indescribable presence in our house that fills the void when everyone else is gone. He is an unquestioning well of love, a constant element of humor. He is a handsome, shiny seventy-pound hulk who brings his velvet-soft ears and mushy nose to my lap ten times a day to be scratched and caressed, reassuring him that he is the best dog in this world. And, of course, he is!

———————————

Marilyn G. Furman does interviews for a market research company. She enjoys free-lance writing and is an active volunteer in the Rochester, New York, community.

Old age means realizing you will never own all the dogs you wanted to.

—Joe Gores

"Deer" Mister Bear

Lou Gramm

A number of years ago, my wife and I were offered a chance to pick a German shepherd puppy from our friends' new litter of pups. Our friends owned both parent dogs, the parents were large boned and great looking and each possessed an even temperament—we could not go wrong. We selected a solid black male pup with unusually big paws and an irresistible face.

The first time we saw him, he was standing in the middle of a large bowl of dog food, growling at his brothers and sisters. He continued to do this between mouthfuls until he had enough to eat. Eventually he sauntered away, allowing the rest of the group to chow down on what remained. We could see that he was very playful, always yapping and nipping his siblings. And he was a little bit of a bully.

This little guy looked like a bear cub, so we called him Bear. He grew to be a magnificent animal with a striking chiseled face, a broad chest and powerful legs. Bear was a great companion and very protective of our family. He certainly could be a menacing presence to anyone he mistrusted. However, we were able to play with him, rough and tumble, without fear.

When Mister Bear, as we now called him, was four years old, we moved to the country. That fall we saw quite a few deer on our property—they came right up to the house to nibble on the shrubbery and look through the window at us on the inside.

*Lou Gramm. "Juke Box Hero"
and voice of Foreigner*

The first time Mister Bear saw these strange intruders staring at him from outside, he nearly threw himself through the window glass.

If Mister Bear was outside when the deer were grazing, he gave immediate chase, sometimes for a few hundred yards through the woods. Of course the deer would stop occasionally to let him catch up. Eventually I sensed it was a game for both the deer and Mister Bear. I never thought Mister Bear could catch a deer, or considered what would happen if he did.

One cold February morning, in the middle of the winter's worst storm, I let Bear out at his usual time and saw him run directly toward five or six deer huddled under the branches of our largest pine tree. Naturally, they all scattered, except for two, a newborn fawn, not more than a day old, and its mother. While they may have been frightened, neither moved. Mister Bear walked right up to them. He sniffed them and walked around them. And he even briefly frolicked with the baby. Then he returned to the house.

His tail was wagging double time and he was wearing his big old dog smile. As relief washed over me, having just witnessed this scene, it only reaffirmed what I already knew.

Mister Bear was a good dog—a very good dog!

———————

Mr. Gramm is the voice of the well-known rock 'n' roll band *Foreigner*. He owns a string of multiplatinum albums and is a Rochester, New York, native.

A Blizzard and a Prince

Ralph A. Hyman

Through the hushed air
The whitening shower descends,
At first thin-wavering, till at last the flakes
Fall broad and wide and fast, dimming the day
With a continual flow.
The cherished fields
Put on their winter-robe of purest white.

—James Thomas, 1776

Like the poet, I see winter as something beautiful and mystical, certainly as no catastrophe from which I must flee to warmer climes. One reason I regard winter as more friend than foe is an unforgettable incident that occurred in the midst of a whiteout in January of 1977.

I was inching my way along East Main Street near the Auditorium Theatre about 5 o'clock that evening when my windshield wipers broke off. In blizzard conditions, I was able to make my way to a gas station where I was greeted by its owner and a four-legged aide whose muzzle was frozen so that he could not bark. Against this cloak of white, all I could discern were two warm, brown eyes.

"Who and what is that?" I exclaimed.

"Do everybody a favor and take him home," said the proprietor. "He's been hanging around here all day, apparently homeless. No tags. No collar. I can't use another dog. Take him. Pay for the wipers; no charge for the dog."

What was I doing? We already had two dogs at home. But heart overruled head. Here was an animal in dire need. I opened the door of my car, and "Pal" jumped joyously into our lives.

Our son, Dan, then nine, named him and "Pal" learned his name immediately.

Breed? Give me a break. The veterinarian who first examined him said dispassionately, "This dog has several different ancestors."

To make it simple, he looked roughly like a mix of German shepherd and golden retriever and indeed had the temperament of both. Once, when a large menacing stray tried to attack our aging cocker spaniel in front of our house, Pal sprang toward the intruder's throat. There was a piercing yelp. Not from Pal. Not from Coco, our cocker. It came from the interloper, bearing a swift retreat. Then, there was the kindly side of Pal. Once, when my wife slipped and fell on the ice, Pal stayed by her side making sure she was all right.

And there was the mischievous side. We were going to one of those pass-a-dish suppers, and my wife had made a tantalizing crock of baked beans. Silently, Pal nudged open the kitchen door, and when we came upon the scene, there was Pal licking his chops in the throes of ecstasy, as if to say, "You've been holding back on me."

We have twelve beautiful years with Pal. The pauper became a prince. We revered him.

He left us as quickly as he came into our lives. One evening in June, he faltered as he headed onto our front entrance. We brought him in. He died at the foot of our bed. We buried Pal at the beautiful Rush Inter-Pet Cemetery. But not the memories. They are with us every day. Along with a handsome portrait of him. A king among dogs.

Editor's note: Pal II, a former Lollypop Farm Animal Shelter dog with a disposition remarkably similar to their first Pal, now resides with the Hymans. He is their unexpected treat—two Pals in a lifetime.

A native of Rochester, New York, Ralph A. Hyman has spent thirty-eight years in journalism as reporter and editor for the Gannett Rochester newspaper. Now "retired," he enjoys free-lance writing.

You can tell by the kindness of a dog how a human should be.

—Captain Beefheart
American rock star

One of the happiest sights in this world comes when a lost dog is reunited with a master he loves. You just haven't seen joy till you have seen that.

—Eldon Roark
Just a Mutt 1947

The Doggie Dictionary

Peg Kehret

I am here as a public service to dog owners. Many dog owners are not aware of the existence of the International Doggie Dictionary. The definitions in this Doggie Dictionary are ancient truths, passed from generation to generation of dogs as part of the folklore of canines.

All puppies are taught these definitions by their mothers. Unfortunately, many humans who *think* they know the meaning of these words, don't realize that dogs interpret them differently.

In an attempt to reduce misunderstandings between dogs and their owners, I will share with you some of the proper definitions from the Doggie Dictionary.

LEASH. A leash is a strap which attaches to your collar, enabling you to lead your owner where you want to go when you're out for a walk.

DOG BED. This is any soft, clean surface, such as the white bedspread in the guest room or the newly upholstered chair in the living room.

DROOL. Drool is what you do when your owner has food and you don't. To drool properly, you must sit as close as possible, look sadly at your owner, and let your mouth hang open. Allow the saliva to drip into a pool on the floor.

SNIFF. Sniffing is a social custom to use when you greet other dogs. Place your nose as close as possible to the other dog's rear end, and inhale deeply. Repeat several times, or until your owner makes you stop.

GARBAGE CAN. A garbage can is a container which your neighbors put out once a week to test your ingenuity. You must stand on your hind feet and try to push the lid off with your nose. If you practice diligently, you will be rewarded by the opportunity to shred margarine wrappers, gnaw on beef bones, and consume moldy bread crusts.

BICYCLES. Bicycles are two-wheeled exercise machines, invented to give dogs a way to control body fat and help their hearts and lungs. For maximum aerobic benefit, you should hide in the bushes near a road and wait until the bicycle is six feet away. Then dash out, bark loudly, and run along side it for several yards. If the person on the bicycle swerves, return to the bushes.

GUESTS. Guests are people who come to your home to see you whine at the table, bark loudly, jump up on women wearing pantyhose, and do other tricks which you wouldn't think of doing just for the family. If the guests put their coats on your owner's bed, it means they want you to sleep there.

DEAFNESS. This is a malady which affects dogs whose owners want them to come in when they want to stay out. Symptoms include staring blankly at the owner, running in the opposite direction, or lying down.

THUNDER. Thunder is a signal that the end of the world is imminent. Owners remain amazingly calm during thunderstorms, so it is necessary for you to warn them of the danger by trembling uncontrollably, panting, rolling your eyes wildly, and following at their heels. If your owner should try to calm you during a thunderstorm, refuse to be comforted. Continue to shake.

WASTEBASKET. This is a dog toy, usually round, which contains discarded tissues, candy wrappers, envelopes and other chewable items. When you get bored because you've been left alone, tip over the wastebasket and strew the contents around the house. It will keep you occupied until your owner returns.

FENCE. A game of skill, the object of which is to get on the other side as quickly as possible. You may be able to go over the top; usually it's faster to dig underneath.

DOOR. A door is a rectangle to scratch on when your feet are muddy, so that your owner will let you in. If your feet are not muddy, don't scratch; the weather is too nice to go inside.

SOFA. Sofas are to dogs what napkins are to people. After eating it is polite to run up and down the front of the sofa and wipe your whiskers clean.

BATH. A bath is a process used by dog owners for drenching the floors, walls, and themselves with water. You can help by shaking vigorously and frequently.

LOVE. All dogs know this last definition, even before their mothers tell them. Love is a feeling of intense affection, given freely and with no restrictions. The best way to show your love is to wag your tail. If you're lucky, a person will love you in return.

Peg Kehret, who lives in a suburb of Seattle, Washington, is a writer, volunteer, and Humane Society supporter. She is a recent recipient of the Pacific Northwest Writers Conference Annual Award.

One of the most enduring friendships in history—dogs and their people, people and their dogs.

—Terry Kay
To Dance With the White Dog

Barry

Norman Vincent Peale

I once read a newspaper article about a German shepherd named Barry. He lived in Bonn, Germany. The landlord of the people who owned Barry didn't like dogs. He told the owners that they would either have to get rid of Barry, or move out. They didn't want to move out or to give up Barry.

But they had to make a decision, so they sold Barry to an Italian ice-cream dealer named Angelini. And Mr. Angelini moved from Germany back to his hometown at the tip of the Italian boot, taking the dog, Barry, with him. Later, he reported to the family in Germany that the dog was missing, and he presumed the dog was dead.

One year later, having traveled twelve hundred miles on foot, walking from the tip of the Italian boot to Bonn, Germany, the dog scratched on his former owner's door—exhausted, unkempt, and footsore. He lay down at his master's feet, and pleaded with him, through those eyes of a dog, *I didn't want to leave you, and I have come back to you*. So the family and the dog moved into another house.

If a dog will walk twelve hundred miles for one year to obtain his objective, why won't a human being keep trying again, and again, and again? Perhaps he doesn't have sufficient *desire*. Now if, with all your heart, you truly seek, you shall find. People who truly try are people who accomplish things!

Dr. Norman Vincent Peale with his family pet at his farm in Pawling, New York. Photo credit: Courtesy of Peale Center, Pawling, New York.

Dr. Norman Vincent Peale, an internationally recognized religious leader who inspired millions of people through his sermons and best-selling book *The Power of Positive Thinking*, died December 24, 1993.

An animal's eyes have the power to speak a great language.

—Martin Buber (1878–1965)
Austrian philosopher, *I and Thou*

Best Friend

Robert Newton Peck

Valor.

This is the name my dog answers.

Years ago, I had only to whisper his name, and he'd come. Now he is almost deaf, so as a courtesy I go to him. Sensing me, knowing my smell, his broken tail thumps the floor in welcome. Then slowly, with groanings of painful age, he forces himself to rise, ready for duty.

Valor is thinner now, almost fragile, no longer the burly coon hunter and bear tracker. I cannot ask him to splash into cold water to retrieve a fallen canvasback. Or drive a deer to my watch.

Frequently he naps indoors, seeking patches of sunlight to ease his stiffness. His eyes, which once shined brighter than horse chestnuts, are now cloudy, a look of winter. I must be careful not to rearrange furniture, for if I do, Valor may bump an uncustomary chair, and then appear to be shamed by his clumsiness.

As a hunter, his bark once sounded with orchestral variety, announcing a rabbit, a fox, or treed coon . . . or that he had found water or my truck.

Valor's body has been bitten by a rattlesnake, raked by panther claws, hit by a car, kicked by a horse as well as by his former owner. Yet pain never soured his rapture of life. Except once, and then only briefly. Valor came whimpering home one night, his soft muzzle bristling with porcupine quills. Head in my lap, he lay trembling as my pliers removed each bloody spear.

He trusted me to do this unpleasant task, somehow knowing it had to be done, licking gratitude upon my face when I told him the last quill had been extracted.

Valor is deaf, blind, lame.

Soon, too soon, I must take a shovel and a pistol, and the two of us will stroll our final outing together. A grave will be dug somewhere in woods where he used to hunt or merely race the wind. Somehow he will know that what I'm about to do for him is just and merciful. One more of my many quirks that he accepts.

No veterinarian's needle will terminate his life in foreign environs. He will not die among strangers. Valor's death must be private and dignified. For my dog, I promise you, death shall be painless.

Only his friend will feel the pain.

Robert Newton Peck has written over fifty-two books, including a long-time favorite, *A Day No Pigs Would Die*, and the *Soup* series. He is a recipient of the Mark Twain Award.

How often do angels kiss our dogs? Just count the pink spots on each nose.

—Mary Clare Goodyear

The Soul of a Dog

Daniel Pinkwater

Once, Jill had fun with our Alaskan malamute, Arnold, by pretending that she was teaching him a nursery song. It was pure nonsense—Jill was tending our old-fashioned, non-automatic clothes washer, and Arnold was keeping her company.

Jill sang him the song about the eensy beensy spider, and indicated where he was supposed to join in. He did so with something between a scream of anguish and the call of a moose in rut.

The next time she had laundry to do, Arnold appeared, and sat squirming excitedly until she sang him the song. He came in on cue. Arnold learned a number of songs. His vocal range was limited, but his ear was good.

It was also Arnold who taught Juno, our other dog, to set up a howl whenever we passed a McDonald's. On a vacation trip, we'd breakfasted on Egg McMuffins for a week, and the dogs always got an English muffin. They never forgot.

I once observed Arnold taking care of an eight-week-old kitten. The kitten was in a cage. Arnold wanted to go and sleep in his private corner, but every time the kitten cried, he'd drag himself to his feet, slouch over to the cage and lie down with his nose between the wires, so the kitten could sink its tiny claws into it. When the kitten became quiet, Arnold would head for his corner and flop, exhausted. Immediately the kitten would cry, and Arnold would haul himself back to the cage. I counted this performance repeated over forty times.

Arnold acquired friends. People would visit him.

My friend Don Yee would borrow Arnold sometimes, and they'd drive to the White Castle and eat hamburgers.

He was the sort of dog you could talk things over with.

But he was not just a good listener, affable eccentric and bon vivant. He was a magnificent athlete. While Juno was tireless and efficient on the trail, Arnold made locomotion an art—a ballet.

Watching Arnold run flat-out in a large open space was unforgettable, and opened a window to something exceedingly ancient and precious—a link to the first time men followed dogs, and hunted to live.

He was a splendid companion—and he would pull you up a steep hill, if you were tired.

In a way, the hardest thing about living with dogs in modern times is related to the excellent care we give them.

Vast sums are spent by pet food companies devising beautifully balanced, cheap, palatable diets. Vet care these days is superb—and most pet owners take advantage of it.

As a result, dogs live longer than they may have done, and survive illnesses that they would not have survived in earlier times. And it very often falls to us to decide when a dog's life has to end—when suffering has come to outweigh satisfaction.

When it came Arnold's time to die, it was I who decided it. I called the vet and told him I was bringing Arnold in.

He knew about malamute vigor. He prepared a syringe with twice the dose it would take to put a dog Arnold's size to sleep. "Put to sleep" is an apt euphemism. It's simply an overdose of a sleeping drug. The dog feels nothing.

"There's enough in here for a gorilla," the vet wisecracked weakly. He was uncomfortable with what he had to do.

Arnold, of course, was completely comfortable—doing his best to put everyone else at ease.

I held Arnold while the vet tied off a vein.

"This will take six, maybe eight seconds at most," the vet said. He injected the fluid.

Nothing happened. Arnold, who had been completely relaxed, was now somewhat intent—but not unconscious, not dead.

"Sometimes it takes a little longer," the vet said. It had been a full half minute. Arnold was looking around.

The vet was perspiring—getting panicky. I knew what he was thinking. some ghastly error. The wrong stuff in the syringe. More that a minute had passed.

A crazy thought occurred to me. Was it possible? Was Arnold waiting for me to give him leave to go? I rubbed his shoulders and spoke to him. "It's OK, Arnold. I release you." Instantly he died.

I swear I felt his spirit leave his body.

The vet and I went outside and cried for a quarter of an hour.

He was an awfully good dog.

Daniel Pinkwater is the author of more than fifty books and regularly contributes to National Public Radio's "All Things Considered." He and his wife, Jill, reside in Dutchess County, New York.

You think dogs will not be in heaven? I tell you, they will be there long before any of us.

—Robert Louis Stevenson (1850–1894)
Scottish writer

My Friend

John T. Purves

We met in the spring of 1977 and started to run together in the middle of the following summer. We soon settled into a comfortable pattern of running at least one-half hour almost every day.

In the beginning, both of us had young lungs and strong legs, and I'm sure that we could have run much farther than our usual four to five miles. But, although it was never discussed, it was somehow clear that turning our runs into a test of endurance would make them less fun. And so, we never did find out exactly how far we could go.

Our runs together were always special. No matter what the day was like, if I said, "Wanna go for a run?" his eyes would light up and his body would visibly quiver with excitement.

On some days, we ran in silence, each of us enjoying the sights, sounds and smells of the season: lush, green plants shining in the warm rain of late April; heat shimmering off the road in July; brown, brittle leaves riding across a lawn on the cold winds of November; our muffled footsteps sounding in soft snows of winter.

On other days, particularly when things had not gone very well at work or at home, I muttered things to him that I would never say to anybody else. He always seemed to listen carefully, reading between the words, to react appropriately to the mood displayed in my tone of voice.

Amazingly, he was never judgmental. Even when I acted less than kindly to him, he would let me know that he wanted to be my friend.

Over the years, injuries and advancing age had forced us to slightly reduce the distance and frequency of our runs. As recently as last September, we were running three to four miles, three or four times a week. But then, his legs began to give out. Several times, he stumbled and fell for no apparent reason. By November, he could run only a mile or two, and then would turn to walk slowly home.

Our last run together was just before Thanksgiving. Less than a mile from our neighborhood, he fell and could not get up on his own. I helped him to his feet and walked him home. I never told anyone what had happened that day. Deep inside, I knew that something was terribly wrong, but, without really thinking about it, I guess maybe I felt that he would get better if I didn't talk about it.

Over the next two months, he lost more than one-third of his body weight. Earlier this week, I learned that his kidneys had failed. Yesterday, the decision was made—no heroic measures were to be taken. I was with him this afternoon when, without a sound, his gentle, brown eyes closed, his head drooped forward, and he stopped breathing. He's been gone only a few hours and already I miss him.

Some people may say that I am silly or even wrong to grieve so over his death. It is true that he was a dog and not a person. I have watched the deaths of family members, and I do not equate the death of an animal with the death of a person. Still, insignificant as it may be in the overall scheme of things, his passing from my life really hurts. A good friend died today.

John T. Purves is an attorney. He resides in Fairport, New York, with his wife and three children.

Dogs love company. They place it first in their short list of needs.

—J.R. Ackerley
My Dog Tulip

Rufus

Chris Van Etten

We opened the door and he came running down the hall. Rufus, our mixed breed dog, always ran up to us when we came home every week day. Rufus was light yellowish and black plus he was jumpy if you came too near to his tail. That was then. This is now.

Rufus died of what my mom said was sickness. It happened around the time when I was five and my brother Brian was three. My brother cried and ran up to his room and my mom went to comfort him. I was heartbroken. It just wouldn't be the same without him.

In the spring, we would go down to Seneca Lake. We liked to bring Rufus down in March a lot when it was too chilly for too many people to be there. On the side of the lake we were on, the shore was sandy and clean. When my dad threw sticks, Rufus would jump up and catch them. Once one of them went into the lake, but Rufus got it out.

One of the reasons I thought Rufus died was we didn't feed him enough. When I asked my mom she said I had always fed him when I was supposed to. I also thought we hadn't given him enough attention. When I thought that over, I knew we had given attention. It was probably old age. I'm not saying Rufus was old. In people years, he was seven. I don't know how old he was in dog years, but it must have been somewhere between twenty-five and forty. For that age, he has done some pretty funny things.

The time Brian jumped on his back and pretended he was a cowboy was really funny. I thought Rufus's back would be broken.

It brings back a lot of memories to look at a picture of him. Only sometimes when I open the front door on a weekday, I can hear his footsteps running down the hall.

Chris Van Etten wrote "Rufus" while in the fourth grade. Now in high school, Chris resides in Fairport, New York, with his family and dog Fergie.

The one best place to bury a good dog is in the heart of his master

—Ben Hur Lampman (1886–1954)
American writer

PART II

Second-Hand Dogs

Their ancestral history often is questionable, their legacy golden for this most popular "breed." Formerly homeless, neglected or abandoned, second-hand dogs can be a low-cost and high-quality acquisition.

In her first-hand narrative, Susan Molinari acknowledges the value of former street dog, George. Other town and country foundlings fortunate to be at the right place at the right time include Stanley, Arnold, Chocolate and Scamp. Even the cartoon world confirms the value of dog adoption as Cathy Guisewite's "Cathy" anticipates, selects, and surrenders to her Humane Society Puppy.

Some of our writers refer specifically to experiences with Lollypop Farm Animal Shelter of the Humane Society of Rochester and Monroe County in Upstate New York. (Lollypop Farm has one of the highest adoption rates in the country.) Dogs are as special as the good folks who welcome them.

Eulogy to Patience

Joan Fingar

She was a has-been. At just five years of age, she lived an isolated existence. Relegated to a remote run during the day, she spent her nights crated with transients. Her only human contact was someone who, always in a hurry, came to replenish her water supply, to drop off her daily meal, and to clean out her run.

Once she was special, living in the warmth of the house, enjoying extra treats, and showered with affection. Her breed had been in favor then and she had produced her first litter. Now there were others who were fancied, small yapping things, bristly and funny colored, with no sense of decorum.

I met her for the first time when I came to acquire her son. She was three, playful, loving, beautiful and happy. She ran into the room where I waited, her silver-grey coat flying in her haste, her jet black ear fringes sweeping the floor, and her big brown eyes reflecting the depths of her soul. I brought home my boy because of what she promised he would be.

Now, two years later, I was afforded the opportunity to own her, a chance I could not pass up. As I drove into the yard, I felt twinges of excitement and trepidation. I walked slowly toward her run to gauge her reaction to me. She raced back and forth along the fence, barking feverishly. I was apprehensive. Was this the dog I had wanted so badly, this fearful thing, now so aggressive? Was I wrong to have thought she would blend into our household?

I was determined to try. I completed the arrangements and loaded her into her crate for the long drive home. During the trip she curled into a tight little ball and quivered and cowered.

When we arrived at her new home, she reluctantly exited the car to be greeted effusively by her new family, her son included. He, still with puppy mentality, sprang toward her, full of curiosity. His exuberance was quickly squelched.

She chose to immediately attached herself to the head of the house, he who had been most disinclined to accept her presence. Whenever he was at hand, she was under his feet, seeking, and most always finding, his favor and attention.

I was concerned that she would find it difficult to adjust to our mad-cap life-style, and, at first, I thought my fears would be realized. She spent much of her time in her crate, even though the door was always open. She was skittish and shy whenever we focused on her.

Four months after her arrival, we returned again to her former home, this time to visit the dog who was to father her pups. I think by then she had begun to like the comfort and attention she received from us, and she was quick to show her displeasure at being removed from it. Being a para-mour was not to her liking, either, and we were both delighted when we headed for home.

Her pregnancy was uneventful. She delivered a litter of ten, two of whom were born dead and two who died within twenty-four hours. The others were a sight to watch. George had a voice like a trumpet and a pushy personality to match. Booberry was a lovely little thing, dainty and delicate, with a sweet face and gentle manners. Mr. Green Jeans was a bumbler, slow and a bit unsteady. Our favorite was Baby Boy, the runt of the litter, who required additional feeding and nurturing. He was the one pushed aside at mealtime and the one shunned by his litter mates because of his preferred care.

She was an excellent mother, teaching all the things they needed to know. From this lovely lady I learned much about raising a family—how best to show disapproval, how to make constructive criticism, how to educate.

After finding good, loving homes for the pups, we settled back to enjoy each other.

Later that summer, she underwent surgery to remove several tumors. The vet, being cautious and forthright, told me they were malignant and might possibly recur, but after two years had passed, we felt we were home free.

As time went by, she became more and more open and loving. She was an integral part of the family and made a lasting impression on everyone. She soaked up love and was grateful for any small attention.

We established a ritual every time she went outdoors. She would stand and wait for her hug, only then going out the door. On her return, she would come as far as the cupboard, waiting for the little pat on her head and another hug before coming all the way into the kitchen.

In December of last year she turned ten. She seemed to be slowing down but we blamed it on age and on a touch of arthritis. She still seemed happy and content. Early in January, she refused her food for several days and had difficulty in moving. One morning when she seemed especially weak, I took her to the veterinarian. She never came home.

Thinking back, I worried that I had not done enough to make her happy and comfortable. I mourned her short life. But he who had once been reluctant to take her made the truest statement of all: "She gave to us more than we gave to her."

For over fifteen years Joan Fingar has shared her home with Skye terriers. Joan lives in Rochester, New York.

Any glimpse into the life of an animal quickens our own and makes it so much the larger and better in every way.

—John Muir (1839–1914)
American naturalist

Cathy

Cathy Guisewite

"This picture is of my dog Trolley who was the love of my life for fourteen years. Cathy's dog, Electra, in the comic strip, 'Cathy,' is modeled exactly on the look and personality of Trolley as a puppy." Copyright © Universal Press Syndicate.

Cathy Guisewite is the writer and artist of the "Cathy" comic strip, syndicated internationally. She is a native of Dayton, Ohio.

cathy®

by Cathy Guisewite

MY FRIENDS ALL HURRY HOME FROM WORK TO BE WITH THEIR HUSBANDS...THEY PLAN EVERY DAY AROUND SPENDING TIME WITH THEIR CHILDREN....

IT MAKES ME FEEL IT'S TIME TO MAKE SOME BIG CHANGES OF MY OWN, MOM. I THINK I'M FINALLY READY TO MAKE A REAL COMMITMENT.

OH, SWEETIE, YOU MEAN YOU'RE... YOU'RE... YOU'RE...

I'M GOING TO GET A DOG!

...MOM??

GO AWAY. I WANT TO BE ALONE WITH MY HAPPINESS.

cathy®

by Cathy Guisewite

CATHY, GETTING A DOG IS A HUGE RESPONSIBILITY.

I KNOW THAT, MOM.

HOW WILL YOU HAVE TIME TO FEED IT? HOW WILL YOU HAVE TIME TO TAKE IT OUTSIDE? HOW WILL YOU HAVE TIME TO TRAIN IT? HOW WILL YOU HAVE TIME TO TAKE IT TO THE VET? HOW WILL YOU HAVE TIME TO PLAY WITH IT?

DON'T WORRY, MOM!

AND WHY CAN'T YOU JUST DO SOMETHING EASY LIKE HAVE A BABY??!

cathy®

by Cathy Guisewite

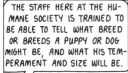

THE STAFF HERE AT THE HUMANE SOCIETY IS TRAINED TO BE ABLE TO TELL WHAT BREED OR BREEDS A PUPPY OR DOG MIGHT BE, AND WHAT HIS TEMPERAMENT AND SIZE WILL BE.

HUMANE SOCIETY

MR. WERNER

ADOPTION COUNSELOR

AFTER THAT, MOST PEOPLE JUST USUALLY GET A SPECIAL FEELING FROM ONE ANIMAL THAT LETS THEM KNOW IT'S THE RIGHT ONE FOR THEM TO ADOPT.

HUMANE SOCIETY

PICK ME. PICK ME. PICK ME. PICK ME. PICK ME. PICK ME. PICK ME. PICK ME. PICK ME. PICK ME. PICK ME. PICK ME.

PLEASE PLEASE PLEASE PLEASE PLEASE PLEASE PLEASE PLEASE PLEASE PLEASE PLEASE PLEASE PLEASE PLEASE

I'M IN BIG TROUBLE.

43

cathy®   by **Cathy Guisewite**

THE HUMANE SOCIETY GETS A LOT OF GORGEOUS PURE-BRED DOGS.

I NEED A BIGGER HOUSE.

WE HAVE DARLING PUPPIES, BEAUTIFUL MIXED BREEDS, AND LOVELY OLDER DOGS WHO ARE DESPERATE TO BE SOMEONE'S FRIEND.

I WILL MAKE A LOT OF MONEY AND BUY A HUGE HOUSE!

NO MATTER WHAT PEOPLE ARE LOOKING FOR, THEY FIND THE SAME SPECIAL THING HERE.

I'LL BUY AN ENORMOUS HOUSE WITH A HUGE YARD AND COME BACK TO RESCUE ALL THE ANIMALS!

THERE'S NOTH-ING LIKE ADD-ING TO YOUR FAMILY TO GIVE YOU A WHOLE NEW SENSE OF PURPOSE.

I WILL BUY AN EN-TIRE CITY AND LET ALL THE DOGS MOVE IN!!!

cathy®   by **Cathy Guisewite**

EVERY YEAR 7 MILLION DOGS AND CATS ARE PUT TO SLEEP BECAUSE PEOPLE DON'T GET THEIR PETS SPAYED OR NEUTERED.

I THOUGHT GETTING PETS FIXED MADE THEM FAT.

NOT TRUE. PETS ONLY GET FAT FOR THE SAME REASON PEOPLE GET FAT. DO YOU KNOW WHY PEOPLE GET FAT?

CERTAINLY. BECAUSE THEY IN-HERITED LOW METABOLISM AND A GENETIC ABUNDANCE OF FAT CELLS, COMBINED WITH A BIG BONE STRUCTURE, IN A SOCIO-ECONOMIC CLIMATE THAT EN-COURAGES THE CELEBRATION OF LIFE THROUGH CARBOHYDRATES!

THEY EAT TOO MUCH.

ALSO A POSSIBILITY.

cathy®   by **Cathy Guisewite**

LOTS OF PEOPLE THINK IT'S "MORE MASCULINE" FOR THEIR MALE PETS TO NOT GET FIXED, AND THAT FEMALE PETS "NEED THE MATERNAL EXPERIENCE."

BETWEEN THE "MACHO MALES" AND THE "MATERNAL EXPERIENCE," MORE THAN A MILLION NEW DOGS AND CATS WIND UP IN SHELTERS LIKE THIS EVERY MONTH WITH LITTLE HOPE OF EVER GETTING OUT.

IT COULD BE AVOIDED SO EASILY IF PEOPLE WOULD WAKE UP TO THE FACT THAT ANIMALS JUST DON'T THINK THE WAY WE DO.

I WANT MY MOTHER.

cathy®

by Cathy Guisewite

cathy®

by Cathy Guisewite

cathy®

by Cathy Guisewite

45

cathy®

by Cathy Guisewite

IT'S NORMAL FOR WOMEN CATHY'S AGE TO TRANSFER CERTAIN MATERNAL URGES ONTO A PET.

WE NEED TO ACT SUPPORTIVE OF HER DECISION TO GET A DOG, BUT ALSO REMIND HER THAT A DOG IS NO SUBSTITUTE FOR A REAL FAMILY. A DOG IS WONDERFUL, BUT IT'S JUST A DOG. A CANINE. AN ANIMAL. A PET.

COME TO GRANDMA!!

MOM'S FINALLY FLIPPED.

I KNOW, CATHY.

...AND GRANDPA'S GOING TO GET SOME PICTURES OF IT!!

cathy®

by Cathy Guisewite

DON'T GET UP EVERY TIME SHE MAKES A NOISE OR SHE'LL NEVER LEARN TO SLEEP THROUGH THE NIGHT, CATHY.

NEVER LET HER HAVE A SNACK UNTIL SHE'S FINISHED HER DINNER... NEVER LET HER GET AWAY WITH SOMETHING JUST BECAUSE SHE LOOKS CUTE...

PUPPIES ARE LIKE BABIES. THEY NEED A MOTHER WHO GIVES THEM RULES, DISCIPLINE AND CONSISTENTLY FIRM AUTHORITY...

...AND A GRANDMA WHO GIVES THEM ANYTHING THEY WANT!!

cathy®

by Cathy Guisewite

THIS IS THE BED WHERE YOU'LL SLEEP... THAT'S WHERE YOU'LL EAT... AND THERE'S THE LITTLE PLAY AREA WHERE YOU WILL KEEP ALL YOUR TOYS.

I AM NOT GOING TO TURN INTO ONE OF THOSE PEOPLE WHO LETS HER DOG SLOWLY TAKE OVER HER WHOLE LIFE!

IT'S SO MUCH MORE EFFICIENT TO JUST CAVE IN AFTER THE FIRST FIVE MINUTES.

CLICK

Hippy Dog Finds Happy Home

Leanna Landsmann

The dean was not amused. It was the second time in a week that we had hit him up for a contribution. Fundraising in the dining hall was frowned upon. Collecting money to free dogs from the local pound and to find them welcoming homes was a nice idea but not on his academic agenda. He tossed in a dollar and a last word: "If you two spent as much time in the classroom as you do in the dog pound, your names would be on my list . . ."

My colleague Gaylord and I were undaunted. The local pound had its deadlines: There were dogs to be freed and homes to be found with students, professors, new families moving into the area. On that particular Thursday a German shepherd pup awaited. "The last unsold pup in a batch. The owners had to move," said the person at the pound. "For eighteen dollars it will make someone a nice watchdog."

Watchdog indeed! This was 1968. The world was coming apart or coming together, depending on which side of the political spectrum you were on. The idea of a couple of college students finding a home for an untrained watchdog was unlikely. We made a few calls. No one wanted a puppy to house train. Not this late in the semester. School was almost out. The families on our list demurred.

A German shepherd puppy proved harder to place than we thought. Gaylord already had two pooches at his off-campus house. His housemates had two more. The solution was obvious: The pup could live with me in the dorm until we found it a home. Why not? The student body was working hard to make the case for coed dorms. I could make a case for pets, too.

I paid the pound, named the pup Geraldine and sneaked her into her new home for the spring semester. We got along fine in the way college kids do. Dorm neighbors were sworn to secrecy. Geraldine didn't lack for affection or tasty morsels from the dining hall.

For a month and a half her residency went undetected. Then the dean who had donated the dollar for her release saw me taking her out on a leash early one morning as he returned from his daily jog.

Caught! In violation of dorm rules, health codes, you name it. The dean, a dog lover, nonetheless laid down the law. Geraldine couldn't live in the dorm.

My mind was set: If Geraldine couldn't live in the dorm then I wouldn't either.

We both moved to off-campus housing and finished off "our" senior year.

During the graduation ceremony I chuckled when I looked at my torn gown, the result of a puppy's plea, "Oh stay home and play instead" that morning as I got dressed.

After graduation I contemplated my options as we all did in 1968 and decided to teach in West Africa. Taking Geraldine with me was out of the question.

I asked my parents (Doc and Katy Abraham) to consider keeping Geraldine until my return. Doc's a soft touch when it comes to pets. But this time he was surprisingly cautious. "I don't know, Lee, she's pretty rambunctious. And she's got some hippy habits." Meaning, I suppose, that she played all day, had not only a free will but an imposing one, and by virtue of having had her own way throughout puppyhood, had shocking table manners.

I started to outline other options, when Doc said, "But don't worry, Lee, she'll be here when you get back. We'll train her to be a terrific house dog for you."

Geraldine indeed was there when I got back, but there was no way that she would move in with me. She was Doc's dog, and Doc's dog all the way. And she had become a terrific house dog. At a hundred pounds, she'd learned to sleep in one place (Doc's favorite couch) rather than on every bed and in every nook. She had stopped snatching food from the table. Instead, she asked politely, as all Doc's dogs are trained to do. And she rode in a car with the ease of a plutocrat in a limo. Doc, Geraldine and Geraldine's black Lab friend, Mirabelle, were a common sight, riding through the streets and hills of Naples, New York, in Doc's Ford Bronco.

Geraldine lived a happy Neapolitan life and died of natural causes on Thanksgiving, 1980. We were crushed by her passing.

After burying her in the family dog cemetery, Katy pulled me aside and said, "The best therapy is to get Doc a new dog as soon as possible."

A few minutes later, Doc pulled me aside and said, "You know, the best thing would be to get Katy a new dog as soon as possible. Probably a small one—easier for Katy to handle than two big ones."

Within days, my nephews and I were on our way to Lollypop Farm Animal Shelter. Our charge? To get Doc and Katy a new dog, preferably a small one that would sit on Katy's lap while she reads.

We went to Lollypop Farm. And we did get a dog, a very large dog, but that's another story and I'll let Doc and Katy tell it.

Leanna Landsmann is an educational publisher and a writer with Landsmann & Schutz, Inc. of New York City. Her parents are Doc and Katy Abraham, also contributors to this book.

Acquiring a dog may be the only opportunity a human ever has to choose a relative.

—Mordecai Siegal
twentieth-century American writer

How We Adopted Singin' Stan

Doc and Katy Abraham

When Geraldine, our twelve-year-old German shepherd, went to Dog Heaven, Mirabelle, her black Lab companion for five years, was devastated. So were our grandchildren.

Our daughter Leanna had the answer. "We'll go to Lollypop Farm and get Mirabelle a friend." They hopped into the Volkswagen and headed for Lollypop Farm Animal Shelter.

They looked over the dogs. The choice was very difficult. One grandchild said, "Grandma wants a little dog." But each time they passed by a black dog, he would whine in a plaintive tone. And each time they'd say, "Look, that dog is singing to us."

"We'll tell Grandma the dog won't get any bigger," they said. (We were told it was half Lab and half Great Dane.)

Aside from the singing, what really caught their attention was a letter attached to the front of his cage. Here is what the letter said:

December 22, 1979

Hi everyone!

My name is Stanley. Though my family will be saddened this Christmas without me, they pray that I'll find a good home. I'm here because my friend, Nancy, is recovering from surgery and she can't tend to me as well as she feels I deserve.

Don't tell anybody, but I do get into a few things because I get so lonely—I wasn't used to her working so long. After four or five hours alone, I bring down security keepsakes. I don't chew anything. I just like having a slipper, a shoe and sometimes both sneaks to lie down with.

Nancy says I'm a good dog and I learn fast. But I'm getting too big and heavy. She can't handle my baths or my style of tug-of-war till she's much better. I'm only six months old and will get even bigger and stronger.

Nancy tried to keep me so I wouldn't have to come here. But I need to play hard and be with someone who works only part-time.

After all I've told you, if you could still love me and be a little patient with me while I'm still learning and getting over a broken heart, then you're the best I can get.

I eat twice a day and am used to dry dog food. I had my D.H.L. and rabies shots in September 1979, at Haller's in Avon. Nancy has my toys. If you need them or if you have any questions, you can call her.

From, Stanley

They brought Stanley to our Naples, New York, home, and you never saw such pandemonium. Doc was lying on the couch, watching the evening news. Stanley jumped up on Doc's belly and nearly knocked the wind out of him. Doc said, "Mirabelle, how did you get here?"

The kids said, "That's not Mirabelle . . . It's Stanley . . . He's your new dog. Better get used to him."

What a great morale builder Stanley was. He and Mirabelle and the Abrahams hit it off instantly.

Each Saturday morning Leanna calls from New York City to hear the two dogs sing a duet over the phone. She says it's the next best thing to being home, just listening to those two dogs sing each week.

Stanley and Mirabelle make a great pair. In mild weather they love to sleep in our Bronco station wagon, dubbed "Doc and Katy's $21,000 Dog Coop" by local citizens.

They're worth every cent of it!

————————————

Doc and Katy Abraham have written nine horticultural books and write the syndicated column, "The Green Thumb." They live in Naples, New York, with Mirabelle and Singin' Stan.

I believe by far the greatest number are owned . . . just for the sheer delight of having a lovely creature round the house to be admired, to admire you, and to keep you company.

—Barbara Woodhouse
English dog trainer and writer

Adopt a Mutt

If you can't decide between a Shepherd, a Setter or a Poodle, get them all.

Adopt a mutt at your local animal shelter and get everything you're looking for, all in one day. The intelligence of a Poodle and the loyalty of a Lassie. The bark of a Shepherd and the heart of a Saint Bernard. The spots of a Dalmatian, the size of a Schnauzer, and the speed of a Greyhound. A genuine, All-American Mutt has it all.

And your animal shelter has lots of All-American Mutts waiting for you. There are genuine, All-American Cats too. Just come to get the best of everything. Adopt a mutt.

—Courtesy of Massachusetts Society for the
Prevention of Cruelty to Animals

Stray Dog

Susan Molinari

There I was, minding my own political business, preparing for the campaign work ahead for the rest of this important day. It was, after all, Election Day 1988.

In less than six hours George Bush would be elected president and my father would win his fourth term to Congress. And in less than six hours, my life would unexpectedly change—I would become a "mother."

On this day a lanky, hungry dog wandered in front of my city council office in New Dorp, Staten Island. She had been beaten, was full of bugs, and displayed pronouncedly bony ribs.

Stray Dog, as she was initially named, was one of five dogs I had found over the last year. I always took them to the vet for proper medical care and had them bathed and fed. From there we always found a suitable home. Clearly, I could never adopt a dog, not with my schedule—not on Election Day—not with Stray Dog.

Stray was released from the vet's office after a three-day stay. The doctor was reluctant in delivering her to me since her starvation was so devastating. She could reasonably survive only three to four months. I assured him that I could care for her for three months.

Stray Dog survived! I like to believe that the love and security that I offered her compensated for all the missed meals, that I soothed all the painful, lonely memories.

My miracle dog was renamed George. Her struggle was as difficult as his, her intentions as noble.

As for me, it is quite fitting that on the day George Bush won the White House, George Dog won my heart and a right to survive.

And one special night I went to the White House for a dinner. While there, I told Millie all about her.

The Honorable Susan Molinari, a native of Staten Island, New York, has a distinguished career in public service. She and her husband, The Honorable Bill Paxton of Amherst, New York, are members of the United States Congress.

If you pick up a starving dog and make him prosperous, he will not bite you. This is the principal difference between a dog and a man.

—Mark Twain (1835–1910)
American writer

Scamp, Address Unknown

Louise Goodyear Murray

The separation of a dog from its master can be unsettling to both. I hope this story of an old dog's final years might comfort her previous owner.

Somewhere in Rochester is a grandmother who cared for a ragged little dog named Scamp. But three years ago, on a cold and overcast November day, Scamp invaded our neighborhood and confusedly roamed our icy streets.

For several days I caught glimpses of this intruder with her downcast eyes, her dragged-down tail and her erratic gait. She was a newcomer, trespassing unknown ground, but I did not realize she was an orphan as well, until she hesitantly responded to my open-door invitation.

Once inside, I was surprised not to find a license tag identification that would allow for a joyful reunion with her master. Instead, a note had been carefully twisted about her worn leather collar. It told the puzzling story of a grandmother who no longer could tend to Scamp, an eleven-year-old dog, protected by shots, and good with children. "Please give me a nice home where I can take care of you," the note pleaded.

And so, a new old dog involuntarily joined our household. Later, we learned that neighbors had witnessed her sorrowful desertion by a blue van that quickly left her, scampering in pursuit. Our veterinarian said in his many years of practice, Scamp was his only abandoned dog patient who came with a personal letter of introduction. Her survival of sub-freezing temperatures amazed him.

With time, her frozen paws regained their feeling. Her ample fleas succumbed to treatment. Her tail reached new heights. And a feisty spirit emerged. Our neighbor's little girl enveloped her with love, our own family dog learned to tolerate her, and our family readjusted routines to accommodate her.

Three years have passed and Scamp is now fourteen, active and comfortable in our home. But we continue to think about her former owner and home. To that grandmother, perhaps this writing will reassure you that your little dog, so sadly separated from you, is well and hardy.

————————

Louise Murray adds that Scamp's remaining years held mystery and magic. Though small and ragged, Scamp scattered love throughout their neighborhood.

To a man the greatest blessing is individual liberty;
to a dog it is the last word in despair.

—William Lyon Phelps (1865–1943)
American educator and critic

A Watchdog Named Flash

Emily W. Owlett

Flash was a beautiful German shepherd given to my husband and me because our friends could no longer care for him. He had been trained as a watchdog. We thought we could give him a good home. He came willingly and became a loving companion.

One cold December day, I took him for a walk before visiting my husband, who was in the hospital following a severe heart attack. But I had the misfortune to step on a piece of ice and I fell and broke my ankle. I sat on the side of the road, wondering what to do.

Since no one was at home to help me, I decided I had to depend on a passerby for aid. A car finally stopped when I signaled.

I cautioned the driver to stay back because I was afraid of how the dog would behave. I asked him to call the police and ambulance, which he did.

After a little maneuvering we got Flash on one side of a nearby fence. Then the police and ambulance could turn their attention to me. They got me into the ambulance and pulled into my driveway because I needed my purse and the house had to be locked.

As this was going on, an ambulance attendant told me to look out the window. Flash was coming down the road at the end of his leash, and the man who had called for help was at the other end. I couldn't believe it. I cautioned everyone to be careful because I was still afraid of what Flash the watchdog might do.

They soon learned that I knew what I was talking about, because when he got near enough, he made one lunge and ripped the policeman's coat from top to bottom. Then they believed me.

I did not know what to do with Flash. The man who had called the police and ambulance asked to keep him. I agreed, but only if he was sure he could handle Flash. I knew it would be months before either my husband or I could care for him.

When this man took Flash home, his wife would not let him keep him. So Flash went to Lollypop Farm Animal Shelter and was there for two months.

He was a very happy dog when we came and got him. He had been beautifully cared for but he wanted his family. Our watchdog and companion lived a long and happy life.

———————

Emily W. Owlett resides in Webster, New York.

Dogs' lives are too short. Their only fault really.

—Agnes Sligh Turnbull (1888–1982)
American writer

Arnold Comes Home

Daniel Pinkwater

"I thought I saw Arnold today," Jill told me. Jill's thought that the dog she had seen might have been Arnold, our Alaskan malamute, was momentary, until she remembered that he'd been dead for a year and a half.

It was a dog running loose in the neighborhood that looked exactly like Arnold. Jill had jammed on the brakes, and spoken to a neighbor. Did he know that dog? He did. It was always hanging around with his dog.

This was the neighbor who had been working for a solid year underneath the truck with "Colorado or Bust" painted on the side—not an ideal person to ask about anything, but it was a simple question.

Jill went about her business, marveling at the resemblance, and muttering about people who let their dogs run loose. That night she told me about the incident.

We were living in an ordinary suburban neighborhood of one-family houses with little backyards. A few minutes away, near the railroad station, was all that was left of the last dairy farm in town. There, in a pasture full of nettles, rented from the retired dairy farmer, Jill kept a couple of horses.

When we moved from Hoboken to the suburbs, we went in to the hilt.

Jill would drive over to the farm three or four times a day to tend the horses. The day after she had sighted the dog that looked like Arnold, she took off as usual, early in the morning, for the farm. I kept sleeping.

I was awakened by the telephone. It was Jill, calling from the deli across the street from the farm. "You'd better get over here," she said. "Something you have to see."

I jumped into our second car—I told you we had hit suburban life heavily—and drove down to the farm . . . where I found . . . well, it was Arnold . . . sitting in the back seat of Jill's car. Arnold—or whoever this was—gave me a friendly kiss on the face when I looked into the car. This dog was a female—but otherwise a ringer in appearance and attitude.

Arnold had a couple of characteristic postures in automobiles. One was sitting facing backward in the back seat. Another was sitting with his haunches on the seat and his forepaws on the floor. This dog assumed both positions while I watched.

"Spooky, isn't it?" Jill said.

It seems when Jill had arrived at the farm, this dog—this Arnold clone—was lying dead in the driveway. It had obviously been run over, and had staggered this far and expired. A small crowd had gathered and were feeling sorry for the poor dead dog, and discussing what to do with the carcass.

Jill yanked the emergency brake and went over and knelt by the body. She lifted a paw, which dropped limply, but not deadly, she thought. Then she thought she noticed a tiny twitching around the eye.

Malamutes, some of them, can sleep like nothing else that's animate. Convinced that there is nothing on earth that wants to hurt them, they can drop off in the middle of noise and crowds and sleep like cinder blocks.

Jill gave the whistle she'd used to give Arnold, and the dead dog sprang to its feet and jumped into her car. Jill got a container of coffee from the deli, thought it over for a while, and phoned me.

We took the dog to the neighbor—the one with the truck. On closer inspection, he allowed that he'd never seen this dog before. There were no tags, of course.

We took the dog home. She trotted right to the front door. Juno, the other malamute, and the housecats gave a sniff, and went about their business. "No big deal," they seemed to say. "Arnold's back, that's all."

We called the various pounds and shelters, read the classifieds, and placed an ad of our own in the paper.

Nobody claimed her. She's with us still, nine years later. We named her Arctic Flake. She doesn't remind me of Arnold as much as she used to. She's got qualities of her own, different from his.

Of course, we've worked up any number of theories about what happened, and how Flake came to us. We're not sure what we believe. For those who are interested, Flakey turned up just a year and a half after Arnold died, and the vet said that, as nearly as he could tell, she was just a year and half old.

Daniel Pinkwater is the author of more than fifty books and regularly contributes to National Public Radio's "All Things Considered." He and his wife, Jill, reside in Dutchess County, New York.

Daniel Pinkwater converses with a friend, a tame deer he met while traveling in Arizona.

Oh, the saddest of sights in a world of sin
Is a little lost pup with his tail tucked in.

—Arthur Guiterman

A Town and Country Dog

Gordon P. Small

Our move to Mendon, New York, proved to be a real change in life for our dogs, Hazy and Fletcher. Both dogs, of mixed ancestry, had been acquired by my wife from the Humane Society when we lived on East Avenue in Pittsford.

East Avenue was not a place to ensure a safe environment for any animal or child. Hazy had been hit by a car and subsequently walked with a pin in his hip. Fletcher had learned to dig under the fence.

Dogs and their owners, therefore, reacted with relief and enthusiasm to the open fields and abundant woodchucks in agricultural Mendon. Leash laws were ignored.

Several years later, one cold January day, Hazy failed to come home. We whistled, called and tramped through crusty snow and ice-covered fields and wooded terrain adjacent to our property. Fletcher was no help.

I walked as far as I thought necessary, calling and whistling. No response.

After several days of zero and sub-zero weather, my wife drew a picture of Hazy and we posted it in the grocery store and gas station.

Another week went by. After twelve desolate days and nights, we received a phone call from a young woman who lived about two miles from our house. It was apparent that the animal she had seen in a field near her might be Hazy.

We drove to her house and saw our emaciated, limping, almost three-legged, but alive Hazy. He had been caught in a steel trap without food or water all that time. We were to later learn the trap had been left unattended by a young man who had gone off to school.

Dr. Smith of Proper & Smith in Honeoye Falls saved the leg, but even after some time in a splint and bandage, Hazy still walked like a three-legged dog.

We now own a Saint Bernard and a Jack Russell who are contained by an invisible fence—but that may not keep the Russell out of woodchuck holes.

Gordon P. Small is an insurance executive. He resides
in Mendon, New York.

Dog! When we first met on the highway of life, we came from the two poles of creation. . . . What can be the meaning of the obscure love for me that has sprung up in your little heart?

—Anatole France (1844–1924)
French writer

The Power of Chocolate

Marge Suplicki

I'm petrified of dogs. Especially strange ones. So when my two sons begged and begged to keep Chocolate just for the weekend so they could find him a home, I consented only reluctantly. He was a dog scheduled to be put to sleep because his owner couldn't keep him and couldn't find anyone to take him.

Chocolate was a nice, quiet dog and had been taught to sit, lie down and shake hands. He had black hair about eight inches long and looked about 150 pounds.

I knew he had teeth, though. On his first day with us, I walked circles around him while he watched me with big black eyes.

That night we had pizza. Before going to bed we left the box of left-over pizza on our coffee table. In the morning when I got out of bed, I stepped on a slice. After investigating further, I discovered that Chocolate had eaten three pieces and then put one slice on my side of the bed, one on my husband's side and one piece by each of my sons' beds. He shared!

Needless to say his weekend stay turned into two weeks. And the begging started again—this time to keep him.

Well, we all know they got to keep the dog. But on one condition. He would have to be checked by the vet and groomed by his groomer. Since Chocolate had been penned in the woods for a week without food, I wanted to make sure he didn't have bugs.

Naturally the boys went to school and my husband to work, so I had to take him.

My heart was pounding. I couldn't believe what a wreck I was. I was alone with him!

I told the vet and groomer to do whatever was needed. He had a few problems that the doctor took care of, then the groomer said to pick him up in two hours. I wasn't happy at this point, but home I went.

Two hours later I returned. The assistant called my name and said my dog was ready. I couldn't find him. She had a skinny, twenty-two-pound black dog on a leash. I sat and waited for her to bring Chocolate out. Well, she didn't move. I didn't move.

"Mrs. Suplicki, your dog is ready," she said.

"I know. I'm waiting for him," I said.

"Here he is," she said.

"The dog I brought was huge. Not that small dog."

She explained that she cut all his hair off and discovered he was a large-boned miniature poodle. Unbelievable!

We've had Chocolate for eight years now. He's between thirteen and fifteen years old and the best friend I've ever had.

Massachusetts native Marge Suplicki lives with her husband in Hilton, New York. They have two sons in college.

A house is not a home until it has a dog.

—Gerald Durrell

PART III

Dogs and the Company They Keep

Long ago dogs chose us, bringing as gifts their house-warming presence. With grace and contentment, they abide with prince or pauper, seeking our company regardless of our income, education or beliefs.

"Dogs and the Company They Keep" presents William F. Buckley Jr., and Phyllis Diller who document the dogs in their lives. Robert G. Wehle and Schuyler Forbes Baldwin affirm their deep respect for the dog. Tales by Sally Ann Smith, Sally Jessy Raphaël and Maxine Kumin entertain us with sprinkles of humor.

You may recognize yourself or your pet.

Gentle Giants
of Orchard Glen

Schuyler Forbes Baldwin

We wanted a big dog. In our search we learned of the English mastiff. Our minister, a Canadian, told us about the Parker Kennels in Aylmer, Ontario. Having investigated, and after some correspondence, we drove up there in the fall of 1941 and returned with our first mastiff puppy, Donegal. This was a choice we would never regret, and when, in the fullness of time Donegal left us in 1950, we knew that the mastiff was the dog for us.

We wrote to the AKC and obtained the names of members of the Mastiff Club of America, including Mr. James Clark of Greenwich, Connecticut. Our letters to Mr. Clark resulted in our getting to know Patty Brill, and in 1951 we made our first trip to Old Peach Farm. As we turned into her place from Papermill Road and drove up a fairly long drive, we were soon aware of two or three mastiffs running alongside the car as escorts. We pulled into the parking area, and lo!—two or three other giants who had been resting in the sun came slowly up to greet us. The deeply scoured furrows in her front door told us that it had withstood the scratchings of many dogs for a long time. Three more huge beasts greeted us once we were inside. This was the beginning of a long friendship with Patty and John Brill.

We left that day with Dougal, a beautiful apricot fawn, our first Peach Farm acquisition. He was by Austin of Chaseway, from Peach Farm

Belinda. It wasn't long before he knew and respected the boundaries of Orchard Glen, our country home.

Feeling that Dougal was in need of a companion, we of course turned to Old Peach Farm and acquired Boudicca in 1955. We named her after Britain's famous queen, but she was officially Peach Farm Cleo (Donaghmore's Arthur x Peach Farm Thisby). This lady from Peach Farm was a lovely brindle, and in her prime became an unusually gentle giant (I supposed "giantess" would be the more correct term!).

Our family enjoyed both Dougal and Boudicca, and we never had a single problem with either. Oh, of course, when Boudicca was in heat, perhaps twice a year, we had to be careful because we did not want to get into breeding at that time. And sometimes when it became particularly "jumpy," we would board her out during that period. But these were minor inconveniences.

Early in 1961, an event took place, the significance of which I would not fully realize until years later. Ray Narramore, the director of the Humane Society of Rochester and Monroe County, called to say he had what he believed was a mastiff which had been left with him for disposal. "A nice dog," he said. I drove right out to see. Ray opened one of the cages and out leaped an unusually joyful dog; the slender apricot fawn bounded toward me! No question but that it was a mastiff. I told Ray then and there I wanted him, and soon my new friend and I were on the road and heading toward Orchard Glen!

Well, now we would have some problems. The newcomer adjusted almost automatically to Mrs. Baldwin and me and to all our family with no trouble at all. But one day I had a call from a man who lived down the road, our newspaperboy's father. It seemed that our new mastiff had bitten the boy. My neighbor was a considerate person and made no trouble, but he didn't like the idea of a biting dog and neither did I.

So we had to put the big fella under some restraints, and I found out later that the dog did have somewhat of a jealous disposition as far as our family was concerned and that we couldn't completely trust him. After some difficulty, I was able to get our rescued mastiff's registration papers from his former owner who had had the same experience as I had with him, except that they lived in a more congested neighborhood and could not have the dog around and feel safe about him.

Our big friend (who we had named Prasutagus, the husband historically of Boudicca) had been purchased from the Castle Kennels in New Canaan, Connecticut. Prasutagus was officially registered by the AKC as King Knight of Beardsley. Well-bred and handsome, he was to become an outstanding sire. Patty Brill brought one of her bitches to Orchard Glen that spring and bred her to him, and we, unwittingly, did the same with Boudicca.

So now, we were mastiff breeders (or so we thought!). Our first whelping came on May 21, 1961; eight little pups arrived, each in a caul. Three were lost simply because we were careless and didn't know enough. But for almost twenty-four hours a day during that first week Mrs. Baldwin and I took turns watching as Boudicca nursed and took care of her littler. Shortly after, we shipped King Knight to Old Peach Farm to become part of Patty's menage.

The biggest pup of Boudicca's litter (he weighed sixteen ounces at birth) was sold to Patty Brill. Named Prasutagus (they called him Gus), he eventually reached a weight of 230 pounds. We sold two others and kept the rest, and then started thinking very seriously of breeding. We advertised in "Dog World," indicating the possibility of having pups later on. To my surprise, I was almost flooded with correspondence—all interested, and wanting to know when we could have anything available.

Well, as breeders of Mastiffs, we weren't. We thought we'd succeeded once, but our vet said it looked like an absorbed pregnancy. And I guess, to be honest about it, we weren't wholeheartedly devoted to the idea. And I suppose, too, the realization of the constant care required during the first week or ten days of puppyhood was also a discouraging factor. At any rate, Orchard Glen Kennels never expanded. Since then, we have simply loved and enjoyed our mastiffs.

In 1963, we purchased another product from Old Peach Farm, Uther Pendragon (Withybush Barguest of Saxondale x Peach Farm Rachel), who enjoyed life here longer than any other mastiff we ever had; he died in his thirteenth year (up till then we'd never had one reach his eleventh birthday).

Another addition to Orchard Glen came in December of 1968 in the form of the three-month-old Pellinore of Old Peach Farm. His sire was Peach Farm Raynor; his dam, Peach Farm Peaches. Renamed Merlin, this pup was the litter brother of Dr. Newmann's champion, Brian. Merlin was with us for a shorter time than any of our other mastiffs; he fell victim of cancer in October of 1975.

Our last acquisitions came in the spring of 1974, again from Old Peach Farm, Maia and Celaeno, born January 16, 1974 (Peach Farm Warlock x Petite Princess Tamora). We'd come intending to get a single puppy, but fell in love with two of them, litter sisters, and so it was that Maia and Celaeno joined our family. For the last seven years they and we have been inseparable. And, of course, their dispositions were as beautiful as their forms. They acted together; when one started something, the other would take it up too!

One of the major characteristics of the mastiff—at least in our experience—is their moderate appetite. Every one of them from Donegal in 1941 to Maia in 1982 was alike in that respect. After some experimenting, the daily regimen included a three pound coffee can of Purina Dog Grain on top of the day's scraps from our table, once a day. But oh, do they drink a lot of water! We have a constant drip of water into their reservoir, winter and summer (heating cables keep it from freezing in winter).

The outdoor kennel is their living quarters. Protected from the breezes, it is about three by six feet, and is insulated and has plenty of straw and cedar shavings. During the day they have a chance to roam.

In the evening we'd have them with us in the library—we read usually and they lay on the rug in front of the fireplace, a favorite spot during the winter months when a fire would burn every night. But around 11:30 or so they'd usually become restless—enough was enough. So I'd let them out and they would go in their kennel for the night. And that was their habit, no matter what the weather, and sometimes we would have sub-zero nights with lots of snow and wind.

For us, it would be unthinkable not to have at least one mastiff. Just their being here makes all the difference. We'd not dare to have a dog of that size who wasn't friendly, and yet their size alone commands respect. In all the years that mastiffs have roamed our grounds, they've harmed no one; and I don't know if they would attack if provoked; but for the nonce, at least, we've never had a problem with prowlers! Traditionally, the mastiff has been the Guardian of his Property; at Orchard Glen, they still fill that role, and as long as the Baldwins are in residence here, they always will.

———————————

Schuyler Forbes Baldwin served on the Board of Directors of the Humane Society of Rochester and Monroe County for many years. Until his death in 1994, he and his wife shared their Orchard Glen home with a mastiff, a Pekingese, and two cats.

What is man without the beasts?
If all beasts were gone
Men would die from a great loneliness of spirit.
For whatever happens to the beasts
Soon happens to man.
All things are connected.

—Chief Seattle (1786–1866)
American Indian chief

Some Budget Director

Chip Block

One day in 1984 when I was publishing director of *The Atlantic*, owner Mort Zuckerman called me to set up a meeting. He said, "Let's meet at my apartment, not my office, so you can meet Stockman."

David Stockman, Ronald Reagan's former budget director, had been the subject of a major article in *The Atlantic*, an article that in retrospect presaged many of today's economic problems. Stockman was a controversial figure and I was glad to have an opportunity to meet him.

The appointed day and time arrived, and I appeared at Mort's door. The butler let me in and took me to the library. Mort was there alone. I said hello to Mort and said I hoped I hadn't missed meeting Stockman.

"Not a chance," said Mort and he let out a whistle. In came an irrepressible chocolate Labrador puppy. "Meet Stockman," said Mort, "an incredibly smart dog."

Chip Block is the founder of *Games* magazine and a consultant to magazine publishers throughout the country.

. . . A species so intimately involved with our own, which has shared our life since time immemorial. . . .

—Alfred Barbou

Almost Nothing Hurts More Than the Loss of Your Dog

William F. Buckley Jr.

My father bred English setters, and there were around the house, at any typical moment, five or six, half of them kept at the farm where we used them in pheasant hunting, two or three around the house, and at age twelve one of these became my own, my first doggie. He was a tall, handsome, black and white freckled beauty, whose pedigreed papers called him Sultan something or other followed by his patronymic, which I have long since forgotten, though I have not forgotten the pride I took in knowing that he had been bred by champions. At first I attempted with some formality to call him by his name, Sultan,but soon gave up, and for some reason, found myself calling him Ducky.

In respect of my liking for dogs, as in other respects, I tended to be taken by enthusiasms. I shared, in those days, a bedroom with my youngest brother, from one window of which a porch began that led along the length of the huge colonial house to a staircase descending to the grounds below. I persuaded the caretaker to substitute for the fixed screen that shielded my brother and me from the mosquitoes and fireflies of New England summers a screen dislodgeable by the merest exertion of a dog's nose. The screen, the dog having passed through it, would return to perform its conventional function through gravity. Ducky could now vault the radiator along the window stool and, knocking the screen out of his way, land on the porch whenever inclined, during the night, to leave my bedside, or more commonly, my bed. When he returned, he would bound up on my bed, and elect to sleep always with his head either over my rump, or over my neck.

Oh how we loved each other, Ducky and I. I had nine brothers and sisters, and my oldest sister, who was sixteen and far gone in cultivated sarcasm, noting the guileful habits of Ducky, who knew instinctively how to endear himself to those who could do him favors—take him hunting, give him food, or simply sit and stroke him—decided one day to refer to him as "Unducky." Some of my brothers and sisters thought this extremely funny. I did not. I managed to rise above it, however, and if anyone, in the course of the day, would say to me, "Bill, where's Unducky?" I would simply continue doing what I was doing, as though I had not heard the effrontery directed at my affectionate, noble doggie, who died one cold night, many years later, when I was a freshman at college.

My first experience with True Grief came when my older sister's cocker spaniel, who was called Peter, was killed by an oil delivery truck one summer afternoon. We rushed him to the vets, but he was DOA. The caterwauling in the household was not surpassed in any Spanish nunnery on Good Friday. It was years later that I heard the awful story, apparently a commonplace in German folklore, which communicates the seriousness of a child's engrossment with his dog. Skipping home late in the afternoon from school, the story has it, seven-year-old Gretel asks her Mother, "Where is Dada?" Her mother has spent the entire afternoon bracing herself for this encounter, because the awful truth of the matter is that Dada was tragically run over shortly after the little girl went off to school. Her mother, consulting friends and professionals, had decided to tell her daughter the plain truth, and take the consequences. Accordingly, she replied, in sober tones, "Darling, I must tell you something: Dada has been killed." The little girl looked up, wrinkled her nose, and then said, "Where are my cookies and milk?" Vastly relieved at her daughter's stoicism, the mother bounded to the kitchen to give her daughter her snack, after which Gretel said, "Mummy, where is Dada?"

"I told you dear, Dada had an accident and was killed."

There followed a lachrymose pandemonium which the mother could not arrest. Finally she blurted out, "Darling, I told you when you came home from school that Dada had been killed."

Little girl: "I thought you said *Papa* had been killed."

I am not saying it was so when our cocker spaniel Peter was killed, that we'd have gratefully exchanged the news that our beloved Father had been run over. But I intend to suggest the intensity of a child's grief, when something happens to the doggie.

My wife also grew up with dogs, and I don't think there was ever a moment when, during our married life, we were without a dog. The highlight of our doggie life together was being introduced to a dog, a dog so special that he and his "heirs," as I delicately call them (in fact, Rowley disdained female company), have brightened our lives consistently, for fifteen years now.

The breed is called Cavalier King Charles Spaniel and thereby hangs a tale.

Rowley came to us in Switzerland. He arrived in a lady's purse: the British gentlewoman, who had bred her own bitch, brought her little puppy as a house present, and it was love at first sight. He was ten weeks old, and when he was twelve weeks old, I flew him back to New York, receiving permission from Swissair to keep him on my lap during the flight. There was something about Rowley that absolutely never failed, at least not during the first two or three years of his lifetime. It was that he was irresistible, and all rules pertaining to dogs and their governance were simply waived when otherwise inflexible executors of the law came face to face with—Rowley.

It happened that the Swissair flight landed at Shannon on that trip, and I decided Rowley needed to be taken off the plane to give him an opportunity to relieve himself. But I was no sooner down the gangplank than four men zoomed up in a jeep with a machine gun mounted on it. I had committed a most awful transgression. Because Ireland, you see, is like England in only one respect: It has the same rules against dogs landing on native territory without first putting in six months in Coventry, in order to discover whether the dog is rabid. When the four Sumo wrestlers skidded to a stop telling me brusquely to take the dog back up into the airplane, I said to them, How could they treat a little dog in this way? They looked down at little Rowley, and—of course—it worked. They permitted me to mount the jeep, Rowley in my arms, and we were driven to a compound. That was the compound where, apparently, immigrating dogs were segregated, before going off to the hygienic dungeons where they sit, forlorn, for six months, before being designated as safe to mingle with the pacific breed of human beings who govern Ireland.

Anyway, there we were, and the leader of the detachment, his eyes furtively looking down at Rowley, waiting for him to do his business, made talk with me. I tried to keep the conversational fires burning, and we talked about politics, Communism, the Pope, and eternal salvation. All Rowley would do was bound about and look endearing. Finally the crisis came: The plane was about to leave. With some embarrassment, I having pleaded the distress of Rowley to the Irish paramilitary, I said we would obviously need to return to the aircraft, never mind that Rowley's little bladder, or come to think of it, immense bladder, was unrelieved. By the time we had got back to the airplane, each of the officials insisted on having a personal valedictory with Rowley, which affectionate embraces Rowley affectionately returned.

Rowley went everywhere with me but as the years went by I had to acknowledge that there was just that slight estrangement that men with such keen perception as mine are bound to notice. He loved Someone Else more than he loved me. He loved Jerry Garvey, who drives for us, better. The seduction of Rowley began when first he rode in the car with Jerry. Sometimes in the front seat, sometimes burrowed in the cavity next to Jerry's legs, sometimes on the magazine shelf behind the back seat, from which he would peer out the back window, or occasionally, down at us: but most often, longingly, toward the front, where Jerry dwelled. But every year, for thirteen years, he was with us in Switzerland, without Jerry, and there his enchantment became legendary.

We welcomed a new little Cavalier King Charles, about whom something very odd needs to be confessed. It is this, that for the first eighteen months, he was a lovely and refined dog, much like Rowley, but there grew a coarsening of body and spirit which my wife identified with the spiritual depression that came on when Beepee, as he was (is) called, was succeeded by Blenhie (after "Blenheim"), the breed colored white and brown. Failing to be the center of attention, and unreconciled to the senior citizenship status of Rowley, Beepee became rather bulbous, and his hair turned matty: and when a Spanish friend who always loved him told us that he would love to give Beepee to his freshly widowed mother to console her, we acquiesced, and as I write, Beepee lives a charmed life in Bilbao.

Blenhie inherited the charms of Rowley, but in due course he, too, faced competition. The circumstances of the new acquisition will amuse all couples, the male member of which is regularly accused of extravagance.

I had come upon a gentleman who lived in Greenwich, Connecticut, and was advised that his wife bred Cavalier King Charles Spaniels. I was informed that they had just bred a fresh litter of beautiful Blenheims. Since, living in Greenwich, they were our neighbors (we live in Stamford), I prevailed on my wife to drive over and have a look at the little six-week-old puppies. She agreed, but on the way to Greenwich, cautioned me: She reminded me we were under no obligation to buy a dog and certainly did not need yet another dog.

All six were brought out—about the size of a man's shoe—and began curling and playing on the carpet in the living room. At one point, the breeders left the room, and my wife looked up at me, from the other end of the room on the floor of which the puppies were playing, and raised her hand inquiringly . . .? She had two fingers raised: and I nodded, and we have been happy ever after, with Sam and Fred.

I have never understood why, when there are beautiful dogs one can acquire, people should go out of their way to acquire non-beautiful dogs. But I know better than to give an example, because nothing arouses owners more than the suggestion that their breed is less than the most desirable in the world. And, of course, it is true that a dog objectively ugly—a cur, a mongrel, a you-name-it—can capture the heart and mind of its owner. I don't know why this shouldn't be true of dogs, come to think of it, since it is certainly true of people: I would rather have spent my days with the Hunchback of Notre Dame, who was very ugly, than with Tallulah Bankhead, who was very beautiful.

But admit it, that the Cavaliers are strikingly attractive. And just as one feels the impulse to stroke them, they feel the impulse to be stroked. Sam and Fred can spend hours being fondled, as you read your book, or talk to your guest. But then they will exhibit their independence. It disappoints me only that they do not like my study. Rowley used to come to my study once every hour or so, to have an extended love-in, during which we would re-exchange our eternal vows. Sam and Fred will accompany me to my study, and then leave, to play elsewhere: or simply to lie, hours and hours on end, in the kitchen, or, preferably—always, if she is there—with Pat. We have constructed those little doggie-doors that give them all but total access to any part of the house, confining them only when they reach a gate outside the pantry compound, where they are barred from frolicking with incoming trucks, and revisiting on my household the trauma I experienced as a little boy, when first Peter, and then Brownie, went off to their greener pastures.

Oh Ducky, how I loved you! And you, Rowley! and Blenhie! And Sam and Fred! Did you know that in China under Mao Tse-tung, owning a dog was a crime? The idea was as simple as this, that if there were dogs about, there would be less food, because dogs consume food. Laid out thus schematically (do you want starving children, or no dogs?) one recognizes the legitimacy of the reasoning. But any legitimate reasoning that means that children can't have a Ducky in the house, or oldsters a Rowley, a Sam, or a Fred, is a regime whose constitution is a fraud, a humbug. Do you need to say anything more about the curse of ideology? Ah, if only my doggies knew the battles I have waged on their behalf! If they did, they would hardly scorn my company in my study, excoriating the evil people who do not tolerate dogs in their kingdom!

———————————

William F. Buckley Jr., is the editor of the *National Review* and host of the syndicated interview show *Firing Line*.

I can't imagine living in a house without a couple of dogs. If I ever got out of bed at night and didn't have to step over a Labrador or two or three, or move one off the covers so I could turn over, my nights would be more restless and the demons that wait in the dark for me would be less easily fended.

—Gene Hill
Tears & Laughter, 1981

Porgy

Mary Higgins Clark

My family (including me) is so allergic that we've not been able to have pets in residence. Our only one, a poodle named Porgy, was Sir George of Washington Township (Georgie/Porgy) and named for the illustrious subject of my first book (the one no one read). Since he had fur not hairs, we were able to have him. We adored him and for the next ten years he took his place as a V.I.P. in the household. Porgy is now in dog heaven. That was a long time ago.

Mary Higgins Clark is the author of mystery, crime and suspense novels. Her recent best sellers include *While My Pretty One Sleeps*, *Loves Music, Loves to Dance* and *All Around the Town*.

Be comforted, little dog, thou too in the Resurrection, shall have a little golden tail.

—Martin Luther
founder of the Reformation

Dogs of My Life

Phyllis Diller

I have a long history with dogs, dogs, dogs. When I was a skinny, freckled little eight-year-old, I visited my aunt and uncle on a big working farm and they had a beautiful collie named Scott who was scared to death of thunder and lightning. They had to let him in the house during storms and he'd slink under the bed and cower and whine till the bad weather passed.

They also had a black and white bull dog of whom I was totally frightened. He had a nasty disposition and I kept my distance.

When I was nine, I was visiting relatives in Toledo, Ohio, and they had a small white terrier. While I was petting him, he went after me like a flash and bit my hand and scared the be-jeezus out of me.

When I was ten, I had a beautiful collie-type shepherd named Jasper, with red and white long fur, a spirited dog. But when he jumped up on a little neighbor boy, they made me give him away. I was heart-broken.

While I was pregnant with my first child in 1940, I had a black cocker spaniel named Mr. Deeds, whom I walked on a country road about two miles every day. It kept us both healthy.

In 1957 I had a huge black Scottie named Joe. He was impossible on a leash—he kept lunging. It would take an Arnold Schwarzenegger to walk him.

Phyllis Diller and Phearless. Without a doubt, "dog owners and their dogs look alike." Photo credit: Courtesy Phyllis Diller

My daughter Suzanne has a little short-haired mongrel named Sasha. The dog is her dear companion and constant comfort.

My daughter Stephanie has the sweetest medium-sized mongrel who was born in the pound and was afraid of grass and just about everything else. The poor dog was a nervous wreck, but through the love and care of a darling family, Theresa is now just a pampered sweet nervous wreck.

My son Perry has a huge black standard poodle named Jeffrey. He is a fine watchdog and gentle with my grandsons, Christopher and Cory.

But the dog-love-of-my-life is Phearless, the pure pedigreed Llasa Apso whose mother was Phyllis Diller. She lived near Dallas in Texas and little puppy Phearless was a gift brought to me at my second symphony concert on New Year's Eve 1971. That precious little pet, the size of a toy, had the softest brownish fur and eyes that looked up at me and melted my soul. When she was full grown she was champagne and white with luxurious fur to the ground.

We had ten great years together and Phearless was photographed, wined and dined by the greats, appeared on television and traveled all over the United States with her adoring mistress.

She sits on a throne in dog heaven, just as regal and uppity as she was in real life. This photo proves beyond the shadow of a doubt that dog owners and their dogs look alike!

Phyllis Diller is a well-known entertainer, actress and author. She is actively involved in animal support groups.

Freckles and Betsy

Curt Gerling

We have owned dachshunds, pointers, beagles and cocker spaniels, but of all the breeds in the dog kingdom, springer spaniels have an irreplaceable hold on my heart. They love you first, then they seek your company by following you about. Their expressive eyes seem either joyful or mournful.

Springer spaniels have many fine qualities, but most of all they love to hunt. They worship your companionship in fields and patiently maintain long waits in duck blinds. They are alert as the quarry nears—it is as though they can hear the flutter of wings and are ready to leap into icy waters at the crack of the gun to retrieve the fallen bird.

Ours seemed deferential and understanding as their master's years slowed them down, and they worked their birds slowly so as not to flush them at too great a distance.

Freckles was our favorite and we hunted together for nearly fifteen years, long after we were both past our prime. When at his death, we were in our sixties, we wept unashamedly as the vet mercifully ended the pain of his debilities.

Freckles's successor and long-time companion was Betsy, a cocker spaniel who from puppyhood was permitted to cruise the fields with the older Freckles. Betsy was a precocious lady and soon rivaled the skills of her running mate.

Betsy had her amorous moments, and her interlude in the driveway with a neighbor's cocker spaniel resulted in her initial accouchement—a litter of six, equally divided in sex. Our wife viewed Betsy's prolific qualities with misgiving—until she discovered that she could get fifty dollars apiece for them. This prompted immediate forgiveness for Betsy's indiscretion and provided a wild afternoon in East Avenue's exclusive shops.

Our long love-in with the animal world ended but a few months ago, when in our semiretirement we selected to move into an apartment and sold our house. The apartment complex is one of the "no pets allowed" ilk and would no doubt frown if we harbored a goldfish. A friend adopted our last springer spaniel and accorded us visiting rights.

If there is a happy hereafter, as the clergy has so long sought to assure us, we presume that our earlier departing friends will be there to greet us, including friends of the canine world. If the latter assumption is correct, we might make an extra effort to join others behind the Pearly Gates. If it would ensure our ascendancy, we would give up our two beers a day, our preprandial martini and forego our tendency to appraise the charms of nubile girls in scanty bikinis.

Anything to assure us a tail-wagging, hand-licking greeting by Freckles and Betsy.

Shortly before his death in 1991, Curt Gerling, age 89, wrote "Freckles and Betsy." Mr. Gerling was a longtime newspaper publisher, columnist and author. He lived in Rochester, New York.

Any woman who does not thoroughly enjoy tramping across the country on a clear frosty morning with a good gun and a pair of dogs does not know how to enjoy life.

—Annie Oakley (1860–1926)
American sharpshooter and vaudevillian

Jim Buck and His Entourage

Olivier Gibbons

The sixty-year-old native New Yorker doesn't like dealing with yuppies or celebrities and only accepts clients living on the East Side. He's demanding and stubborn. He's also New York's premier dog-walker. He's Jim Buck.

"We don't do the West Side. They don't pay their bills," says Jim, who has been raising, training and walking dogs professionally since 1955. "We deal with old-family money."

Old-family money apparently doesn't include celebrities. "Those are the people who won't pay their bills," says the outspoken Jim. "They think they're doing you a favor." Jim doesn't like revealing present clients, but contends a number of show business personalities didn't pay their $50 a week bills.

He first started the business by accident when he agreed to walk a friend's dog. Jim, who trained dogs and horses while growing up, noticed a need for a dog-walking service and took advantage.

President, CEO and chief dog-walker of Jim Buck's School for Dogs, Jim officially begins his day at 4:30 A.M., waking up to a strong cup of coffee and a Pall Mall cigarette. He wears gold-rimmed glasses and has a full head of gray hair and a prominent moustache. He is sporting a blue sweatshirt with matching cap, sneakers and khaki pants. Written in bold white letters on both sweatshirt and cap reads, "Jim Buck's School for Dogs."

By 5:30 A.M. he picks up his first dog at 98th Street and Fifth Avenue and embarks on what will be a four-hour, seven-mile course from Park Avenue to East End Avenue to Fifth Avenue; and from 98th Street to 56th Street. He hasn't missed a day in twenty-nine years.

By 7:30, on a warm, sunny spring day, he and an assistant have picked up nineteen dogs, ranging from a 160-pound Great Dane to a 20-pound miniature poodle.

That's when the adventure starts. Picture Jim, cigarette in mouth, walking twelve dogs at a time, all on separate leashes he holds in both hands. He maneuvers them across busy streets, filled with rush-hour traffic.

When the huge, black Great Dane bends down to poo, Jim abruptly stops the dogs. He waits until the Dane is finished, bends over, removes newspaper from his back pocket and scoops the poop. (He first checks for worms and then discards the newspaper in the nearest garbage can.) "It's a lot like leading a pack of horses. But you have to worry about deranged people and crack addicts messing with the dogs," said Jim, a real-life version of an urban city cowboy.

As Jim waits outside an East Avenue high-rise for yet another dog, he ties the dogs' leashes together. They are lying on the concrete, forming a circle, calm and exceptionally well-behaved.

Jim himself is resting. He lights up a cigarette. "I tried giving up smoking years ago. Went from 160 pounds to 230. It was the last time I tried that."

An Irish setter suddenly emerges from the building. Jim unties the leashes and resumes walking at a pace faster than most people jog.

In the summer, Jim regularly walks the dogs through Carl Schurz Park at East End Avenue and 85th Street and winds up near Gracie Mansion. Frequently, he would run into former New York Mayor Edward Koch, who would wave at him.

In the winter, Jim must brave a windchill of ten degrees as he walks up Fifth Avenue. "As long as you're moving, it's not bad. It's beautiful to see the dogs playing in the snow. They really enjoy it."

For all his troubles, Jim says he charges clients only $50 a week, the same price he collected a decade ago. But Jim has several employees walking dogs for him. He won't tell how many employees he has nor how many dogs are walked each week.

Jim, who plans to retire in ten years, says he is under constant surveillance by dog owners and their friends who monitor the way he handles the dogs.

"Everybody who drives by here knows an owner," Jim says while walking along East End Avenue. "You gotta watch out. Can't be too rough with the dog. Someone will call and complain. Working the East Side is tough. Make one mistake and you're ostracized."

"Hi Jim," a jogger yells out, passing dog-walker and his entourage at 86th and Park Avenue.

"How are you?" Jim replies. This scene is replayed at least half a dozen times each morning, Monday through Friday.

He is a constant among the old-family, Park Avenue crowd, having grown up in a Park Avenue high-rise. Jim, who divorced ten years ago, now shares a one-bedroom apartment off Park Avenue with one of his three grown sons.

"He's great. I've seen him for twelve years every morning," says a woman who identifies herself only as Louise.

Jim's job doesn't begin and end each morning. He is more than just a dog-walker. He helps clients pick out dogs, recommends veterinarians, even rushes to homes to subdue unruly dogs.

He keeps a portable phone in his front left pocket in case of emergency. (When he gets a call while dog-walking, he must shift all the leashes to one hand.) Jim recalls one woman calling him at eleven at night, begging him to stop her dog from attacking a friend.

"I had to run down the street with a bat in my hands. I finally got there and got the dog off this man. . . . The woman had just broken up with her husband and I don't think the dog wanted a new boyfriend," Jim says matter-of-factly.

But Jim doesn't accept just any client or any dog. He first interviews both dog and owner to determine the dog's character, he says. "We'll refuse a dog that is a rogue. We'll take a dog that's rough. We'll take a dog that's shy. But we will not take a rogue. We don't tolerate bullies," he says firmly.

Jim maintains that dogs will take on characteristics of their owners. "If I see a bunch of spoiled children, I know what to expect from the dog."

He says yuppies don't make good dog owners because they are too busy and "irresponsible" and, he adds, "Their dogs are out of shape."

That's not the case with Buck's dogs, who walk up to thirty-five miles a week. "My dogs come back all charged up and full of energy," says Reverend Frances Mercer, who owns two golden retrievers named Daphne and George. Reverend Mercer says that she tries to emulate George, who she describes as secure and comfortable with himself. "It's always been my hope that my personality would be like his. He's a good model for me."

Jim describes his own dog, Samantha, a ten-year-old French shepherd who accompanies him on his walks, as a "no-nonsense sort."

That's probably the best way to describe Jim Buck.

———————

Olivier Gibbons is a staff writer for Gannett Rochester newspapers.

We are alone, absolutely alone on this chance planet, and, amid all the forms of life that surround us, not one, except the dog, has made an alliance with us.

—Maurice Maeterlinck (1862–1949)
Belgian naturalist and poet

Man, Bytes, Dog

James Gorman

Many people have asked me about the Cairn Terrier. How about memory, they want to know. Is it I.B.M.-compatible? Why didn't I get the I.B.M. itself, or a Kaypro, Compaq, or Macintosh? I think the best way to answer these questions is to look at the Macintosh and the Cairn head on. I almost did buy the Macintosh. It has terrific graphics, good word-processing capabilities, and the mouse. But in the end I decided on the Cairn, and I think I made the right decision.

Let's start out with the basics:

MACINTOSH:
  Weight (without printer): 20 lbs.
  Memory (RAM): 128 K
  Price (with printer): $3,090

CAIRN TERRIER:
  Weight (without printer): 14 lbs.
  Memory (RAM): some
  Price (without printer): $250

Just on the basis of price and weight, the choice is obvious. Another plus is that the Cairn Terrier comes in one unit. No printer is necessary, or useful. And—this was a big attraction to me—there is no user's manual.

Here are some of the other qualities I found put the Cairn out ahead of the Macintosh:

PORTABILITY: To give you a better idea of size, Toto in "The Wizard of Oz" was a Cairn Terrier. So you can see that if the young Judy Garland was able to carry Toto around in that little picnic basket, you will have no trouble at all moving your Cairn from place to place. For short trips it will move under its own power. The Macintosh will not.

RELIABILITY: In five to ten years, I am sure, the Macintosh will be superseded by a new model, like the Delicious or the Granny Smith. The Cairn Terrier, on the other hand, has held its share of the market with only minor modifications for hundreds of years. In the short term, Cairns seldom need servicing, apart from shots and the odd worming, and most function without interruption during electrical storms

COMPATIBILITY: Cairn Terriers get along with everyone. And for communications with any other dog, of any breed, within a radius of three miles, no additional hardware is necessary. All dogs share a common operating system.

SOFTWARE: The Cairn will run three standard programs, SIT, COME, and NO, and whatever else you create. It is true that, being microcanine, the Cairn is limited here, but it does load the programs instantaneously. No disk drives. No tapes.

Admittedly, these are peripheral advantages. The real comparison has to be on the basis of capabilities. What can the Macintosh and the Cairn do? Let's start on the Macintosh's turf—income-tax preparation, recipe storage, graphics, and astrophysics problems:

	TAXES	RECIPES	GRAPHICS	ASTROPHYSICS
Macintosh	yes	yes	yes	yes
Cairn	no	no	no	no

At first glance it looks bad for the Cairn. But it's important to look beneath the surface with this kind of chart. If you yourself are leaning toward the Macintosh, ask yourself these questions: Do you want to do your own income taxes? Do you want to type all your recipes into a computer? In your graph, what would you put on the *x* axis? The *y* axis? Do you have any astrophysics problems you want solved?

Then consider the Cairn's specialties: playing fetch and tug-of-war, licking your face, and chasing foxes out of rock cairns (eponymously). Note that no software is necessary. All these functions are part of the operating system:

	FETCH	TUG-OF-WAR	FACE	FOXES
Cairn	yes	yes	yes	yes
Macintosh	no	no	no	no

Another point to keep in mind is that computers, even the Macintosh, only do what you tell them to do. Cairns perform their functions all on their own. Here are some of the additional capabilities that I discovered once I got the Cairn home and housebroken.

WORD PROCESSING: Remarkably, the Cairn seems to understand every word I say. He has a nice way of pricking up his ears at words like "out" or "ball." He also has highly tuned voice-recognition.

EDUCATION: the Cairn provides children with hands-on experience at an early age, contributing to social interaction, crawling ability, and language skills. At age one, my daughter could say "Sit," "Come," and "No."

CLEANING: This function was a pleasant surprise. But of course cleaning up around the cave is one of the reasons dogs were developed in the first place. Users with young (below age two) children will still find this function useful. The Cairn Terrier cleans the floor, spoons, bib, and baby and has an unerring ability to distinguish strained peas from ears, nose, and fingers.

PSYCHOTHERAPY: Here the Cairn really shines. And remember, therapy is something that computers have tried. There is a program that makes the computer ask you questions when you tell it your problems. You say, "I'm afraid of foxes." The computer says. "You're afraid of foxes?"

The Cairn won't give you that kind of echo. Like Freudian analysts, Cairns are mercifully silent; unlike Freudians, they are infinitely sympathetic. I've found that the Cairn will share, in a nonjudgmental fashion, disappointments, joys, and frustrations. And you don't have to know BASIC.

This last capability is related to the Cairn's strongest point, which was the final deciding factor in my decision against the Macintosh—user-friendliness. On this criterion, there is simply no comparison. The Cairn Terrier is the essence of user-friendliness. It has fur, it doesn't flicker when you look at it, and it wags its tail.

Writings by James Gorman, an editor of the *New York Times Magazine*,
have been published in magazines across the country.

[A dog is] a liberal. He wants to please everybody.

—William Kunstler

Dogging the Walk

Donald Hall

Dogs provide an excuse for walking; they love us, we love them, and we walk them because it makes them happy. Gus is a golden/sheepdog cross, affectionate and agreeable, handsome and guilty, who presides over the walkable acreage of our hearts. Like most dogs Gus is an enthusiast, not least for perambulation. In our house as in many, when Jane and I plan the day, we are reduced to spelling our words out: w-a-l-k.

For us it may be walking; for Gus it is running and halting, often combined in a cartoonish maneuver, as Gus skids stopping in mid-sprint, scattering gravel: his acute olfactory sensor has bleeped him information of irresistible fascination. Some woodland creature, seldom encountered, has decorated this bush with an odoriferous Kilroy: coyote, skunk, bear, moose, otter, badger, raccoon, beaver, fisher, fox . . . Who knows?

We live in the country but Gus cannot run loose because our old house sits by a busy two-lane blacktop, Route 4 in New Hampshire, which killed my grandfather's dogs as early as the 1920s. Good walking, however, waits all about us: Our house sits like an egg in a nest of twenty dirt roads, from which old logging trails slant up-mountain. Often we walk Gus on New Canada Road, which lopes its cursive path along the side of Ragged Mountain, up and down—mostly *up*, in both directions. As we trudge onward, Gus will flash into the woods after a flickering chipmunk, disappear into hemlock or birch or ash, and reappear fifty yards ahead, calmly sitting in the ditch to wait for us while we absurdly whistle for him into a dark shade.

Watching him run is one of my favorite activities. I walk doggedly ahead while Gus loses himself head over heels in rapt contemplation of something about a stone which I lack equipment to contemplate. As he applies five minutes of intense rhinal analysis, acute ecstasy of nose, I pump ahead uphill, puffing, making tracks which Gus will cover in one-eighth the time. At the top of the hill, where I can see his whole trajectory, I whistle. Having catalogued five hundred items about examined stone, he looks up and remembers me. He enjoys the game we play: *You walk ahead, I race all-out to catch up.* He coils himself like a spring, flattens on the air, and breaks the all-world up-Ragged hundred-meter record—every afternoon, all over again.

While I trudge, or while I pause for him, my eyes perform like Gus's nose. On New Canada Road I can walk the same path, day after day, and always uncover new glories of the creation. Over the sharply divided seasons I study the stone walls, that used to keep sheep out of corn, as they extend into dense woods. I contemplate the thick-waisted matronly birches, dark hemlocks, and every spring the fragile indomitable ferns. Streams hurtle after rain and turn into the dry stony gulches of August. Snow decorates, leaves fall, moss blossoms—and I walk each day through an anthology of natural growth, change, and stasis, pausing to stare at mossy granite as Gus pauses to inhale.

Six legs walking provide pleasures for two grateful eyes and one lengthy learned nose.

New Hampshire resident Donald Hall's books of poetry include *Here at Eagle Pond* and *Life Work*. He is a highly honored and versatile writer whose most popular work is *Writing Well*. Most recently, he published the children's book *I Am the Dog, I Am the Cat.*

Usurper

Craig B. Hanlon

It was springtime in the city. "Time for work," I said to myself. I locked the side door and headed for my 1972 green Ford parked by the curb in front of my house. It seemed like a pleasant morning until I tried to enter my car.

First, I was met with a snarl-like sound, then a grooowl!

After close inspection, I discovered a small, white, mixed-breed dog about the size of a terrier. He had climbed through a half-open window and was now exercising squatters' rights in my car!

When I opened the door, the dog showed his teeth. Gently, I tried to coax him out, but after several unsuccessful attempts, it occurred to me that one should fight "fire with fire." So I gave the dog my fiercest look and then growled my fiercest growl. It worked! The dog jumped out and I jumped in; I rolled up the window and began to drive away with the dog barking and jumping alongside the car.

I never did see that usurper again. One can only surmise he found a nice big Cadillac.

Craig B. Hanlon resides in Rochester, New York.

They are the only species in the animal kingdom to have truly embraced human beings.

—Jon Winokur
Mondo Canine

Call Waiting

Esther Rudomin Hautzig

Our Brussels griffon dog, Jasper, was so "human" that several times during our years together I actually asked him, upon returning home from the office (albeit late at night and tired), "Did anyone call, Jasper?" This was before answering machines and electronic gadgets. His tiny wiggling tail and head, tilted to the side, were somehow more personal, if less informative, than a flashing light on a brown box.

Author Esther Rudomin Hautzig is the recipient of the Jane Addams Children's Book Award and the Lewis Carroll Shelf Award.

His name is not Wild Dog any more, but First Friend, because he will be our friend for always and always and always.

—Rudyard Kipling (1865–1936)
English author of *Just So Stories*

A Day Gone to the Dogs

Maxine Kumin

Today the mason appears to repair one of the elderly chimneys this house is blessed with. The house is a center-entrance, twin-chimney Colonial of authentic design, built nearly 200 years ago. The chimney has been leaking creosote inside on the second floor for most of that time.

This is a skilled and expensive mason who was expected a month ago. He arrives complete with dog, an aging black part-Labrador bitch who rides in the back of his pickup. She is just enough dog to tantalize our two Dalmatian puppies, who are trouble enough without an accomplice.

Our houseguests from Middlebury arrive *in medias res* with their dog too, a mutt from the local pound and smarter than the three aforementioned animals. His name is Byron, which does not necessarily have anything to do with the poet Byron. The husband wanted to call the dog Clank. The wife protested that you can't go around calling a dog, "Here, Clank!" It doesn't work, one harsh syllable like that.

She wanted to call the dog Guido. The husband said that you can't go around calling a dog Guido, for Pete's sake, it sounds like a restaurant. So they compromised on Byron, with equal accents on both syllables, which makes a spondee, and is a very callable name.

While we are conducting this amiable discourse, large, tricolored (part Great Dane?) Byron sits grinning. Evidently he has heard this explanation before.

The mason is on the roof by now, ripping out bricks and casting them down at a great rate. He is also ripping out the original authentic ancient chimney tiles and dropping them. He finds the offending leaky tile and begins his repair.

The situation gets a little heady on the roof, what with his shifting the ladder, lifting bricks in great clusters, hauling up cement by the bucket-load. Before any of us can think to mention what may happen, the mason puts ladder and self through an upstairs storm window. The sound glass makes as it shatters is quite musical.

In the midst of all this, or perhaps as a result, the two Dal puppies disappear with Byron. The visiting wife and I are selected to go find them. We hike up the hill toward the strawberry farm, our nearest neighbor in a westerly direction. Grueling through clouds of mosquitoes and almost visible humidity, we call Byron and the puppies, whose names, if they paid any attention to them, are Gus and Claude. Byron at length appears. The puppies have gone disobediently elsewhere.

We return. There is no long confab as a result of the fallen glass, which is everywhere. The puppies materialize out of the woods stickered with burdock burs. We close the dogs on the porch, turn our backs on the work scene, I get lunch on the table, and we enjoy a relaxed meal. It is pleasant to entertain old friends. We push back from the table in a mood of mutual self-congratulation.

The houseguests now pack to depart, as the husband has a lesson (he sings) in Middlebury and they will just get back in time for it if they hurry. Consternation hits: Byron is missing, and along with him, the black Lab belonging to the mason.

Leaving the mason on the roof to contend with the remnants of bricks, tiles, glass, and the like, the visiting husband and my husband, Victor, set out to find the missing Byron and Ophelia (the less pedigreed the dog the more elegant its name). They decide to search the strawberry fields of the neighboring farmer, one alp above our own, but will do so by driving down to town, cruising under the highway, and up the other side of the hill to the berry farm.

The visiting wife and I, after a conference in which we agree we can

Maxine Kumin with Appendix Quarter Horse Duffy, dog Josh and Dalmatian dog Gus. Gus has since died and is very missed. Photo credit: Craig Blouin.

do nothing, decide to lie in the sun and have a beer. Just as the men vanish downhill Byron reappears, dripping wet from the pond. We leap into the visitors' car and take off to intercept the men in hopes that the husband can leave early enough to have his music lesson after all.

Halfway down the hill the car feels sluggish, unwilling, lumpy—flat tired. Byron, panting in the back seat, threatens to approach heat prostration. We feed him ice cubes out of a cooler and lean back, waiting for the men to return from their fruitless search for the dog now in our possession.

Four or five hours later, our houseguests depart. The mason leaves with his rediscovered Ophelia. He does not clean up behind himself; he is too highly skilled for that. Less highly skilled, I sweep up half a ton of cement dust, pick up several shards of glass that have escaped his casual scrutiny, and find a safe place in the barn to store the broken storm window frame.

The chimney is clean and does not leak. Inside the house at the chimney cleanout—a little trap door that would be eye level for a mouse—there is an additional pile of creosote and dust. Thank you, expensive mason. This chimney is now certified for winter. The cost of certification would possibly have paid for installing an oil burner and filling it for a season.

A day later, the next house guest arrives two hours after the time agreed on for a carefully planned Saturday picnic lunch. He comes carrying a huge floral arrangement from the last place he visited. It's too late. Victor and I were so hungry we have already eaten, but we go through the motions.

This guest is not allergic to poison ivy. His annual house present is to pull up great swatches of it all around our pond, where it is creeping luxuriantly. We celebrate its removal with the first swim of the season. The puppies stand on the diving rock and bark frantically as their master and mistress disappear into the enormous drinking-water dish. They will not be coaxed into this element. If God had intended them to swim, they say they would have webbed feet, right?

Suddenly Ophelia appears, crashing through the underbrush, and does a racing dive off the rock. It is clearly a rescue situation. She is intent on saving any one of the three of us she can reach. As the houseguest is the closest to shore, she goes for him. Only our vigorous intervention keeps him from drowning in the grip of her enthusiasm.

The expensive mason has refigured his bill and wishes now to adjust the amount he was paid downward by $12.75, which he judges to be the replacement cost of the fractured pane. He was in the neighborhood anyway, so he thought he would just drop by. Finding no one at home, he adduced that we might be using the pond. His words exactly. As for Ophelia, it is in the breed to fetch things from the water. The long scratch down our houseguests's forearm attests to her zeal. The mason promises he will clip her toenails tonight.

After only a brief palaver, we all repair to the house for iodine. Victor seems to think the situation calls for beer, and the mason is right behind him as he peers into the refrigerator. Before either of them can straighten up, Ophelia is gone again, and with her the puppies.

Maxine Kumin, a recipient of the Pulitzer Prize for Poetry in 1973,
is an author, poet, lecturer and nature enthusiast. She lives
in New England and has two dogs.

A person who has never owned a dog has missed
a wonderful part of life.

—Bob Barker

Pushkin

Jerre Mangione

I had a most cheerful relationship with a dog named Pushkin, a French poodle who came with a previous wife. He was most likable and far more humorous.

I remember two demonstrations of his humor. On a Fifth Avenue shopping trip in front of Saks Fifth Avenue, his need for attention and admiration caught up with him and, standing on two paws, he did a dance near the doorway, evoking shouts of admiration from the shoppers.

His other antic took place when we were in the living room with a number of guests. Feeling left out, Pushkin went to my bedroom, found an old sock of mine and, rushing downstairs, deposited it in the very center of the circle of guests.

Jerre Mangione is a professor emeritus of English at the University of Pennsylvania. He is the author of *Mount Allegro* and ten other books of fiction and nonfiction.

A dog coming and staying in your house is an omen of wealth.
A dog has no aversion to a poor family.
To be followed home by a stray dog is a sign of impending wealth.

—Proverbs of China and Japan

The Dog, the Stars,
the President

Rick Marsi

When was the last time the President woke up on a January night and had to let the dog out? It's probably been years, and more's the pity, because the poor guy is missing out on some great astronomy.

I had such an opportunity not long ago—it was garbage night, a Thursday—and came away deeply enriched.

It all started when a dog nose appeared on the pillow and nudged with obvious insistence. These nudges, I have learned through years of trial and error, mean, "Let me out, I am plagued by gastrointestinal irregularity."

My usual response is to bolt upright, make with great haste for the front door and facilitate in any way possible this canine flight to freedom. On garbage nights, however, the routine is fraught with added responsibility. On these occasions, I, too, must venture outside, there to serve as chaperone.

For the wind on garbage night is laced with tempting innuendo. Pork chop bones from up the road, potato skins from down—the siren scent of sin is everywhere. The self restraint of well-intentioned pets melts upon contact.

So outward into the darkness I plunged—in pajamas, overcoat and rubber boots—to contemplate what the President was missing. He missed Orion, mostly, and a feeling of relative human insignificance.

Often called the Mighty Hunter, Orion is a constellation of sprawling brilliance, more beautiful than any other in the winter sky. On frigid nights, it beams through the southern heavens with breathtaking clarity.

People who enjoy picturing things say the stars in Orion show him standing with a club raised in one hand and a lion skin shield in the other. They also say his right shoulder is marked by a giant star, Betelgeuse. I would tell you how to pronounce Betelgeuse but am not sure. I tried "beetle juice" once and wasn't rebuked by a nearby cluster of serious sky watchers, so maybe "beetle juice" is right.

In addition to possessing a shield and large shoulders, Orion also is reputed to own a star-studded belt and a left ankle dominated by a blue-white star called Rigel. Looking up, I really couldn't catch all this. I just saw dazzling pinheads, beautiful and far away.

After staring at the Mighty Hunter for awhile, thinking about light years, specks of cosmic dust, and other humbling things, I drew an imaginary line from his belt toward the southeastern horizon. There, just over the top of a hill, I found Sirius, the most dazzling of all winter stars.

Blazing away from a distance of eight or nine light years, Sirius is universally known as the "Dog Star," a name supposedly derived from its location in the constellation Canis Major, or The Great Dog.

Out there on garbage night, I saw things differently. Watching my own dog sniff the breeze, I pegged Sirius as the patron saint of earthbound canines, lighting their way toward pork chops and potato skins.

Gazing out at this brightest star, absorbing the vastness of its celestial medium, I easily could have lost myself in a sky beyond dimension. I might have, too, had it not been for a tiny window of vulnerability between the bottom of my overcoat and the top of my rubber boots. This single weak link was allowing brutally cold air to infiltrate my defense perimeter and gnaw away at flannel pajamas.

There was a whistle for the dog and a retreat over snow that glowed eerie white. Sirius remained behind, sparkling through the branches of a large Scotch pine.

"That's the only trouble with astronomy in January," I mumbled, now inside and fumbling with large boots. "It takes place outdoors, at night, when most people prefer being indoors, gazing at television."

My last reverie before drifting off was about the President. Do you think he ever goes out late at night and stares up at the winter sky? If he had a dog around the place, he might. Otherwise, probably not.

Naturalist Rick Marsi is an author of books and an award-winning, nationally syndicated columnist. He writes for the *Press & Sun-Bulletin*, Binghamton, New York.

Not Carnegie, Vanderbilt and Astor together could have raised money enough to buy a quarter share in my little dog.

—Ernest Thompson Seton (1860–1946)
American writer and naturalist

Birthday Party

Thomas S. Monaghan

In regard to dogs, my most memorable thoughts concern my daughter's dogs and her fondness for them. In fact, one day while working at the office, she hosted a birthday party for one of her Newfoundlands and the party was attended by dogs of other coworkers. It was a hectic few hours, but I believe the guests enjoyed themselves.

Thomas S. Monaghan is the Chairman of the Board
and owner of Domino's Pizza, Inc.

You should keep dogs—fine animals—sagacious.

—Charles Dickens
The Pickwick Papers

Chaucer's Tale

Barbara Murphy

Chaucer's my name; protection, my game.

I, of course, didn't pick my name—my owner chose it. As an English teacher, she thought that given my elegant posture and imposing nature, I needed a distinguished name. Besides, she has commented that the original Chaucer had not been able to finish writing his ambitious *Canterbury Tales* and that maybe I could find the time to do so. When I was young, she placed papers and pens all over the house when she left for work. I suppose that was what the papers were for, but I found other uses.

I weigh in at ninety-six pounds. My original color was a chocolate brown, but over the years, even my roots have turned to taupe. Standard poodles are rare in this area, especially those of my light brown color, so I do attract attention wherever I go.

I was born in a farmhouse near Lockport, New York. When my owner visited the farm, she chose me instead of one of my five brothers because I was the most lively. I've been told, often, that as we drove away, my dog mother could be heard issuing a sigh of relief.

My job is to protect my house—and, in fact, all four houses on Lewis Street—from all who dare to pass by. This includes mailmen, delivery boys, meter readers and sundry cats, dogs and squirrels. Fortunately, because of my size and basso profundo, I have never been forced into a confrontation.

A few well-chosen warnings and no one touches our door. I really am not aggressive—in fact, I would hold the flashlight if they wanted to take the silver.

Since we live across the street from a park, my second role is that of greenskeeper. This self-appointed job is time-consuming, but most important in keeping up the appearance of the neighborhood.

Every season brings its own problems with this second job. In the spring the four baseball diamonds are swarming with activity. My first task involves traffic control and the mothers of the future Hank Aarons who must drive their cars to see their offspring perform. Needing to park as close to the action as possible, these fanatic Mario Andrettis race down our little street for the few spaces available, creating much ado about little. A cacophony of horns jangling with sounds of crunching metal keeps me alert as I bark parking instructions and driving rules from my front window vantage point. Our driveway is never still, for the mothers, vying for parking spots, need to turn around to re-enter the fray.

After the game I police the scene of battle with my walker. Since the midget ball players save all their throwing prowess for the cylindrical orb, all manner of their trash is tossed carelessly on the ground. Wonderful fast-food boxes, pizza crusts, and bubble-gum wrappers never reach the green trash cans stationed at each of the four diamonds. My job is to examine each abandoned article, and then let my walker properly dispose of the debris.

My perk, however, is that in today's affluent society, the young see no need to search for lost balls, so they are just left there for the harvest. I have the best collection of hard and soft balls in Fairport. Since I take three walks a day and am on constant lookout for good specimens, my ball collection is enormous.

Summer brings the men's softball league. They leave behind softballs that are more challenging for me to pick up. I have been known to carry a softball all around the block, if I find it when the walk begins.

The tennis courts yield the greatest booty. Fuzzy yellow balls fit my mouth beautifully and can be spotted easily, even when the grass needs mowing.

Fall deposits piles of crunchy leaves for me to plow through and scatter, plus they abound with summer smells and forgotten treasures. This also is the time for activity on the soccer field. Once I found a soccer ball and refused to go home without it. My walker emphatically said no, but I was steadfast. I tightened every neck muscle and she tugged on my leash and choke collar. But I stood my ground. I tried to maneuver the ball but by mouth was not large enough to get a good grasp. I knew that she would not pick it up for me, so I dribbled it home using my nose and front paws. Frustrated and defeated, she did lift it into the house. Such fun I had with that treasured soccer ball.

In winter, activity slows down in the park. I romp in snow drifts and try to remember that a leash attaches me to the old lady. She, looking not unlike Nanuk of the North in layers of scarves, boots and such, valiantly mushes through the deep snow behind me.

My life is good. I eat table food and have a dish of dog treats each morning. I get three twenty-minute walks a day and, since I usually retire before the eleven o'clock news, I get the choice spot on the bed.

Of course, this relationship is not all take, for I also give. I give my walker a lot of exercise. I force her to eat decent meals. I maintain her neighborhood and park. I give her lots of love and attention. And most of all—I give her protection.

Barbara Murphy, a retired high school English teacher, is a part-time instructor at local colleges in upstate New York.

Nor does anyone who ever owned a dog need to be told the sound a man makes as he bends over a dog that has been his for many years.

—Eric Knight (1897–1943)
American writer and drama critic

For the Love of Fame

Sally Jessy Raphael

With an endless assortment of children and animals living under one roof, there was always some absurd crisis that gave comic relief to my problems.

None was more absurd than the day our jet black jumbo poodle, named Fame, walked out the apartment door and disappeared for an entire morning. To me, the incident has become a parable of my life in broadcasting. Maybe it's because I've always had a special attachment to fame, in all its forms!

We had gotten the dog in Puerto Rico, and for a while we had two dogs: Fame and a dachshund named Fortune. We gave Fortune away and were left with Fame; that tells you something about our sense of priorities.

Fame was a rare creature, a huge Argentine breed that was the size of a St. Bernard. We loved him dearly, but he was too big to take with us on various family outings. That's how it happened that we left Fame behind one weekend when we went off on a trip. With him in the apartment was fifteen-year-old Alexandra, the daughter of a good friend of mine from Puerto Rico. Alexandra was one of those kids who happened to drop into our lives for a year or two and become part of the family.

Since I didn't want to leave Alexandra and Fame unattended, I had asked my friend Sandy Keay, who lived in New Jersey, to come stay and look after them. Actually it wasn't Alexandra I was worried about. It was Fame.

Early Saturday morning Sandy was awakened by a loud buzz over the intercom.

"Your dog has just run out the door!" said the doorman.

As it turned out, Alexandra had gone to the laundry room, leaving the door ajar. Fame, seeing his opening, walked down the hall, threw himself against the door to the stairwell, climbed down the stairs, and ran through the lobby before anyone could do anything about it. The front doors to the building open automatically, so Fame just kept going.

The last the doorman saw him, he was trotting down Seventy-second Street, probably singing to himself, "Free again, I'm free again."

When Sandy heard from the doorman that the dog had disappeared, she threw a coat over her pajamas and raced out the door to look for him. Like a maniac, she ran up and down the streets of the Upper East Side, asking everyone she saw, "Have you seen a dog?"

Finally, in desperation, she spotted a police box and called for help. But when the cops pulled up in the squad car, they were less than thrilled.

"Lady, in New York City you don't ring the police if your dog is gone."

"Please," she begged. "I'm watching this dog for someone. You've got to help me."

It must have been a slow day at the precinct because the cops put her in the squad car and then drove up and down the streets, canvassing the neighborhood.

At every block Sandy stuck her head out the squad car and yelled, "Fame! Fame!"

After a fruitless search the cops dropped her off on the street and left her to her wanderings. Four hours later, demoralized, she returned to the house. But when she opened the door to the apartment, there to her astonishment, was Fame. He jumped on her with delight and started barking with joy.

Sandy, of course, was more confused than ever. Was it all a dream?

Was she going nuts? Had the dog been in the apartment all the time, while she had searched the streets for hours in her pajamas?

Later the police filled her in. Soon after they had left Sandy on the street, Fame had trotted by. They brought him home in the squad car, and the doorman had let him into the apartment.

Sandy was so overwhelmed by the whole experience that the minute she saw Fame, she just sat down and sobbed.

When we returned from our weekend trip and heard about Sandy's ordeal, I started laughing and crying at the same time. Her search for Fame was the story of my life! I might as well have been in the squad car, yelling out, "Fame! Fame!"

Sally Jessy Raphaël, a 1989 Emmy Award recipient for best day-time talk show host, is a popular television and radio personality. She is passionate about causes involving animal rights.

Never have I experienced a serenity and sweetness of disposition as with my Chocolate Lab.

—Mortimer B. Zuckerman

Me and My Coauthor

Alfred Slote

I showed this picture of my fox terrier, Freddie, and me to a class of kids in Kansas. I said, "Here's a picture of me and my coauthor." And this one kid, a boy, said, seriously, "Which one is the coauthor?" I was stunned. Now I just tell kids I go around the country taking credit while Freddie does the writing.

Alfred Slote. Photo credit: Suzanne Coles.

Alfred Slote is a novelist and children's fiction writer. Mr. Slote resides in Ann Arbor, Michigan.

Great men always have dogs.

—Ouida
English novelist

The Chance of a Lifetime

Sally Ann Smith

Cassie, our chocolate Labrador, got another piece of junk mail today—she's been getting a lot lately. A while back I filled out one of those long questionnaires that appears in your mailbox promising great riches if you will only give them a mass of data on yourself.

Six months later when your free gift box of goodies arrives it turns out to be three Alka-Seltzer tablets and a mini tube of toothpaste. I got so aggravated by them I STRUCK BACK and filled one out for Cassie L.(ab) Smith, and one for Cory B.(asenji) Smith. Old Cory must not have looked too promising since he said he drank at least a six pack a day, and smoked two packs a day.

Cassie's I don't remember as clearly, but she appealed to the bronzed baby shoe folks. She kept getting bi-monthly offers to have her baby shoes bronzed. After two years of this, I decided whoever owned the original questionnaire must not be selling names and addresses actively. I almost wrote back to tell the company Cassie was still using her baby shoes.

Good thing I didn't because a couple months ago, she received a huge pack of post cards with offers for great bargains in gold and silver. She returned every one with postage paid. Each said literature would not be sent unless a phone number and time to call was included. Yeah, sure!

The cards further insisted a "convenient time for them to call" be given. Only the fear of mysterious computer-generated numbers also on each card could trace the source prevented me from giving to at least twenty-five of these firms the names and phone numbers of a couple of my least favorite people. (I would have also told them the ideal time to call my hit list was "between 2 A.M. and 4 A.M.")

Cassie coped with the phone number situation like this:

Home Phone—yes
Work Phone—no

Her occupation was "companion." Several companies, one from Texas, one from Canada, and one from Colorado, sent her glossy expensive mailings. They must have decided "companion" sounded promising. Especially one who doesn't read small print well enough to realize a phone number was being asked for.

But Cassie has decided not to invest in mining stocks or gold coins. Today she got a much better offer from a gentleman who will sell her a way to get rich quick in the pyramid mailing game. Just send twenty dollars to this guy, and mail one hundred letters to the addresses he will provide on preprinted labels.

Cassie will be rich beyond her wildest dreams in six months. Then she'll be able to afford a classic motor car. There's a company in Florida offering her this chance of a lifetime.

The only problem will be that these cars have to be assembled by the purchaser. Right! After a lot of glittering prose about an "amazing investment in design and engineering," and capturing "a windblown memory reborn as a modern motoring adventure" comes the bad news—you have to "assemble your own classic."

Since Cassie is all paws when it comes to anything mechanical, I suppose she'll have to pass up this opportunity too. Besides, she'll need to have a little something stashed away for her old age.

We tell Cassie we'll still love her if these great opportunities don't work out and she has to stay a companion the rest of her life. So far she hasn't expressed an opinion about all this, but the other day I did see her inspecting the financial pages of the paper with some interest. It was a relief to find a chew bone buried underneath the pile.

So that's how Cassie's investment opportunities are progressing at the moment. Just wanted you to know.

Sally Ann Smith is a teacher and writer. She resides in Jasper, Georgia.

They give unconditional love and undying loyalty in return for regular meals and an occasional pat on the head.

—Jon Winokur
Mondo Canine

Dogs and an Old Tree

Robert G. Wehle

Imagine what this great old water oak tree has experienced over its many years—surely three hundred or more. Probably saw the camp fires of the Creek Indians living in the area before it was decided they had to leave.

In the winter of 1836, the United States Army forcibly marched these native Americans from Alabama to Oklahoma. Few survived the ordeal. Hunger, thirst and cold took its toll. Today their route is known as the Trail of Tears. Our society shall bear its blight forever. Hard to conceive a peace-loving people could behave in such a primitive fashion.

Think of this old tree's association with other forms of life. Hundreds of quail fed on its acorns and used its shade on hot summer days. Mourning doves enjoyed its security and shelter for many years.

Now again in primitive fashion, we are destroying. We are destroying beautiful quail and are possessed to shoot the last dove in our frenzy to consume or destroy everything good on earth.

Soon nothing will be left for those coming behind us. Should we not protect and preserve the great gift of natural wonders we are blessed with and so many of us cherish?

At a time when most people of the world have discovered peace and are learning to live in a democratic society, we need to give up our primitive behavior to shoot the last grouse, to catch the last trout and to kill the last wolf. Will our next generation remember us for destroying wildlife as we remember those who allowed the Trail of Tears?

Far better if instead, with a fine bird dog, we enjoyed the presence of the grouse and watched it fly off to reproduce, to be enjoyed again and again. Or should we put a stop to all this splendor forever?

The essence of the great sport of bird dogs is not the killing of the game but the pursuit of it. It's the joy of watching a finely bred, carefully honed pointer performing his artful skills and proudly displaying grand qualities inherited over the centuries.

It pains me when I hear tales of these wonderful animals being mistreated in their training. It doesn't seem possible that people can be so abusive to the undisputed aristocrat of the bird dog world. Rather they should enjoy and respect his great hunting qualities, warm personality, intelligence and unwavering loyalty. These are the characteristics that make the pointer so responsive to kindness and good treatment.

We should be forever grateful for inheriting such a magnificent animal as the English pointer. Six or seven hundred years of selective breeding have resulted in great attributes that we take for granted today.

Historians claim the pointer was carried throughout Europe in the days of crusades and later bred and enjoyed generation after generation by royal families, noblemen and aristocrats.

Eventually they migrated to the English Isles, where for the last few centuries they were bred and enjoyed by British aristocracy. From this source most of our early imports originated. It is exciting to think that the very pointer sleeping in your kennel tonight has such an illustrious heritage.

Let's enjoy and respect this great dog and respond to his warmth and devotion. And let's have this great old tree be witness to us as we spare the bird.

———

Robert G. Wehle divides his time between his business interests and Elhew Kennels located in New York and Alabama. For over sixty years, he has bred, trained and campaigned some of the world's finest English pointers.

Let's have this great old water oak tree be witness to us.

PART IV

Early Childhood Education

Writer Claire Romanof said it best: "There is something almost mystical between children and dogs"—the wooly coats of our childhood.

The dogs of yesteryear are recalled with humor, joy and appreciation by Chip Block, Norman P. Leonardson and Leonore R. Mandelson. Surprise awaits us in the writing of young Emily Dysinger.

Mary Stolz presents a complete and never-before-published dog story for children. "Fifi Sue" leaves readers cheering for one determined little dog.

Fred Rogers and Ruth E. Hyland recommend the child and dog-as-mentor combination. Alice R. Barletta, Nancy M. Charcholla and Beverly M. Chizek document the unique partnership.

Gaga

Alice R. Barletta

According to my storytellers, I was only a year old and in my buggy when the black puppy came to live at our house. I looked down and uttered the famous words of a one-year-old: "Gaga."

Obviously my parents doted on my every word because that's what they named the innocent puppy. And that wonderful Scottie never knew what an incredibly foolish name she had! She gave the name great dignity. She elevated the infantile muttering, Gaga, to great stature. To me, my family and our friends, Gaga was just about the absolute epitome of doghood.

Through all her thirteen human years, the little Scottish terrier remained forever a lady. I never remember her growling or showing her teeth. The perky little black dog with the ridiculous name Gaga is prominent in all the many pictures of my childhood.

My earliest memories include crawling with Gaga on a scratchy rug and cuddling together under the dining room table.

Alice Marie, a large-as-life doll, and Gaga were my first playmates. Often our gentle and unsuspecting pet was dressed in her doll clothes. My unbridled love cost Alice Marie most of her hair and the loss of an arm. The black Scottie fared not much better: Her sway back was reminiscent of my toddler days when I would plunk down on her soft black fur. Her tail forever drooped, the result of my constant tugging.

Because my father loved to take pictures, there are many photographs of my brother and me growing up, and Gaga is in most of those old snapshots. There I am, a towheaded three-year-old, instructing the black Scottie to sit up; and there's another shot with my doll buggy and Gaga. Whenever the family gathered, whenever there was a birthday party or a holiday, Gaga was always conspicuous. She was as loyal as an indulgent grandparent and as constant as the changing seasons.

I grew up. Gaga aged, grew gray and moved more slowly. I went off with friends and started eyeing boys. Though often neglected for more exciting pals, Gaga still waddled to meet me at the front door, always delighted at any crumb of affection.

As she grew older, my loyal pet started sleeping a lot. She had trouble with her short arthritic legs. We began to carry her up and down the stairs, or out to the backyard and back into the house.

Quietly and with little fuss, Gaga died as she had lived. I came home from school one noontime, and through tears my mother told me Gaga had died that morning. My first true friend in this world was no longer with me.

Over forty years have passed and I can still feel the pain of that first major loss in my life. Gaga was my wonderful teacher of patience, kindness and unconditional love.

———————

Alice R. Barletta is an executive secretary. She is a long-time supporter of the Humane Society of Rochester and Monroe County.

Not the least hard thing to bear when they go from us, these quiet friends, is that they carry away with them so many years of our own lives.

—John Galsworthy (1867–1933)
English writer, *Memories*

The Case of the Missing Rib Roast

Chip Block

Buddy Boy was my first dog, a bright red Irish setter. I was two years old, living in Phoenix, Arizona, when my father opened a box and out popped Buddy. It is my very first memory of a very happy childhood.

The year was 1947. Buddy was about two months old when he arrived at our house. He and I were crazy about each other. He was very protective of me, which was a good thing, since we lived on the edge of a desert called Dreamy Draw.

As we grew older together, Buddy and I chased jackrabbits, gila monsters and other desert creatures. We tried, without much success, to pluck grapefruits from our neighbor's orchard. He went everywhere with me, to the barbershop, to my friends' homes, even to parochial school, where the nuns tolerated his waiting for me after classes.

Buddy was a very smart, athletic dog. He could run like the wind, he was courageous (he scared the daylights out of our neighbor's fierce billy goat) and he was always getting into trouble. His problem was that he was both hungry and curious all the time. Everything was interesting to him, especially where food was concerned. He was a hearty eater, not at all picky, and his taste ranged from roses to gila monsters and scorpions.

Nothing made Buddy's eyes light up, however, like a nice piece of meat. Usually that meat was part of something like the Andersons' chickens or the aforementioned goats. Buddy became famous around the Draw for his persistence in pursuing his quest for gustatory satisfaction.

One day, Mrs. Anderson, who set a fine table, was cooking a rib roast for her family and guests. Now, we all knew when she was cooking because the hot desert wind carried the delicious aroma from her kitchen for miles around. Buddy got a good whiff of that rib roast.

Mrs. Anderson made very few mistakes in her kitchen. But she made one that day. She left the roast cooking, went out to do some errands and came home a few hours later. Her biggest mistake, however, was in not shutting the door tight. When she arrived, the oven door was open, the pan was on the floor and a trail of drippings was all that was left of her beautiful roast.

She suspected that a hungry passerby might have made off with her dinner, so she began to canvass the area to see if anyone had seen a stranger around the neighborhood. When she came to our house, my mother told her that she hadn't seen anyone. I was playing cowboys and Indians with Buddy and my friend Tommy Marian in the backyard. Buddy was the Indian.

Mom asked Tommy and me if we had seen anyone. We had not. Now, Buddy had been an especially happy and frisky Indian that day. Mom looked at the erstwhile Apache brave with a questioning glance. Buddy looked back, like Cochise under his war bonnet, and ran for it like Mom was the U.S. Cavalry. Must have been a guilty conscience.

Mom found what was left of the roast (a few cloves of garlic) in her rose garden and went to explain to Mrs. Anderson. Buddy came back, thinking the coast was clear.

Mom and Mrs. Anderson negotiated whatever solution adults contrive under such circumstances. I suggested rather urgently to Cochise, er, Buddy, the he head for the hills. My empathy was all for him. When Mom came out, carrying a hoe, I feared that Buddy was headed for the Happy Hunting Ground. But Mom was laughing so hard that she couldn't catch Buddy, who was running in circles, making happy war whoops. Mrs. Anderson never forgave Buddy, but everyone else loved the story of the enterprising Irish setter who opened the kitchen door, the oven door, took the roast and had a feast. Buddy, already famous, had become a legend.

Chip Block is the founder of *Games* magazine and a consultant to magazine publishers throughout the country.

Zenda

Nancy M. Charcholla

She was a roly-poly, beautiful puppy with white and tan colors. We got her at the Humane Society way back when it was located at Henrietta. She was only a few months old but had that wonderful dignity and regal bearing associated with collies. She looked purebred but her nose wasn't long. There was shepherd back in her heritage.

She was smart and well-behaved except when left alone. Then she chewed all the cushions on the glider.

I wanted a unique name for her and when I saw an old magazine ad for the movie *Prisoner of Zenda*, Zenda fit.

Our oldest son was two years old when we got Zenda. We were living on a farm in Henrietta. He liked to wander around while I was busy with his six-month-old brother. One day I heard him crying. I finally found him in one of the big barns with Zenda by his side. He said a big mouse had frightened him. I'm sure it was a rat and that Zenda chased it away.

When our second son started to walk, Zenda stayed by his side and if he started to fall, he would grab her.

When we moved to the city, she followed all the neighborhood kids to school.

Our next move was to a small village. Next to our home was an empty lot where all the kids played baseball and football, depending on the season. When anyone tackled one of our boys, Zenda took the tackler's arm in her mouth to gently warn him not to hurt her boys. She protected them and followed them everywhere.

As she got older, she had to have some teeth extracted. We brought her home from the vet before she was completely out of the anesthetic. We laid her in the back hall, but she heard the kids leaving and struggled to get up to follow. She was staggering so she couldn't walk. We had three sons at this time, and her life's work was to watch and protect them.

Her bad habit was chasing cars and trucks. We lived on a corner with a road going to the left of our house. Zenda would lie in the front yard and she knew when a car was going to turn left before the directional was even put on. She would cut across the lot and catch the car at the top of the hill.

One day a man came into the backyard where I was hanging clothes and he said, "I just hit your dog." And there she was, standing beside him, just fine. She was blessed.

The whole town knew Zenda. On Sundays when we went to church, she would walk quietly down the center aisle looking for her boys. When we gave her a frown, she'd go back and lie in the vestibule.

Zenda was loved and loving. She went on all vacations with us; she would have been broken-hearted to be left home. She was family.

Our next move was to a larger house, one in the village, and it had an upstairs. Zenda was getting on in years (she was fourteen at the time). She always slept next to our beds, but someone had to boost her from behind up the stairs and carry her down in the morning.

The day came when we had to make a tearful decision. We think she had a stroke. She was no longer living with dignity. We went to the vet and we all had our hands on her as he gave her the shot. She just closed her eyes and was at peace. We brought her home and buried her in the backyard.

We still live in this small town. Our boys have grown up and left home. Our middle son lives next door through the woods with his four sons, and I wait for the day when they get a little older and have a friend and companion as their dad had in Zenda.

Nancy M. Charcholla lives in Bergen, New York. She recently adopted a part miniature collie named Bandit from the Humane Society.

With Allegiance to Sam

Beverly M. Chizek

Born in the bicentennial year, 1976, and appropriately named Sam, he was an independent, rollicking, lolloping, good-natured dog of uncertain lineage but predominantly Doberman and hound. His smooth, black coat, broken up by the "copper penny" above each eye and corresponding shirt front, gave him a formal and formidable appearance—belied by the floppy ears and long, wagging tail.

We should have known from the day we met him at Lollypop Farm Animal Shelter that he would be a part of our lives forever. This eight-week-old pup pushed himself to the front of the cage, barking, whining and pressing his paws against the wire mesh while his sparkling amber eyes begged, "Take me, take me! I'm the one for you." He and our son exchanged glances and for the next ten years he was ours, or rather, we were his.

He became a legend in his own time and, even now, five years after his passing, we still remember and tell "Sam stories" whenever the family is together.

He became the "drop out" of the obedience class because he never completed the final class, but he never forgot the basics. Sam loved to show off his training and at the end of a leash he became a truly noble beast—heeling, wheeling, dropping, stopping, and snapping to attention like a Marine recruit. Off the leash he ran like a deer, stretching out as flat as any Derby winner and flying over field and stream.

Sam was at once the best of dogs and the worst. He was bright, lively, full of fun and the most well-behaved of canine companions; but left alone in the house while everyone went off to work and school, he became a monster—wreaking destruction upon anything in the basement that he could sink his teeth or paws into. We still have the tooth marks and torn wood scars to remind us of his anger at being left behind.

Sam was the Houdini of the dog world—scaling fences, opening doors, going out windows and otherwise squeezing his fifty-five-pound body through unbelievably small places to effect an escape from captivity.

He was our family pet but had special affection for our son and his friends. Sam became "one of the boys" and followed faithfully wherever and whenever he was allowed. In this fashion, he became a neighborhood pet as well.

After our son left for college, Sam canvassed the neighborhood looking for the boys. He entered the back door of our neighbor's house and just walked in—absolutely sure that he would be welcome. It came as a great surprise to him when the neighbor's cat took umbrage at his invasion of her territory and boxed his ears smartly.

Another neighborhood mother, who didn't know Sam, was prevented from hitting him with a frying pan when her son yelled, "Don't hit him, don't hit him! That's Sam!" as though that explained why this dog had suddenly appeared in her kitchen, uninvited.

Sam gallantly and chivalrously accepted our daughter's cat, which we were prevailed upon to adopt when she moved across the country. Actually, after the first few days, chivalry turned to fear as the cat proceeded to take over the house, as cats usually do. From that point on, there was a special relationship between them. They had some unspoken but clearly defined rules of their own making, and the rest of the time they were playful and tolerant companions. They raced through the house one way—dog chasing cat—and returned the other way—cat chasing dog.

Sam's wanderlust led him into trouble many times. He was pursued by the police, returned by the dog warden and had many narrow escapes from oncoming cars, but it never deterred him from seeking adventure wherever it might be found.

He had only one fear—that of loud noises, particularly thunder and fireworks. These noises drove him absolutely frantic. Every Fourth of July we had to give him medication or take him to a boarding kennel in the country to try to alleviate his panic. This terrible fear eventually led to his demise. In the midst of a lengthy and especially fierce electrical storm, when no one was at home, he tried, in vain, to escape through a basement window and fell back onto the basement floor to his death.

During the heartbreak that followed, we told all the familiar stories over and over again—and there were many.

Sam will always be a part of our happiest family memories. We know that somewhere his spirit still survives, running smoothly across some distant meadow—flying free.

———————————

Webster, New York, resident Beverly M. Chizek is an animal enthusiast and a supporter of the Humane Society of Rochester and Monroe County.

Give a boy a dog and you've furnished him a playmate.

—Berton Braley

In his grief over the loss of a dog, a little boy stands for the first time on tiptoe, peering into the rueful morrow of manhood. After this most inconsolable of sorrows there is nothing life can do to him that he will not be able somehow to bear.

—James Thurber (1894–1961)
American writer

My Dog Duffy Ate My Bird

Emily Dysinger

My Westie dog, Duffy, was thirteen years old when it happened (he ate my bird). My bird's name was Stewart. He was one year old. When it happened I was in first grade. Now I'm in fourth grade. I was at school waiting to be picked up. When my mom picked me up, she left me alone with the bird and the dog. The bird was out of the cage ('cause he didn't like to be in his cage). And normally my dog didn't go after my bird. But all of a sudden the dog ran right toward the bird. I started after him. And I grabbed his collar. But it came off of him. So I put my arms and legs around him and waited an hour for my mom and brother to come back.

The next day my mom put my dog in the basement, but the door wasn't closed all the way. So when my mom left, he pushed the door open and got the bird.

For Christmas my brother got my mom a pair of slippers that are bird feet because when my dog ate my bird, he left his feet.

Emily Dysinger wrote her story in 1991 when she was
nine years old. She lives in Fairport, New York, with her family,
a kitten, two birds and Duffy.

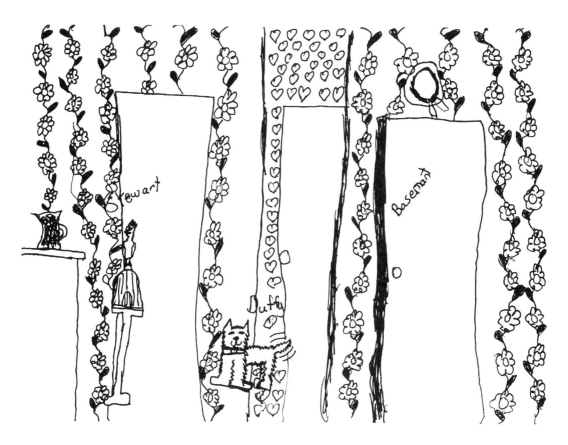

"But the door wasn't closed."

—Drawing by Emily Dysinger
age 9

Hallmarks of Holly

James R. Glynn

We had hoped for a springer somewhat larger than she turned out to be. (My father continued to call her "small stuff" well into her adult years.) My sister had requested, if we were to finally decide on a dog of this breed, one colored liver and white. (Two years beyond my eight, she recognized the importance of this choice more than I—akin to a late adolescent selecting the shade of his or her first car.) Holly was, however, definitely black of coat, in majority, with speckled white thrown in as an apparent afterthought.

Since she was first located and then purchased long distance, her shortcomings could not actually be considered her fault. She did not appear at all remorseful regarding such alleged flaws upon our first meeting.

A man brought her to us in one of those big trucks that used to have ships as insignias on the side. The delivery man, in matching dark green shirt and pants, held out a semi-small crate with lots of spaces for air to move in and out.

The box was placed on the dining room floor (no carpet), and my mother provided her illegible signature on a clipboard that was originally slung from his hip. An acquaintance of mine, more a neighborhood bully than a close friend, stood near the spot where our packed puppy had been deposited, and I figured him to be as excited as I was. (My sister may have been there, too, but after the years that have passed I can't quite place her on the scene.)

After my mother unlatched something, Holly exited from the crate with a bound, peed and grabbed my mother's closest hand. Her teeth, of course, were then of the little variety, and my mother laughed and squealed some, which sounded okay, even if she was all grown up. The delivery man chuckled low and informed us that it looked as if we had our hands full. He left soon after, which was a relief to me, since I had planned on enjoying such a momentous occasion with just family and grateful friends.

Holly roamed around her immediate setting with abandon, sniffing here and there. Her tail had been cropped and moved about in a stubby but convincing wag. An at least six-hour trip from somewhere in Pennsylvania had not seemed to affect her strength or stamina. We soon learned, however, that her actual level of energy far exceeded this display.

My father arrived home and gave his general approval, although dog selection and care were most often left up to my mother. He noted that our new pet was a bit husky compared to a famous dog from his childhood, also a springer. (I believe my mother may have brought a spaniel into our home as an attempt to appease my father, in the event that he chose to object to another pet. Earlier on, we had had a high-strung Irish setter that had ripped down curtains and disrupted the contents of bureau drawers whenever she was left alone.)

Holly was assigned to the kitchen/dining room area for the first few evenings. My parents were justifiably fearful of what she might do to dacron-polyester carpeting if not closely monitored. Attempts at containment proved to be futile. Head bowed, Holly first backed up and then galloped toward a selected barrier at full speed, employing her girth to knock aside the adjustable screens that had been placed between doorways.

What made Holly memorable was that she proved to be close to unmanageable. She swam like a fish and frequently rolled in them to test our allegiance. (Due to this particular predilection, she was shaved in summer and then resembled a stout cow.)

I can clearly recall our collective family pride when Holly would jump from a raft where, say, full-blown Labor Day revelry might be in full swing, swim to shore, relieve herself and then attempt to doggie paddle back. The river current usually proved to be too strong, because she failed to move above us, on land, before re-entering the water. I was then selected to bring her back. Holly would continue to slap her paws about as I gingerly grasped her and unsuccessfully tried to avoid the negative impact of her nails across my sunburned skin.

On one occasion, after discovering and partaking of an especially pungent carp, Holly headed through the neighborhood in search of entertainment. Mrs. Hawkins, a fifty-something school secretary, had opened her front door for a reason I do not know and our dog headed inside. Brushing by Mrs. Hawkins's startled legs with speed, Holly failed to notice Mrs. Hawkins's even more surprised face. According to later reports, Holly romped about most of the downstairs rooms and chose to rub her recently conditioned fur against various pieces of recently purchased furniture. (That was how it went: Other families got new material items, we got another dog.)

My mother was later full of strangled apologies and provided the Hawkinses with many cans of Glory Carpet and Upholstery Deodorizing Cleaner. My father avoided the Hawkinses for a significant period of time.

Even when functioning fishless, Holly had moments that remain in infamy. A particular favorite of ours is when Mrs. Tidd, a fussy lady across the street, set up an elaborate outdoor buffet on a long picnic table and then went upstairs in her home to freshen up before a tasteful summer gathering. A good view of the Tidds' backyard was provided from a bathroom, and Mrs. Tidd's high-pitched screams were heard for blocks. Holly had perched herself in the exact middle of the table and was enjoying potato salad and a relish plate—after a brief struggle with Saran Wrap.

After a Halloween during which I dressed as a peace protester but was mistaken for a Mexican, I was till quite proud of my candy haul. Everyone carried plastic pumpkins then, with black straps that look like ironed licorice, and mine was almost to the point of overflowing. I awoke that November first, earlier than at any other time of the year with the exception of Christmas morning, certain I could manage a few Sweet Tarts and at least one Mounds Bar before official breakfast.

After heading downstairs, however, my attitude underwent severe readjustment. Holly slammed around near the dining room table and breakfast bar. Her head was firmly caught in my plastic pumpkin, but she had managed to keep herself busy while stuck. My sister was later allowed to demonstrate her generous side by dividing half her candy with me, after my wailing subsided.

We kept one of her daughters after Holly was accidentally with puppies at three years of age. (Her heats were legendary in scope and drama. Male dogs fought long, loud battles on our front porch until blood was drawn, and those approaching the house were wise to pass through the melee as passively as possible.) Holly's third puppy, Joy, was the only mostly white one, and I, because I had sort of predicted this and just liked her best, whined enough that she was selected from five others, although a curly haired male was close in the running from others' points of view.

Joy was more reserved, overall, but she did inherit some of her mother's resolve. When less than a year old, she returned home with a whole chicken, still tepid from its first few minutes on somebody's grill. (The Idels' was suspected.) My mother grabbed Joy's prize and had it in the outside trash before witnesses were available. We had a few laughs about this event, during our own dinner, even if we were a bit guilty. Secretly, I think there may have been some sense of approval for Joy's accomplishment. We had come to expect such feats.

Aware as we were of leash laws, Holly saw fit to find freedom and commit misdemeanors at an alarming pace. Chains were broken, collars slipped, and, even after a fence was constructed, she proved expert at slipping out of almost closed doors. Holly's physical being, like her spirit, could not be effectively contained by any ordinary means.

I hold this fond image of her, running after our grandfather's Model T car, which we drove across dusty roads during weekends spent at his camp. Her tongue hung long from her mouth, and her legs moved so fast as to blur, but she would have nothing of sitting inside the vehicle. She drank sloppily from many bowls of water at the conclusion of these runs, and she was stiff the next morning from such extensive exercise.

Most certainly, however, while she chased us through the woods, never flagging despite the hopelessness of ever passing us, or even catching up, Holly was smiling.

———————————

James R. Glynn is a school psychologist. He resides
in Fairport, New York.

Rolf

Lydia Parker Hartman

With legs outstretched in front and behind, he could jump over the garden fence without touching. It was a pretty sight. Using the crossbars on the front gate, which must have been about twelve feet high, he could even clamber over that.

I don't know how old I was when Rolf, a Doberman puppy, came to join our family in my native Germany. But I remember he was very acrobatic as well as intelligent. He was a one-family dog, and woe to anyone who had mischief in mind.

My older brothers, Willy and Eugene, in their teens, managed to get into various kinds of mischief. One winter they decided to use Rolf as a sled dog. They made a leather harness for him similar to the one used on the horse. But when they put him into the harness and got on the sled, Rolf just turned around and looked at them. They kept trying to think of some way to get him to pull them.

They knew Rolf seemed to hate one man from the village, so that winter when this man came to buy our bread, the boys hastily got out the sled and put Rolf in the harness while the man was walking back to the village. Rolf, who had been tied up while the man was at the house, immediately took off before the boys could get on the sled. When they finally caught up to the man, he was using the loaf of bread as a weapon to fend off the dog. It was a funny sight, but Willy and Eugene were reprimanded for putting the poor man in danger.

Rolf and Fuchs, our horse, were an inseparable pair. They were always used when the wagon was hitched up to sell bread in the neighboring town of Gruenberg. It was a covered wagon, just like the ones used to cross the prairie, but lighter. Rolf knew that it was his job to guard the wagon while it was left in the street. He would lie on the seat as though he were sleeping; but woe to anyone who tried to get near that wagon while the master was away. The boys told of egging on their friends to try to get past Rolf. No one ever succeeded.

There came the day when his love of horse and wagon had to be used to get him off the roof of the barn. Rolf's shelter was through a hole in the wall of the stable, where he could keep warm along with the horse. He was tied to a chain, which in turn was tied to a steel loop in the wall on the outside. He could be inside or out as he pleased.

In the summer we had barn swallows nesting in the barn. They loved to tease Rolf by swooping low over his head while he was chained. He would become more and more agitated. This had been going on for some time when the boys decided to let Rolf loose and watch what would happen.

Barking as loud as he could, he jumped onto the pile of manure in front of the pigsty, onto that roof, and then to the ridge of the barn next to it. There he ran back and forth barking furiously until he realized that he could not get at the swallows there either. His barks turned to wails, and nothing could induce him to come down. Finally, the boys decided to hitch Fuchs to the bread wagon and start out as though going to town.

It worked. Rolf now barked furiously for them to wait for him, intermittently wailing at his predicament. They had the horse go slowly. Finally, when they had nearly reached the village, Rolf scrambled down the barn roof onto the pigsty and jumped from there to ground to race after the wagon, barking all the way.

Nothing was going to stop him from going along!

Lydia Parker Hartman came to the United States from her native Germany at the age of eleven. She is a student of the German language and enjoys writing. Mrs. Hartman resides in upstate New York.

Like St. Francis

Ruth E. Hyland

Like St. Francis,
I love them all and
Cannot turn a hungry one
From my door.
They are your creatures, God,
That, we know;
And I believe you
Created them
For children to know.
You cannot have anything on
Earth forever, and so
Their pets too must go!
Tears they shed are
Soon forgotten, as their lives
Find new meaning in
Another pet to love.
But the seeds of loving grow
Within their hearts, and
This is a start to understanding
Life and Death.

The family of the late Ruth E. Hyland donated her poem.
Mrs. Hyland taught school for over twenty-five years.
She loved children and animals.

The only animal who has seen his god.
                                    —Anonymous

Family Circus

Bil Keane

"When dogs are happy they don't have to bother smiling. They just wag their tails."

For over three decades, Bil Keane has chronicled American life in his cartoon "Family Circus." Mr. Keane resides in Arizona.

Dennis the Menace

Hank Ketcham

"RUFF IS A LOT EASIER TO UNDERSTAND THAN HOTDOG. DOGS ARE SORTA LIKE KIDS BUT CATS ARE LIKE GROWNUPS."

Hank Ketcham created "Dennis the Menace" in 1950 and, ever since, Dennis has been amusing his readers with his antics. The cartoon appears in newspapers and books.

For Barking Out Loud

Rosemary L. Leary

Over fifty years ago an Irish setter named Nancy lived in Fairport, New York, with my parents, my brother and me. She was my wonderful friend and true companion from the time I was about three until my twelfth year, when she had to be put to sleep because of an incurable heart problem. Nancy had a sweet disposition, always loving, ever devoted. I still have a bit of her lovely red fur.

One awful day in the early 1930s Nancy was hit by a car on South Main Street in Fairport. We lived on nearby Orchard Street then, and I can still recall her terrible scream of pain. I raced to an upstairs bedroom window and saw her limping home across our lawn on three legs.

The veterinarian put her broken front leg in a cast, and she spent much of that summer lying down while her leg healed. Ever afterwards Nancy limped because one front leg had become shorter than the other. But that never impaired her cheerful spirit or her joyful eagerness to accompany my father pheasant hunting or to explore or hike with me through the countryside.

So it happened that one winter Sunday in the 1930s after our family had moved to the George B. Hart Farm on Mosley Road, Nancy and I went for a hike.

My father was a foreman at the George B. Hart Greenhouses. Even in the midst of widespread unemployment during the depression, somehow

143

people could still afford the beautiful, perfect long stem roses and fragrant gardenias grown at Hart's. The greenhouses were located at the southern edge of the Fairport village.

About one mile further south, at the top of the next high hill, stood our house. No one lived between the greenhouses and our home, so there was no one to hear a little girl if she screamed.

On that winter Sunday afternoon I set out with Nancy to visit my dad at work. We came to the valley we called "The Hollow," where the Niagara high tension lines cut across the countryside, and I decided to walk across it to reach the greenhouses. Suddenly I dropped straight down in snow up to my chin.

Later I learned I had plunged into a drainage ditch. Snow had completely hidden it. I was pinned in the ditch by snow all around me. I could not move. Nancy immediately began barking, barking, barking.

My father said later that while in the north-most section of the greenhouses he had heard a dog's distant barking and said to himself, "That sounds like Nancy."

He left work and following the sound of Nancy's frantic barking, he found me with only my head protruding from the snow. Quickly he freed me from my snow trap.

Nancy had barked her alarm when she realized that I was not playing and that something bad had happened. With canine wisdom, she saved my life.

Oh Nancy, my dear friend of childhood, you are not forgotten. I love you still.

———————————

Rosemary L. Leary retired from the Rochester Police Department in 1977. She enjoys art and local history of upstate New York.

But ask now the beasts,
And they shall teach thee.

—Job 12:7

A Christmas Message, 1940

Norman P. Leonardson

With our fox terrier dog, Rex, my big brother and I were exploring the frozen river across from our Indiana home. Our dog ventured too far out and fell in that river, through the thin ice, out near the middle. His paws kept slipping off the sharp edges of the ice, and although we tried in vain to get out near him, the ice creaked and cracked in front of us.

Just at that critical moment a hunter came along and leveled his big shotgun at the struggling dog. We nearly died of apprehension. The hunter blasted away with both barrels and reloaded his gun.

The two shots were so neatly placed in the ice, to the right and in front, that our dog was able to swim in much closer. We grabbed him by the ears and nose and pulled him out of the icy river.

We hollered our thanks and ran home with an exhausted animal. It was the day before Christmas, so my brother and I bought a box of shotgun shells and wrapped it with red ribbon. We took it to the hunter's house and gave him our heartfelt thanks.

Our mother gave the shivering animal some whiskey and warm water and bundled him in a blanket. He slept most of the day.

He lived and enjoyed many more years, to the fine old age of sixteen.

We told the story of his rescue that Christmas, and many more times since. It embarrassed our mother when we told the part about the whiskey to "church folks."

He enjoyed many more years.

That fox terrier is buried in the yard of our old family home, with a small carved marble stone. It says, "To Our Beloved Dog—Rex." I look for it when I go back to visit.

My Christmas wish for you and yours is to be loved as much as our old dog Rex.

Norman P. Leonardson lives in Sun City, California. He adds that Rex is a grand part of his boyhood memories.

I suppose there's a time in practically every young boy's life when he's affected by that wonderful disease of puppy love.

—Wilson Rawls
Where the Red Fern Grows

Canine Comments

Art Linkletter

I don't have a favorite dog story, just the usual pet owner's enthusiasm for his particular animal. I like big dogs; King was a beautiful collie that helped raise my five children, and now I have Max, a German shepherd and very much a member of the family.

Art Linkletter is one of America's well-known radio and television broadcasters and authors.

No one appreciates the very special genius of your conversation as a dog does.

—Christopher Morley

The Dachshund Lady

Leonore R. Mandelson

Long ago, when I was a child growing up in Mexico City, I visited The Dachshund Lady. I have known all kinds of animal lovers but none like her. She was one of Mama's best friends.

She lived in a fine house, attended charity events, was educated, intelligent and otherwise quite rational. But when it came to her dogs, she took all leave of her senses.

The Dachshund Lady was a distinguished-looking woman with a passion for dachshunds. She had seventeen of them. They sat on her luxurious brocaded sofas and chairs, they hid under her tables, they piddled in her foyer. They were all shapes and sizes—big, small, fat, thin—and they were all dogs with pedigrees. There were long-haired dachshunds and short-haired ones. Like Queen Victoria's dachshunds, they ate off fine German china and sprawled on antique sofas.

And they were greatly adored, to the point of excess, living blessedly indulged lives. My mother, who always found *le mot juste*, described The Dachshund Lady as *eine melancholische Mutter ohne Kinder*, "a melancholy mother without children." Instead of children, she mothered her dogs, often at the expense of her husband.

Mama took me with her to visit The Dachshund Lady. The door swung open and a long dog ran out and began to lick my hand. The lady of the house called, *"Komm her, Maximilian."* Then the mother of the dachshunds came in, singing a German greeting with a whiskey baritone. I was fascinated.

Behind Maximilian were sixteen other little brown pooches. The puppies were pawing and knocking each other over, trying to jockey for position with their mistress.

"These are my babies," she said, meaning her dogs, and she proceeded to introduce every one of them: Hildegarde, Ingrid, Ingeborg, Wilhelm, Baumeister, and so forth. Some of her dachshunds had names like Ludwig I, II, III, IV up to X. But one she called El Jorobado, "the hunchback," because being so long and low slung, he had trouble with his back, and he had turned into a bit of a hunchback.

We looked over the dogs, but didn't get all their names straight because they kept shifting positions, climbing up and down the sofas, hustling in and out of the back door and running back and forth into the yard. They swarmed everywhere. The Dachshund Lady had a half-dozen photographs of her dogs perched on the piano. She showed us a photo of her Brunnhilde, who had died of old age the previous year.

"Would you like some coffee and *Kuchen*?" she asked, and was on her way to the kitchen before we could reply. Then she hustled us out the back door and into the garden and soon we were sitting together having refreshments at a little white table under the Cyprus trees. I watched the *zensontles*, the mockingbirds, and drank lemonade and got licked by her seventeen dachsies.

The Dachshund Lady talked with my mother about anything that came to her mind. She told her of life in Germany ("Dresden was a spiritual experience") and of Mexican markets ("The sanitation—isn't it awful?").

And then, as she was telling my mother about how she prepared her *Leberknödel*, she suddenly remembered her husband and broke into tears.

"Detlef is so unfaithful," she sobbed. "He has this string of woman friends . . ." She had no intention of talking about her husband but it just burst forth involuntarily.

Mama tried to comfort and talk sense to her. "That is a cross many women have to bear," Mama said. "But see?" she continued, trying to cheer her. "Your house is so beautiful. You have a good life. Take comfort in that. And you have all these dogs to keep you company."

Indeed, she had all that canine company. In my six-year-old eyes, that made her worthy of envy.

The only bad phrase I ever learned in German in childhood was one I overheard The Dachshund Lady say in a conversation with my mother: "*Verfluchter Schweinehund*," damned dirty dog. I thought it had something to do with her seventeen dachshunds, but Mama told me she was referring to her husband.

Mama told me the Germans bred the dachshund hunter dog some time back because they had a need for a dog that could slither into burrows and, with powerful jaws, hold its quarry while the owner pulled it out by its long, tough-rooted tail. The dog had to have short legs, be low to the ground and have a lean nose, plus intelligence and lots of courage.

As we walked out, I heard Mama say, "*Die Arme*," poor thing. But I thought that the lady was lucky to have all those dogs with their friendly expressions.

The smooth-haired dachshund is my favorite dog to this day.

Leonore R. Mandelson, a retired teacher, grew up in Mexico and California. She resides in Pittsford, New York.

Nature teaches beasts to know their friends.

—William Shakespeare (1564–1616)
English dramatist

Dad, the Depression and a Dog

Andrew P. Meloni

When I was a child, my twin sister and I owned a beautiful white Eskimo spitz dog named Whitey. He was supremely protective of Terri and me.

We're talking about depression days, folks! I can vividly recall doing something to irritate my dad. I was about five years old. My father moved toward me in anger and the dog sensed he might do me harm (which, by the way, never happened). But Whitey grabbed my father's pant leg (his only suit) and ripped the heck out of it.

My dad didn't find this incident too amusing at first, but all of us soon broke out in hysterical laughter. A suit was not easy to come by in those days, but neither was a dog as faithful as Whitey.

Andrew P. Meloni has spent his entire career in law enforcement.
He is the Sheriff of Monroe County, New York State.

And sometimes when you'd get up in the middle of the night you'd hear the reassuring thump, thump of her tail on the floor, letting you know that she was there and thinking of you.

—William Cole,
Man's Funniest Friend

A Love Story

Louise Goodyear Murray

Christmas 1988 held no joy for Melissa Mae Kieffer. As she slept Christmas eve night, her small seven-year-old hands clung to a worn, red dog collar. Next to her damp pillow rested treasures—a plastic dog statue, a dog book, and a wrapped Christmas gift. The unopened gift was a surprise present, a chewy dog bone, for Scamp.

Scamp was my foundling dog of the streets. After she had been abandoned at age eleven, our home became her home. At the same time my four-year-old neighbor, Melissa, began her solo visits to our house without the escort service of her older sister Jennifer. Her special bonding with Scamp developed—strong and steady.

This feisty little dog of unknown heritage tolerated all of Missy's attending activities. One Christmas season Scamp endured the restrictions of a child's red jacket with white fur trim and played the role of Mrs. Santa Claus for two long weeks.

And there were the hunting lessons. Only Missy, and perhaps Scamp, understood the intricacies of these: Tethered to a leash attached to our hallway newel post, Scamp was instructed in the art of hunting.

Summers saw Scamp harnessed to Missy's red wagon. They were engaged in the relocation of rocks, the delivery of merchandise and the exploration of new frontiers.

Our house routines became Missy's. If Missy wasn't at my door when

I came home from school, I would miss her greeting. Her smile could throw wall-to-wall light in any room. Our boys' calls from college often included their asking and laughing about these inseparable two and their antics.

Soon enough the predictable request evolved. Missy wanted to own Scamp. My fast-thinking husband had, we thought, a satisfying answer. Half of Scamp could belong to Missy. But faster-thinking Missy, with dazzling eyes, urged total possession. We compromised. Missy would own Scamp. Scamp would be housed with the Murrays.

The following years saw Missy's love for Scamp only grow. Scamp was Missy's dog, and Missy was a constant visitor.

When Scamp's energy gave out that December 23, 1988, a seven-year-old experienced the hurt death brings. Together, we talked, reminisced, cried. We laughed, too, as we remembered Scamp's funny dances, her barking dinner-demands, her possessiveness of her orange ball, her five-minute-flat devouring of a chewy bone.

She still visits, almost daily. But this Christmas, Scamp's worn, red collar adorns Missy's very own little dog. And our new dog—predictably, he will soon be only half ours.

Editor's Note: As an addendum to her story, Louise Murray adds that where Missy and Scamp once tread is now the path of Missy's dog Pierre and the Murrays' dog Kaycee. In this case, good "dogs" make good neighbors.

Dog is the only animal in the world who ostensibly likes another breed better than his own. Man.

—Ted Patrick
The Thinking Dog's Man

The Forbidden Dog

Florence H. Prawer

He was not really my dog. He belonged to a neighbor, a baker, whose store was adjacent to the women's and children's clothing shop my parents had in Coney Island.

Spotty was small, quiet, white with black and brown markings. When I rode my tricycle on the wide sidewalk, he padded alongside. When I sat reading on my little stool in front of the store, he lay beside me peacefully, looking up at me occasionally, yawning contentedly from time to time. When I was sent to the corner newsstand to buy a newspaper, Spotty was alert to accompany me. He was the best friend a lonely only child of four could have.

One afternoon, my parents were working on stock. They had unpacked some imported, dainty, white embroidered children's cardigans to display in the glass showcase. Afterward, as I stood admiring them, I had a brainstorm. I went outside, scooped up Spotty in my arms, and carried him into the store. Very carefully I slid open the glass door of the showcase, removed a sweater, unbuttoned it, put it on the dog and rebuttoned several buttons. After patting Spotty proudly, I set him on a shelf and closed the door of the showcase. I stepped in front of it to admire the new live canine model.

My mother soon returned to the front of the store and discovered my deed. She put on her serious mother's expression, quietly undressed Spotty and placed him outside the store. She rebuttoned the lovely sweater, refolded it, and replaced it on the shelf, sliding the door closed.

Then still wearing the stern mother's face, she looked at me and led me to the back of the store where we had our apartment. In very few quiet words, my mother explained that what I had done might have damaged an expensive item of merchandise that then could not be sold.

As punishment, I was banned from the store for several days. I stood woeful and weeping behind the door between the apartment and the store, leaning against its oval, beveled-edged glass, suffering the silent, reproachful looks of my mother.

Never again did I take Spotty into our store. but I enjoyed his company outside in the street. He never blamed me for what I had done to him.

Even now, when I recall this experience, feeling him warm and soft in my arms, tears come again easily to my eyes, just as they did during that exile from my parents and the store.

Some years later, my mother allowed us to have a small tank of guppies. But they could never replace Spotty.

Florence H. Prawer, a retired teacher, has a translation business and teaches adult education in Monroe County, New York.

To err is human, to forgive canine.

—Anonymous

Mitzi

Fred Rogers

When I was little and didn't have a sister yet, I did have a dog whose name was Mitzi. I got her as a present for taking some terrible-tasting medicine. My parents had promised me a dog if I took the medicine; so I took it without a fuss.

Fred Rogers. Photo Credit: Family Communications.

Mitzi was a brown, wire-haired mongrel, and for a long time I think she *really* was my best friend. In each other's company, we learned a lot about the world. We explored our neighborhood and beyond. I remember feeling a little braver whenever Mitzi was with me. We shared times of particular excitement, joy and sadness. We got scared together when there was thunder and lightning and often crawled under the bed and quivered together.

When Mitzi died, I was

156

very sad. For a long time afterwards I played with a stuffed toy dog, pretending it would die and then come back to life, over and over again. Only little by little did I stop playing out that drama.

My friendship with Mitzi was like the friendship that many children have with their pets. My mother and father thought it was "good for me" to have a dog for a companion. Well, it *was* good for me, but it was only many years after she died that I began to understand how good it was . . . and why.

————————

Fred Rogers, an ordained Presbyterian pastor, is the television producer and host of the well-loved *Mister Rogers' Neighborhood*.

*Blessed is the person who has earned the love
of an old dog.*

—Sidney Jeanne Seward

The Promise

Bonnie J. Shirley

My husband, Al, had insisted that every boy needed a dog and since we already had the boy, I cautiously agreed. But I also distinctly remember saying, "Since this will be a pet, let's do it cheaply."
He nodded.

"And we'll only consider short-hair dogs."

Again, he nodded.

I tried one more time. "And please, let's get a male."

"Anything you say, dear."

We went to Lollypop Farm knowing our cute little puppy was only a heartbeat away. Scott ran in ahead of us and then quickly dashed out saying, "They don't have puppies here!"

Naturally, we knew he was wrong. But inside the shelter we found a nice selection of older dogs and many empty cages. We asked about puppies.

"July is our busy season," came the reply. "We're temporarily out of puppies."

We left, assuring Scott that there were puppies to be found. My husband even promised Scott that he could pick out the puppy.

Our local newspaper came to the rescue. The ad read, "Puppies: Beagle and Basset mix, $5.00." We called and learned that most of the puppies were males with short hair. The price, of course, was fantastic. My three conditions for owning a puppy would be met.

We found the correct address and made our inquiry. The first dog we saw was the mama, a proud-looking beagle. She pranced from the garage in grand style, picking her feet up like an aristocratic show horse. The eight little puppies, in single file, marched out with as much dignity as puppies can muster.

I nudged my husband, "Great, all of them have short hair."

Then a ridiculous-looking thing dashed out from the garage and caught up with the tail end of the procession. The funny sight made us laugh. Certainly, this last one couldn't belong to Mama Beagle.

"Do you have two litters of puppies?" I asked.

"Everyone thinks that, but the last puppy belongs with the litter," came the answer.

I looked at that last puppy, the funny-looking thing, and had a feeling I knew which puppy Scott was about to take.

Scott made his choice—the funny thing at the end of the line. *She* had *long* hair. I tried to point out how cute the other boy puppies were, but a decision had been made, and we knew we would never go back on our promise.

Leaving, I whispered to my husband, "Why did you promise Scott he could pick the puppy out?"

"At least she's cheap," he said. "One out of three isn't bad, you know."

Scott named her Tinkerbelle Elizabeth and in short time she wiggled her way into our hearts. At exactly six months of age, we took her to the vet to make absolutely certain she would never know the joys of motherhood.

As she grew, she confirmed what we had suspected from the beginning. Her brothers and sisters may have been a beagle-basset mix, but we firmly believe that her mother was a beagle and her father a handsome traveling man. At full growth she has a beagle face, a basset body, a collie coat, and a beaver tail thump.

She eats anything from Brussels sprouts to the current brand of dog food on sale for the week. She's gentle and loving and is always thrilled to see us at the end of a long day.

She's also living proof that promises should never be broken.

New York resident Bonnie J. Shirley teaches fifth grade in the
Rochester City School District.

Skippy

Suzie and Mark Spitz

Most little girls play with dolls, dressing them up and taking them for rides in doll carriages. My wife's friend, however, played with Skippy, a beige and white toy fox terrier.

The best play time for Skippy was to be taken for a ride. A ride in anything—the car, a bicycle basket, a wagon. It really didn't matter what. However, her really favorite activity was to have someone dress her all up in a little doll dress and bonnet, put her in a doll carriage and wheel her up and down the street.

Occasionally, folks would come along and look into the carriage to compliment the pretty "baby." To their delighted surprise, looking back at them with big brown eyes, all dressed up, bonnet, dress, blanket and all, was Skippy! A happier, more contented pup you couldn't find.

Former Olympic swimmer Mark Spitz owns a total of nine Gold Medals won in the 1968 and 1972 Olympic Games. He and his wife, Suzie, live in California.

A dog teaches a boy fidelity, perserverance, and to turn around three times before lying down.

—Robert Benchley (1889–1945)
American Humorist

The Perils and Pleasures of Fifi Sue
A Story for Young Children

Mary Stolz

Here is Fifi Sue, sitting in the bay window, looking at the world outside.
Fifi Sue has a small garden in front of her house, and a long road going
   past it.
That's it. That's all. That is what's to be seen outside her window.
Houses, trees, and telephone poles in the early morning light.
No people.
No other dogs.
No cats coming home from a night out.
Here comes a robin, looking for breakfast!
Fifi Sue watches until the robin flies away.
This is how it is for Fifi Sue every morning.

She's an early riser.
She wakes before Mr. Tumble has stirred in his bed.
She gets out of her basket with the cushion in it, takes her wooden doll, and
   goes to sit on the window seat in the bay window.
Then she waits.

She has not been outside yet.
She has not had her breakfast.
She does not have her ribbon on.
She waits, and watches, and wishes she could get out in the garden.

She wishes Mr. Tumble would get up and fix her breakfast, and put her ribbon on.

Across the street is the house where Klio lives.
Klio is a fox terrier with three legs.
He can run faster with three legs than Fifi Sue can with four.

Fifi Sue is a very little dog with a great many interests.
She likes to scamper in the garden.
She likes to walk to the park with Mr. Tumble.
She likes little biscuit dog bones, and cheese.
She likes to look out at the rain when the wind tosses the trees around.
She likes to watch snow falling, and to dash about in the fluffy flakes.
She loves her wooden doll.

Klio, the fox terrier who is so fast on his three legs, has only two interests.
He likes to chase his ball and bring it back to his person, Mrs. Marley.
Mrs. Marley often says to Mr. Tumble, "Klio would rather chase that chewed up rubber ball than eat. He'll chase that ball till the cows come home."

Fifi Sue has never seen a cow come home. She has never seen a cow at all, and thinks they probably look like cats, who come home in the early morning.

The other thing that Klio likes to do is this: He likes to chase Fifi Sue.
It is Fifi Sue's belief that Klio would rather chase her than his chewed up rubber ball.

Once, long ago, he chased her and caught her, without any trouble at all.
He did not bring her back to Mrs. Marley, oh no.
He took off down the street with Fifi Sue between his teeth, and who knows what would have happened if Mrs. Marley hadn't blown her whistle and called, "Klio, come back! Come back this minute with that poor little dog!"

Klio raced back and dumped Fifi Sue at Mrs. Marley's feet.
Then he waited, panting.
"My goodness," Mrs. Marley said with a laugh. "He wants me to throw Fifi Sue for him!"

Mr. Tumble, with a very strong word, took Fifi Sue home where he gave her a bath and an extra little biscuit dog bone and a piece of extra special cheese that she usually only got on Christmas and her birthday.

Since then Mr. Tumble and Mrs. Marley never let their dogs out at the same time. Not even when they are on leashes.
When Klio is on a leash and sees another dog, he strains on his two back legs and waves his front paw and shows his sharp teeth and growls like a buzz saw.
Klio is one fierce fox terrier.
Mrs. Marley says that with people he is gentle as a lamb. "No harm in him at all, with us," she says. "And he really *likes* cats. Oh my, yes. A real little lamb. Most of the time."

Fifi Sue has never seen a lamb, and thinks they probably look like robins, in whom there is no harm.
Except to a worm.
Fifi Sue, who is not a worm, and not a person, and not a cat, is terrified of Klio. All of the time.

And now the door opens in the house across the street, and out dashes Klio!
He speeds down the driveway, over the road, into Fifi Sue's garden.
He plants himself in the flower bed, looking right up into Fifi Sue's face.
His lips are curled back, his teeth glisten, the scruff of his neck rises stiff as a hairbrush.
He growls.
That'll show her what he thinks of her.
He barks his shrill sharp bark, and he can bark till the cows come home.

Fifi Sue, behind her window, shivers and turns her head away.

She picks up her wooden doll and goes back to her basket where she curls up with her nose in her paws.

She picks up her wooden doll and sneaks off the window seat, back to the bedroom and her basket, where she curls up with her nose in her paws.

"Oh, my goodness," says Mr. Tumble, waking up at last. "He's at it again, is he? That dog is a hoodlum."

He picks up Fifi Sue and holds her close. After a bit she stops trembling.

"And you want to go out, poor thing, don't you?"

He goes to the telephone. "Mrs. Marley," he says, "Fifi Sue needs to go out, so will you please whistle your roughneck in for a while? No, no, of course I didn't mean it . . . but just the same, will you—thank you."

He turns to Fifi Sue. "She's going to call him in. And between you and me, I certainly did mean it. Klio is a roughneck and a ruffian and a bully. But we have to get along with the neighbors, don't we?"

Fifi Sue knows that she will never get along with that neighbor, but all she wants now is to get outside.

She gives her piccolo bark and rushes to the front door.

When she comes back, Mr. Tumble fixes her breakfast before he gets his own.

After breakfast, he brushes her neatly, and ties a scarlet ribbon in her hair, on her forehead, just between her two small silky ears.

Now they are ready to go for their walk.

Mr. Tumble gets her harness and leash, Fifi Sue gets her wooden doll, which
   she carries carefully in her mouth.
They set off.

The agreement is that while Mr. Tumble and Fifi Sue take their morning
   walk to the park, Klio will remain in his house.
When they return, Mrs. Marley will take Klio for *his* walk to the park.
This is how they keep the peace.

The park is a wonderful wide grassy place where dogs can run free.
Except for Klio, who has to be walked all the time on his leash while he
   strains and growls and barks at all the other dogs.
He can't even chase his ball in the park, since the time that a spaniel tried
   to pick it up.
The spaniel spent three days in the hospital.
A policeman came to call on Mrs. Marley.
Now Klio can only chase his ball down his own street, when no other dogs
   are out and Mrs. Marley has the whistle that he always answers to.
Come to think of it, Klio's lot is not a happy one.

Now Fifi Sue and Mr. Tumble have returned from a happy hour in the
   park.
She is not on her leash, as she's a very timid small dog who would never
   run off.
She trip trip trips beside Mr. Tumble, carrying her wooden doll, dreaming
   of little biscuits.

But what's this?
What's gone amiss?

What is Klio doing, untethered on his porch?
Before Mr. Tumble realizes what is happening, Klio is across the road, and
   into the garden, barking through his terrible teeth.

Fifi Sue, with a flutey shriek, leaps into Mr. Tumble's arms.

In the scramble, her doll drops to the ground.
In a trice, Klio has grabbed it and dashed back to his house.
There he is on his porch, with the wooden doll at his foot.
He is smiling his doggy smile.
He is growling a low, satisfied growl.

Next to snapping up Fifi Sue herself, Klio finds snatching her wooden doll
    away from her the best.
In a minute he will start chewing on it.
And what now?
Another surprise!
Surprise after surprise this morning and where will it all end?
Fifi Sue wriggles out of Mr. Tumble's arms and hurtles across the road,
    straight up the porch steps, straight up to Klio.
She pushes her nose up into his.
She growls.
She shows her tiny teeth.
She yips!
She yips and yips some more!
She yip-yip-yips right in Klio's horrified face!
And then . . .

She picks up her wooden doll and prances back, head high, to Mr. Tumble,
    who is standing in the garden with his mouth open.
He is saying, "Will wonders never cease?"
Klio, on his porch, nibbling at his rubber ball with a dazed expression, is
    probably thinking the same.

The fact is—wonders never will cease.

Mary Stolz, a National Book Award recipient, is the author
of many popular books for children, including *The Bully of Barkham
Street*, *A Dog on Barkham Street*, and *The Noonday Friends*,
a Newbery Honor Book.

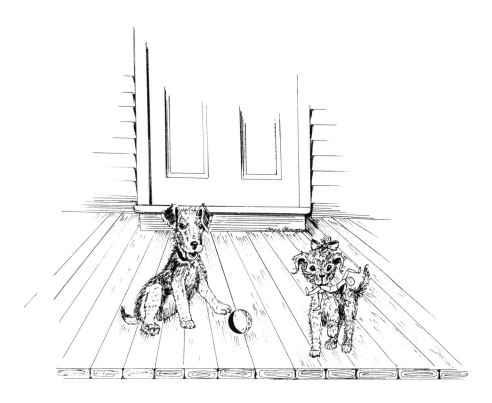

She picks up her wooden doll and prances back.

PART V

In Dogs We Trust

Dogs—our sentinels, companions, shepherds, therapists, guides and life savers—are good for our souls.

Dogs provide security at its best. Some people train service dogs. Other professionals use dogs in therapy. The hearing and sight impaired enlighten us with tales of their companions.

Dogs have found their way into nursing homes and hospital rooms. They comfort the ill and console the bereaved. They provide vitality where before there was none. At a police officer's side, they offer reassurance and protection. For a lost child, they afford guidance.

Bandit, Duke, Blackie, Anna, Kelly and Lucky are honored.

Petting Hour

Paul Barsell

At one o'clock on a Thursday afternoon, the Wilson Litski Home for Adults had scheduled "petting hour." Volunteers randomly handed out pets to patients. But eighty-six-year-old Alfred Young opted as always to stay in his room. Having dealt with Alfred for almost a year, nurses had all but given up, knowing well his answer if asked to participate.

For Alfred had seen it all—how little four-legged varmints were being brought into nursing homes as a means of therapy—and he wouldn't buy it.

"Oh, look, look at this one," he'd snickered, peeking at the group from behind his door. "No better than the damn varmints themselves, cuddlin' and gropin'."

Vaguely he remembered reading something about the elderly reverting to their childhood stage, and refusing to believe such rubbish, the memory only angered him.

"I'm just as sharp as I've always been," argued Alfred, reciting at once his entire alphabet. Having successfully pronounced all twenty-six letters, he would then begin his multiplication table, fully convinced such simple practices would ultimately prevent his own decrepitude.

". . . Two times two is four, two times three is six . . ."

Just outside, old Herbert Crenshaw was petting a fluffy Pekingese. Alfred was too busy to notice.

". . . Two times eight is sixteen, two times nine is eighteen . . ."

Pacing once again past the door, however, he saw them, sitting around like members of some gosh darn puppet convention.

"Pitiful," he'd say, pausing between tables to watch Henry Jones stare off into space, his right hand tenderly stroking some mangy crossbreed.

Next to old Henry, Alice Morgan was carrying on a one-way conversation with a Dalmation. Crazy Alice, Alfred had named her. Every morning she'd ask if it was Thursday yet, always worryin' and waitin' on them smelly little varmints. At ninety-four, Crazy Alice had a habit of bothering and chasing after the other residents. Presently, she had lost her pup while trying to stroke a French poodle cradled by Clara Bitterman.

". . . Two times ten is twenty," he grumbled. "Three times one is three, three times two is six." He stopped occasionally to take another peek.

". . . Three times three is nine, three times four is twelve, three times five is . . ." He briefly hesitated while concentrating. "Three times five is . . ." He searched but couldn't find the answer, breathing heavily while trying to remember. "Three times f' . . . five is . . . f' . . . just . . . s' . . . sixty . . .

"No, wait . . . ." He tried his fingers once but somehow they'd lost their magic. "Th' thirty . . . I . . ." Then he felt dizzy, drawing a blank just as he'd done the week before with his fours, and the week before that with his fives. "Th', three times . . . f', five is th', thirty . . .

"No, no I . . ." A dog began barking in the background. Another dog joined in, adding to his confusion. "Five times six . . . is . . ."

Someone was crying—a woman. But on his way to take a peek, Alfred lost his train of thought. He panicked, forgetting to look after all. Guiding himself to the mirror, a sudden terror gripped him, the sort of terror that proclaims it's too late, nothing matters, no one cares.

The face, at last recognized, would never grow young again. He shivered with a sudden chill of loneliness.

"I have no one, no one. They're all strangers," he cried, referring to his fellow residents. No one heard him. Slowly he sank onto his bed.

Then something pounced onto his mattress, startling him at first.

The mangiest of mutts, some sort of mongrel escapee none of the others must've wanted, greeted him. Having no choice, Alfred reached to restrain the energetic dog, its tail wagging as it affectionately slobbered him.

"Hey, now," he mildly protested. The mutt broke free and danced up and down Alfred's bed. "Now you get down from there," ordered Alfred, halfheartedly. "Go on now before they come in here lookin' for ya."

The amused dog tilted its head and tried to understand.

"Did you hear me?" asked Alfred. "Get outta here." He nudged the pup, which in turn tackled him. "Now c'mon . . . I . . . hey now that's enough . . . do . . . do . . .

"Do ya hear . . . me . . . I . . ."

Who knows what suddenly caused Alfred to stop protesting. Perhaps it had to do with the relentless shower of dog kisses. Or maybe the mere sense of youth the pup conveyed as it playfully trampled over Alfred, forcing him to pay attention.

Something came over Alfred, something he hadn't felt in years. The pooch gave him no time to figure it out, flooding him suddenly with a second wave of overwhelming affection. The animal sent a jolt of warmth over Alfred's rusting bones. He took hold of the dog, and pulled it close to him.

"Okay, hey. Here, c'mere." The dog had dropped onto its side panting from exhaustion. "Sure you little runt, look at you, can't even keep your eyes open now, can ya?"

And though Alfred seemed amazed by how sleepy the dog suddenly became, it wasn't long before he too felt the day's toll.

Later, Head Nurse Martha Wiggins would come across the most amusing discovery. Calling Nurse Brady, they took turns peeking in on Alfred.

"Surprised old Alfred's snoring doesn't wake the poor thing," whispered Nurse Brady.

Several other nurses gathered.

"You think he even knows the dog's there?" asked Nurse Macky.

"Oh, I'm sure he does," said Wiggins. "Perhaps we'll have to work something out next week."

"Think old Alfred would join the session?" asked Brady.

"I certainly don't. But if a particular little fella strayed from us this afternoon," she raised a brow, "who's to say it can't happen again next week?"

And while the other nurse nodded, Nurse Wiggins closed Alfred's door to mute his snoring.

Paul Barsell enjoys writing essays and short fiction. He resides in Rochester, New York.

'Tis sweet to hear the watch-dog's honest bark
Bay deep-mouth welcome as we draw near home;
'Tis sweet to know there is an eye will mark
Our coming and look brighter when we come.

—Lord Byron (1788–1824)
British poet, *Don Juan, I*

Anna

Barbara Landon Biggs

The generator that provides electricity for our home here in the foothills of the Cascade Mountains is growling away, masking all other sounds by the strength of its roar. There was a time when a knock at the door, the ringing of the phone, the voices of my family members calling my name, and the urgent screeching of the smoke detector would have gone unnoticed by me, generator or no generator. Thanks to Anna, my Hearing Ear Dog, I no longer wonder what I'm missing.

Anna, snuggled into a little ball at my feet, is ready to alert me to whatever sounds I may not hear. She is a shadow—no, a silhouette— always dogging my steps wherever I go, her beautiful expressive eyes looking searchingly into mine and inquiring, "What next?"

She would rather be chasing a ball or playing with her tug toys but she understands that there must be quiet moments, too.

Anna came to me two years ago from Dogs for the Deaf, Inc., an organization of caring people in Southern Oregon. Just before placement I received a photo of my new "ears" and I remember thinking, "What a funny looking little thing!" She reminded me of an overgrown fox with only half a tail and ears that stuck out like airplane wings at attention.

Anna was described as a fawn-colored Australian cattle dog/Labrador retriever mix, standing seventeen inches high and weighing thirty-five pounds. She was stocky and tough-looking but her eyes gave her away;

they were as gentle as a doe's and as deep as craters. When I got my first look at Anna on placement day, I fell into the bottom of those eyes and I'm still there.

Doubtless there are those who would not understand such attachment to a mere dog. What is so wonderful about this partnership of ours? It's difficult to explain because it's an emotional one based on both her needs and mine. As I once remarked in a letter to Dogs for the Deaf trainer Karen Hall, "I'm finally beginning to understand what a bond is. No matter where we are, Anna is happy as long as she's with me." And, I might now add, vice versa. It's almost unthinkable that I should go anywhere without my "ears."

Besides presenting me with a security that I never dreamed could be mine after losing ninety percent of my hearing at the age of six, Anna has aided me in becoming an emotionally complete person. I have always, despite my ability to lip read, feared personal contact with the hearing community. There has always been that feeling of not fitting into society. As long as I had no reason to speak to someone, my handicap truly was a silent one.

Nobody knew I was hearing impaired until they spoke to me. I spent years dealing (not very functionally) with anxiety over the possibility that the checker at the supermarket or the teller at the bank might say something I couldn't grasp, and then—horrors! I would be forced to reveal my secret, usually in front of onlookers. I avoided public places whenever I could. I feared being stared at because I was "different." Hearing people may think I made a mountain out of a molehill, yet it happened to me and it happens daily to countless thousands of people like me.

With one friendly wag of her tail, Anna began to crumble my emotional Berlin Wall against the hearing world. Because she goes everywhere with me, I've had to explain her presence in public places to security guards in hospitals and department stores, to restaurant managers, supermarket employees, librarians, teachers, fellow Christians and curious onlookers. Anna has made it necessary for me to communicate with hearing persons in order for us to gain access to public places, and because she is very conspicuous I can no longer hide my handicap. I've had to reveal it and learn to be comfortable with it at last.

Because of her beautiful manners and lovable personality, Anna has done much to help people appreciate Hearing Ear Dogs and allow them a place in society beside their teammates. Many individuals have approached me to compliment her outstanding behavior. This usually leads to a conversation that marks the beginning of another acquaintance. Anna has more friends than most humans do. She is simply irresistible. We can all take lessons from her in impartiality; she is unfailingly polite to all she meets.

She has her comic side, too. When the alarm clock rings at 6:30 A.M., she staggers out of her bed, as red-eyed as anybody who's been rudely awakened from a sound sleep, and throws herself on top of me. She wiggles her body and shoves her cold wet nose into the back of my neck, making my head flop around on the pillow until I respond with a "good girl!" Then she yawns in my face until I'm fully awake. She is also far more effective at getting the rest of the family out of bed than I am—they don't seem to mind her prodding as much as they do mine.

I get much more exercise now than I did before Anna came along. She is a high-energy dog who requires a playmate that is anything but sedentary. She will also play with the rest of the family, much to their delight, without forgetting to keep an ear cocked in case a sound goes off in the meantime.

Anna and I receive many invitations to demonstrate our working relationship. She and I both love this as audiences are always appreciative and enthusiastic. Anna makes everyone laugh when she "Annaticipates" sounds before we have a chance to set them off. She knows what a demonstration is and enjoys the applause.

Will there ever be a perfect dog? No matter; Anna is proving to be the perfect dog for me. Anna's trainers had the skill and the intuition to pick us out from all the available applicants and dogs, and bring us together. For that I'll always be grateful.

There is a saying, "Handsome is as handsome does." Some working dogs would not win any beauty contest, but the beauty that radiates from the special relationship they share with their handicapped partners outshines any other human/animal bond. Anna has fit into our family, perfectly filling the gap left by my hearing loss. She shares her unconditional love with all five of us and though we can't tell her in so many words how much we love her, it's obvious she already knows. You can see it in her eyes.

———————————

Barbara Landon Biggs's teammate Anna won Delta Society's Hearing Dog of the Year Award in 1990. Barbara and her beloved Anna reside in Oregon.

The only creature faithful to the end.

—George Crabbe (1754–1832)

English poet

The Human-Canine Bond

Paul R. Black, D.V.M.

A large volume of material has been written regarding the human-animal bond, the emotional connection between a person and a pet. The pet in this pair can vary from horse to cat to exotic animal, but the most studied animal in this bond is the dog.

We all have read and seen the images of a "boy and his dog" and "man's best friend." We have personal experiences with our own dogs and with those of friends and family, so we are aware of the love that abounds in this relationship.

Yet there is a unique bond that exists between man and a trained working dog. These are the guide dogs for the blind, the hearing dogs for the deaf and the helper dogs for the physically handicapped. The bond between these dogs and their human partners is based on mutual dependence, respect and love.

Over the years I have had the privilege to provide veterinary care for a number of these working pairs. Each time I care for them, I am once again amazed by the versatility and intelligence of our canine friends.

Perhaps this special relationship is best described in the following lines from a letter written by a client whose guide dog had recently died from cancer:

> *He gave me freedom, independence and dignity that I never*
> *dreamed possible. He dedicated his entire life to serve me.*

Not only was he a guide, but a dear friend, therapist and companion. I shall cherish the many happy memories of our time together.

I am fortunate to be able to spend my days working with dogs and other animals in a profession I enjoy. My life has been enriched by the many canine companions I have had the opportunity to help.

———————

Paul R. Black, D.V.M., has a private small animal veterinary practice in Pittsford, New York.

A dog is not "almost human" and I know of no greater insult to the canine race than to describe it as such. The dog can do many things which man cannot do, never could do and never will do.

—John Holmes

A Dog Named Bandit

Ronald "Scotty" Bourne

For the past ten years I have been placing a little figure of a dog next to the infant Jesus in my Nativity set at Christmas. Some people raise their eyebrows, but when they hear my story, they feel differently. For it represents a real dog, named Bandit. Whether he belongs there, you judge for yourself.

I got Bandit in 1967 when I was working as an animal trainer for Walt Disney Productions. We were filming *Three Without Fear*, a TV movie about three children and a dog trekking across a desert. We needed an animal that looked like a starved Mexican street dog.

At an animal shelter in Glendale, I found a part German shepherd. His ribs protruding through his mangy black-and-gray fur, he fit the part. Bandit was what local children had called him for stealing food.

Bandit turned out to be a natural actor. He took direction well and was always ready to play. Sometimes the play got out of hand. When we were filming near Scammon's Lagoon In Mexico, someone threw a stick into the ocean for him to retrieve. A strong undertow carried him along the shore. As he struggled to keep his nose above water, I raced along the high sandbank, trying to reach him before he was carried out to sea. At the last second, I managed to grab his collar and pull him to safety.

Another time, in Arizona, a little raccoonlike animal called a coatimundi, which was appearing in a scene with him, bit Bandit's leg. The

Ronald "Scotty" Bourne's Bandit starred in the Disney TV movie,
Three Without Fear.

animal's razor-sharp teeth severed an artery, and two crew members and I made a mad dash by car sixty miles across the desert to a Tucson veterinarian. As I held Bandit in my arms, I realized how much my friend meant to me. Thank God, a fine vet helped pull Bandit through. I decided then it was time he retired from the movies.

For a while Bandit lived with my sister's family in Simi Valley. He thrived on domestic life and became a neighborhood hero: As his movies appeared on television, there was a constant demand for him to "speak," "shake hands" and pose for pictures. Bandit loved the attention and had infinite patience.

Moreover, he had an almost human understanding of people's needs. For example, one of my sister's boys was born with splayed feet. The doctor prescribed braces and told her not to expect the child to walk at the normal time. However, one day to everyone's surprise, Bandit was seen walking very slowly across the yard with the baby toddling behind, hanging on to the dog's bushy tail!

Then came a time when everything in my life fell apart. After a broken romance, I was at my lowest ebb. Bandit and I got back together again, and during long reflective walks on the beach, he was my only companion. Though now graying at his muzzle, he still wanted me to throw a ball and play with him. This was my therapy, for Bandit coaxed me out of my melancholy solitude.

As my outlook improved I deepened my relationship with the Lord. This led me into many new areas, one of which was a juvenile prison ministry. Bandit accompanied me on my visits to the teenage boys; they loved to hear his story, especially about my finding him in "prison."

However, by 1979 Bandit was old and painfully stiff; I sensed it would be his last Christmas, and I asked the Lord to help me make it especially significant, not only because of Bandit, but because of my new life with God.

By mid-December I was afraid Bandit would not even make it to Christmas. One day while praying over him, I envisioned myself going to the stable at Bethlehem. Carrying my old friend in my arms, I presented him to the infant Jesus. I explained to Jesus that my gift was the only treasure I had left. Slowly, I placed Bandit beside the baby Jesus, then turned and walked away.

The picture I had while praying became a reality on Christmas Eve. Bandit lay on the lawn, unable to stand. His brown eyes, glazed with pain, looked up at me imploringly. In anguish I called the animal shelter, and I placed Bandit in my car for the last time. The man at the shelter took him gently, and I stood waiting outside until he brought me Bandit's collar; he put his hand on my shoulder and told me it was all over.

All the way home I begged, "Lord, I know he was just a dog, but he meant the world to me and I loved him. Please let me know if he is with You."

I was still grieving the next morning as I arrived at the detention camp to conduct a Christmas communion service. I really didn't feel like being there. The boys were at a low point too, for they had nothing to give their families, who would be visiting later in the day. Our service was held in a small television room, the only decoration being a simple Nativity set on the table which served as an altar.

As I talked to the boys about the spirit of giving, I said, "People place too much emphasis on expensive gifts. The greatest gift you can give is what you seem to place the least value on. While we're taking commu-

Bourne with the figure of the dog he found in the Nativity set at the boy's home.

nion, I suggest each of you offer Jesus the one precious gift that no one else can give: yourself."

When it was over, as the boys started filing out the door, I happened to look down at the manger scene. I stared transfixed. Standing beside the crib of the baby Jesus was a little statue of a dog. A dog that looked like Bandit—in the exact spot where I had placed him in my prayer.

With a tight throat I asked, "Who—where did the dog come from?" The boys all shook their heads.

No one at the center had any idea who put the small figure of a dog there or where it came from. So I gently put the figure in my pocket, looked up and silently thanked God for answering my prayer.

And that's why I have a little dog next to the baby Jesus in my creche.

Ronald "Scotty" Bourne is a native of Scotland. In California he served as a chaplain for juvenile detention facilities. For over twenty years he trained animals, and wrote and directed for movies and television.

My Eyes, My Friend, Part of My Soul

Adria Burrows, M.D.

The first time I saw Sara Jones was not in my office, but on the beach. I saw her figure at a distance, standing on the edge of the waves. She was particularly noticeable because there was a dog standing next to her and I knew dogs were not allowed on the beach. I came closer, wondering why the lifeguard nearby hadn't chased the dog away.

Then I knew why as I watched her, the waves lapping at her feet. She threw a ball into the water and, though the dog jumped through the waves to retrieve it, she stared blankly ahead, laughing as the dog put the ball back into her hands. He was a black German shepherd with soft eyes and a wagging tail—a seeing-eye dog. He put his head into the woman's lap and she sat down on the dry sand and looked up at me as I approached. As an ophthalmologist, I was curious.

She looked up as she scratched the dog's ears.

"Can I help you?" she asked into the wind, obviously sensing my presence. This unnerved me a little, as I had approached silently.

"I couldn't help noticing how well you and your dog get along," I answered. "I'm an ophthalmologist, so I have a special interest in eyes."

She smiled, saying, "This is Lucky." The dog perked its ears up, hearing his name. "He is my eyes, my friend, part of my soul. He watches over me." She paused. "As to my eyes, I wasn't always blind. Used to come to this beach as a little girl. I knew every rock, every inch of the beach. That's why I'm not afraid to come here, though all I see now is shadows. Lucky watches me too. I have retinitis pigmentosa."

I nodded and then remembered that she couldn't see my sympathy. Retinitis pigmentosas is a disease that often slowly chokes the vision from the eyes, first working on the peripheral vision and then on the rest.

"Do you know what it is like, Doctor, to slowly lose your vision? To look at something steadily and try to memorize it in your mind, knowing you won't see it someday? I've memorized this beach."

"I'm sorry." That was all I could think of to say in response.

"Lucky is the best thing to come into my life. Now I can go anywhere I want to."

"Would you like me to examine your eyes sometime?"

"Have there been any new discoveries?"

"No."

"Well, why not? Haven't been looked at for a very long time."

I told her my office was not far from the beach; it would be a short cab ride.

Lucky got up with the ball in his mouth and put it in my hand. Did he think I was blind too? I threw the ball into the water and he retrieved it joyfully, but dropped it into Sara's lap. She laughed as he gave her cheek a quick lick. He was a very special dog and clearly adored her.

Sara Jones was her name and as she got up to say good-bye, her eyes looked through me. She was about thirty-five years old, thin, and had a warm smile. Lucky, on the other hand, stared right into my head with his deep green eyes, but smiled at me as his tongue hung out of his mouth. I had the approval of mistress and dog.

"You know," she said before she turned around to go, "I can often tell someone's fortune—or at least part of it—by the ocean. Would you like me to tell a piece of yours?"

She held out her hand and lead me into the waves till they licked our ankles. Lucky followed by her side. "The waves have different ways of rebounding off people. The way they are coming off of you and toward me, I can see good fortune. You must be a good doctor. Yes, Lucky and I will see you for an examination."

They came the next day and I noticed her immediately in the waiting room, sitting with Lucky's head in her lap. He kept one front paw over her foot, as though to reassure her that he was near. She patted his head now and then.

When the receptionist called Sara's name Lucky got up first—did he even know her name?—and walked with her. She sat down in the examining chair and stared straight ahead as Lucky stood near her and put his head in her lap again. This was my first opportunity to watch the interaction between a blind person and her dog.

The retinae of Sara's eyes were covered with hyperpigmentation and bone spicules and her optic nerves were waxy yellow instead of healthy pink. There was no hope for vision ever again and she knew this.

"If there is ever a cure, will you call me?" she asked. "Even if they need a volunteer for a drug trial, let me know."

I assured her I would.

Lucky seemed to realize that we were done even before either of us made a move. He turned his head and gave my knee a quick lick, as if to thank me, and then began to walk with Sara. He stared back at me for a moment with his soothing eyes and they were gone.

After that I went to the beach often and noticed Sara frequently. I would watch from a distance as Lucky ran circles around her when she sat down. Her laugh sounded truly joyful. She would throw the ball into the water and coo at the dog as if she saw him. Sometimes they just sat quietly together, Lucky resting his head in her lap, enjoying a soothing ear scratching. The beach seemed to be their friend, the water their company. I enjoyed watching them in my invisible silence.

One day she came to the beach without Lucky, holding a cane by her side. She had a bag with her, into which she put broken seashells and rocks. She was so much more helpless without Lucky, walking hesitantly, seeming to count her steps. She also looked around more, as if searching for something in the sound of the sea. I approached her.

"Sara, hi. Where's Lucky?"

She looked toward me and her eyes dimmed with sadness.

"He's very sick. He will die soon, I expect." A silent tear trickled down her cheek. "I noticed he lost his energy and the veterinarian said it's leukemia. Poor dog . . . where will I be without him?

"I'm bringing him some shells he can sniff. It will help him think of the good times we had here. All he does is lie on the floor all day. What can I do? He's a part of me."

She paused. "You know how true that is. You've been watching us, right?"

I was amazed she knew.

"I know I get a lot of attention with Lucky. People marvel at us. Even though you are an ophthalmologist, you marvel at it too. I can't live without him. Before I had him I barely went out. I only came here today to bring him back a remnant of the beach."

"Can't you get another dog, if you'll pardon me for asking?"

"There's a waiting list."

"If I wrote some kind of a letter, would it help?"

She nodded no. She doubted it anyway. Sara thanked me for my concern and gave me half of a smile. "How many eye doctors take such a personal interest in their patients? I told you the right thing when I read your fortune in the waves."

But I felt helpless. I wanted to make her life easier. Was there any hope for Lucky? No. He should be put to sleep.

But Sara sat with him day after day, never leaving his side, holding food for him that he wouldn't eat, letting him sniff a seashell now and then for what she thought was comfort.

I called her once at home to see if anything had changed and even spoke to her veterinarian who could offer no hope. I didn't see her on the beach and felt sorry about the whole situation. Lucky was a part of Sara's being. She would never have him put to sleep, but would sit with him day and night.

She dropped me a note when he died, telling me that his head was in her lap as she sat on the floor. He sighed heavily and then the deep green eyes closed forever.

I didn't see her on the beach anymore either and the sand seemed barren without her and Lucky. I pictured them playing and smiling at each other but only saw the empty waves.

I became engrossed again in my work and didn't think about her for a while; now and then I remembered her and thought of calling, but something stopped me. Maybe I would be a nuisance or would make her sad, reminding her of Lucky. One day I broke down and rang her number, getting it from her chart, but the line had been disconnected. Now she was surely lost and I would never find her.

A year later I was walking on the beach after work and saw a figure in the distance with a dog prancing about. Sara?! I quickened my step and there she was, playing fetch with a golden retriever. She stopped, sensing my presence.

"Someone is sneaking up on us, Ginger."

"Yes, it's me," I responded happily. "I'm so glad you're back."

"Have you been looking for us? But of course, you used to watch us. This is Ginger, Doctor. My eyes, my friend, part of my soul. I am complete again. I just got Ginger . . . took almost a year. I have to tell you, I was so lost without Lucky. Never went out, rarely even got out of bed. The world is such a formidable place without a set of eyes. Now I don't feel alone or lost anymore. Not with Ginger." She patted the dog as he panted happily.

"But you should join us, not watch from a distance." She reached for my hand and placed the ball in it. "Go ahead."

I threw it into the water as Ginger dove into the waves and the sounds of our laughter echoed in the wind.

———

Adria Burrows, M.D., is an ophthalmologist practicing on Long Island, New York. She writes as a hobby.

The dog has been esteemed and loved by all the peoples on earth and he has deserved this affection for he renders services that have made him man's best friend.

—Alfred Barbou

In Good Company

Nancy Watson Dean

My husband was in bed with a bad back, and his secretary had come to take some urgent dictation. My three-year-old son, Tony, begged to go out to play in the snow, which was about four inches deep and newly fallen.

We lived high above Irondequoit Bay, on the western side, with a marvelous, wild view. I let Tony and our five-month-old standard French poodle, Clovis, out and watched them delightedly roll and gambol in the snow.

Thinking I could now do some housework, I washed the breakfast dishes and took coffee up to the sickroom. Then I went to bring Tony and the poodle in.

They had disappeared completely. Snow had begun to fall again, and their tracks were obliterated. Fear struck. I ran as far as I could imagine possible in every direction, calling and listening. Muffled silence filled the landscape as snow continued to fall.

Returning to the house, I saw the secretary to the door. I was afraid to tell my husband about the missing child, hoping he would turn up any minute and nobody would ever know what a careless mother I was.

Lunchtime came and went, with many trips to look outdoors. After settling my husband for a nap, I put on outdoor clothes for a thorough search. As I clumped through the snow toward the bay, I saw a young woman climbing the steep hill, carrying Tony. Clovis was bouncing around her, occasionally pulling at her coat sleeve.

Through tears of relief, I asked the woman where on earth she had found my son. We went into the warm house where she told me . . .

Her father was a muskrat trapper. She and her mother lived with him in a cabin on the edge of the bay. They had heard crying and thought one of their chickens had gotten out. Instead, when she went outdoors to rescue the chicken, she found Tony and Clovis.

At first they took Tony into the cabin and fed him. But the poodle barked constantly and threw himself against the door. They thought possibly he was trying to tell them something. So the daughter dressed for outdoors. They zipped Tony back into his snowsuit and went out.

The terrain was so rough she had to carry Tony. The poodle repeatedly ran ahead, then returned to tug at her coat sleeve, and thus they arrived at our house.

Imagine how impressed I was with Clovis, who at five months was only half grown. We rewarded the young woman (my story was out, now that there was a happy ending) and I drove her home, or as nearly home as the deep snow at the edge of the bay allowed.

Saved by a smart puppy! Tony can still remember being in that trapper's cabin, being fed bread with tomato sauce and seeing the father fling bloody muskrats onto the table, though over fifty years have passed.

Nancy Watson Dean lives in Rochester, New York.

There is no faith which has never yet been broken, except that of a truly faithful dog.

—Konrad Z. Lorenz (1903–1989)
Austrian naturalist

K-9 Duke, Fighting Crime and Cancer

David Friedlander

He had not yet spoken a word, but the face of the police veterinarian told me I was about to hear bad news. The thing I recall most about the conversation that ensued was, "Duke has cancer."

Those three words and the three days that followed embarked Duke and me on an arduous fight against lymphosarcoma, cancer of the lymph system.

Duke is a German shepherd police dog and together we are a working K-9 team with the City of Rochester Police Department. I brought Duke to the veterinarian that day after finding a lump alongside his rib cage. Golf-ball size and newly formed, the lump troubled me, yet the thought of it being cancerous never entered my mind.

Within a few hours of the diagnosis, Duke and I were at an animal hospital in Pittsford, New York, in the office of Dr. Robert Rosenthal, a canine oncologist. Being one of only a few such specialists in the world, Dr. Rosenthal has developed an experimental protocol to battle lymphosarcoma using chemotherapy and bone marrow transplantation. During our first meeting with Dr. Rosenthal, I learned that without treatment my seemingly healthy partner would most likely have been dead within thirty days. Accordingly, our best chance was to begin the chemotherapy immediately. This was easier said than done.

Like any tried and true dog lover, there is little I would not do for Duke or, for that matter, my other dog, a Chesapeake Bay retriever named Maggie. Yet decisions about Duke and his care are laden with bureaucratic procedure. For Duke is owned by the City of Rochester and only *assigned* to me. As with all city property, no one person can decide what can or cannot be done with Duke. The City of Rochester, in essence, the police department administration, has control over the purchase and care of its police dogs. I hated to see that even before we began our fight against the disease, we first had to confront the practical dollars and cents issue. The chemotherapy drugs cost anywhere from $15 to $85 per dose. Several meetings were quickly arranged between veterinarians and police officials to discuss expenses, benefits of treatment and the prognosis for Duke. While the expenses run high, the effects of treatment remain uncertain and the long-term prognosis is poor. I am told that 90 percent of the dogs will go into remission once chemotherapy is given. Once in remission, 50 percent of the dogs will survive up to one year, 48 percent will live up to two years, and 2 percent will live beyond that and thereby be considered "clinically cured."

The projected costs associated with treating lymphosarcoma range between $1,000 and $12,000 using chemotherapy alone. Should the dog be a qualified candidate for bone marrow transplantation, the additional cost is $2,500 for that procedure. While that is a great deal of money, it is important to consider the amount of time and money necessary to invest in a dog just to establish a working police K-9 team such as we are.

Initially there is the purchase of an adolescent dog, preferably between eighteen and twenty-four months old. That means that a person or kennel needs to care for the dog prior to its life of service. This can be a costly endeavor. Duke, for example, was obtained from a kennel in Liverpool, England, untrained, for $1,800. Next, Duke and I attended a fourteen-week course in police K-9 tactics. This was a full-time assignment for me, eight hours per day, five days per week. Also, the lead instructor for the course, Sergeant Thomas Stiles, was assigned to train with us. Now it may be easier to see how the investment of time, money and provisions can add up quickly. All told, the approximate cost of establishing a police K-9 team is roughly between $8,000 and $10,000. The additional expenditure for cancer treatment in a young dog may not be too outlandish.

Officer Dave Friedlander and Duke. Photo credit: Jonathon Friedlander

The City of Rochester has nine working K-9 teams. Each team consists of one dog handled by one officer. A dog is assigned to one handler with whom he lives and works. The dog becomes part of the officer's family. Because of this, I have grown very attached to Duke and would do anything for him. And, through his training, Duke has learned to do many things for the City, the police department and for me. For example, Duke is able to track criminals and lost people, search buildings and protect me on the street. This he does eagerly and with great courage.

I have no doubt that, if necessary, Duke would give his life to protect me. Therefore I feel a great need to do everything in my power to help fight his cancer. We are a team and we are fighting the disease together. Through the surgical procedures, radiographs and chemotherapy treatments I have been with him, as I knew he would be there with me had I been the one with cancer. As of this writing, the disease in Duke has gone into remission. For as long as he is able, we will continue to work together, fighting both crime and cancer.

There are many times, particularly after chemotherapy, when Duke does not feel well. Yet, as I prepare for work each day, Duke is there, watching as I dress in uniform. As I pick up the keys to our police car, I find him standing next to the door, eager to get to work.

It is this strong will that led me to bring Duke to visit Camp Good Days and Special Times, a camp for children with cancer. Always true to form, Duke showed off his police stuff and quickly won the hearts of the kids. They related well to Duke's predicament, asking questions about the different medicines he takes, the testing he has had and the effects of the treatment on him, and then making comparisons to themselves. The children spoke of hospitals and needles, losing fur and losing hair, and of being sick. Most of all they gently petted him, tugged at the badge he wears on his collar and listened intently to our story.

My hope is that they were inspired by his strength and courage. I know I am.

Editor's note: Duke ultimately lost his battle with the disease. He died shortly after completing a bomb detection school with Officer Friedlander, having added yet another facet to his service to the City of Rochester. All told, Duke missed only three days of work due to cancer. And as expected, David was with Duke when he died.

_____

David Friedlander is a police officer for the City of Rochester and is assigned to the K-9 Unit. He is a 1984 graduate of Cornell University and a native of Rochester, New York.

The fidelity of a dog is a precious gift.

—Konrad Z. Lorenz (1903–1989)
Austrian naturalist

Puppy Love

Paul Humphrey

Some things you wish would happen won't
    And fortune treats you ill;
When those who used to greet you don't
    The welcome waggin' will.

Paul Humphrey is a commercial writer residing
in Spencerport, New York.

Blackie

Kathleen MacInnis

Dorothy wasn't long for this world. And knowing that made bringing her black Labrador up to the floor seem more okay. We toyed with the idea of wearing sunglasses and somehow rigging a harness to simulate that of a guide dog. But Dorothy smiled at our plans and warned us that Blackie, being an eighteen-month-old "wild and crazy teenager," would tangle himself and us, sniffing all around. So we went cold turkey, up the back stairs.

Blackie knew he had to behave. His ears went back, his nose stretched out in wonder at this unusual smelling place: a potpourri of scents, from the sterile smell of alcohol to the acrid one of urine. His nails clicked against the floor tiles. People looked and smiled, some reached out to touch his fur. But the nurse who brought him from the car walked quickly, purposefully, straight to Dorothy's room. Blackie took one crooked-eared look at his mistress, gave one happy sniff, and climbed right in beside her. IV's in both her arms were carefully wrapped in long white cuffs of gauze. Blackie burrowed in, snuffling his way from her hip to armpit, obviously repeating some playful preliminaries Dorothy had encouraged before— antics that led to ear scratching, to "good boy!" and treats.

Dorothy was too sick to scratch his ears, though; her pressure had been hovering in the eighties. When she told us what he wanted, we obliged. As we scratched his ears, his eyes rolled part way back into his head in ecstasy. This pleased Dorothy the most.

But there was her chest pain. She tried too hard to talk. Even with the nitro drip and frequent morphine injections we still had to balance her precarious blood pressure. We'd talked about this with Dorothy the night before. It was more important to her to see Blackie, never mind the pain. Actually, the dog was great for her blood pressure. Her delight at having him beside her helped her peak one hundred.

Once I asked our infection control physician why we were so strict about animals in the hospital. "Is a dog really all that dirty?"

"Oh no, not nearly as dirty as a cat, for instance, with the way their nails carry the . . ."

"What animals *are* OK?" I interrupted.

"Mice, hamsters, gerbils are really quite clean. Dogs are pretty good," he added. "Now ducks, in water are . . . and beavers . . ."

Again I interrupted him, "I don't mean *all* animals. I mean animals that could visit patients in the hospital; pets. What are the worst?"

"The really *worst* animals from the standpoint of infection control are humans," he answered with an air of finality.

Later that week Dorothy died in her sleep. After the coma. After the balloon pump, the ventilator. . . . And after her visit with Blackie. We felt good about that, but wondered if we had waited too long for her to enjoy the visit, to scratch his long black furry ears.

So much—too much—of what medical science does for people isn't really *good* for them. At least it doesn't bring them happiness. Doesn't really comfort them. It only allows them to breathe or have a heartbeat for another day or month or year. It seems to come down to a matter of semantics: the difference between a dying myocardium and a broken, lonely heart. When a colleague argues asepsis, as we measure yet another dismal cardiac output, or increase the oxygen delivery to lungs that cannot heal, I reflect on all the things I cannot change or help my patients with. But I will remember with pride the evening Blackie spent with Dorothy. And how, in the face of incurable disease, her broken heart was healed.

———————

Kathleen MacInnis, R.N., is a primary nurse on the cardiovascular
unit at a Michigan hospital.

History of Hill Haven's Kelly

Karen W. Wasserlauf

Imagine, if you can, a few people sitting around hoping to find a way for a dog to live at Hill Haven Nursing Home. The desire and need for a resident dog inspired a group of dedicated employees to work with the New York State Health Department to make their wish come true. It took tremendous effort to convince the Health Department to allow pets in nursing homes, but New York's State Assemblywoman Audre T. "Pinny" Cooke and State Senator Paul Kehoe sponsored a new law permitting pet therapy programs. Then-governor of New York State Mario Cuomo signed the law in June 1983.

Once the law went into effect, the real work began—the search for Kelly was on. Hill Haven consulted with vets and breeders trying to identify the most appropriate breed. We needed a good companion dog that would be able to cope with lots of hands, love and general confusion. Finally a Labrador retriever was chosen.

Kelly was born at Kresland Kennels in Victor, New York, on August 21, 1983. She was given special training to teach her how to behave around the elderly, and after receiving her Companion Dog Certificate, she came to live at Hill Haven in February 1984. She was only six months old.

Kelly works very hard to help visitors and residents feel welcome. One resident used to come to the lobby every morning to smoke a cigar and sit with Kelly on the couch. Another resident, who had difficulty speaking, began saying a few words to Kelly and later was able to speak with other residents and staff. Kelly continues to bring much joy to visitors, residents

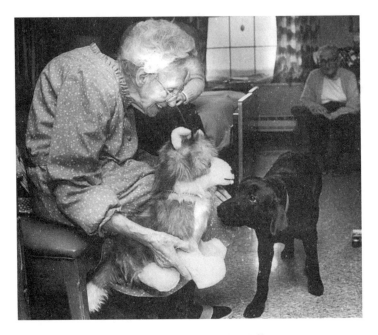

Residents at Hill Haven Nursing Home enjoy Kelly. Photo credit: Michael Schwartz. Reprinted courtesy of the *Democrat and Chronicle.*

and staff. She enjoys walks in the nursing home's apple orchard, visiting residents, greeting visitors and having her belly rubbed.

Stop by and say hello to Kelly—she loves to make new friends.

Karen W. Wasserlauf knows companion dog Kelly well since they both work at Hill Haven Nursing Home in Rochester, New York.

The psychological and moral comfort of a presence at once humble and understanding—this is the greatest benefit that the dog has bestowed upon man.

—Percy Bysshe Shelley (1792–1822)
English poet

I Desperately Need a Sheepdog

Jane Worthmann

It was a miserable sheepdog day—three inches of rain had fallen and the weatherman promised at least one more. I was preparing to meet prospective new owners for an eight-month-old welfare puppy from the pound. Bathed and examined, she waited at the vets. Surely, her new owners were sincere to wade through deep puddles to see her.

While making my last minute house check, the phone rang. I answered.

Brad Smith's voice followed. "I'm in desperate need of a sheepdog," he said, "and it can't be a puppy. Is your welfare dog still available?"

I explained I was about to meet her prospective owners and, in fact, needed to leave shortly, but I expected a grown male named Churchill, also from the pound, to be available in a few days.

As I listened to his story my heart went out to this kind and gentle man. He explained that he and his wife had owned six sheepdogs over the years and that their five-year-old had just died following 3 A.M. surgery for torsion. Then he told me his wife had Alzheimer's Disease. She couldn't understand why her dog wasn't there.

"Sometimes she calls the dog by one of the other dogs' names. But that doesn't matter. Only that she has her dog to love and walk with on the beach. She keeps asking, 'Where's my dog?' I tell her that we don't have the dog now—we'll have the dog again but we don't have her now.

Then she takes the leash and withdraws upstairs. So you see, I desperately need a sheepdog."

Yes, I could see that. After the proper questions about housing and care, I promised him Churchill when he was available.

But it would be three to five days before this dog could be released to me. His owner had finally been located after a long search, and rules mandated this waiting time for her to either sign him off or pick him up.

Our volunteer auxiliary talked to the owner. She was "tired of getting him out of pounds" after he jumped her fence, visited people and then got picked up by animal control. She acknowledged that he was friendly but too big for her house and yard. She didn't want him anymore.

The auxiliary workers asked her to sign him off. Hoping for an earlier release, they even offered to take her to the pound. But to no avail.

Brad Smith would have a four-day wait before he could drive the six-hour trip to get Churchill.

We did get his shot record and age (eighteen months) and learned he had been neutered, which was a help because I require all welfare dogs to be spayed or neutered before going to new homes.

My next concern was his coat. What could be saved after a life outdoors and, by release date, thirty days in the pound with urine and chemical cleaners? Co-Old English sheepdog welfare worker Jim Lord offered to get him the morning of his release (the pound knew to release Churchill only to Old English Sheepdog Rescue but we did not want to chance a mix-up). I told him to use his judgment about a bath.

I met Jim, Brad Smith and Churchill that afternoon, and knew the placement was right.

Churchill had been groomed out as much as possible, and bathed out of absolute necessity. He looked adorable with about three to four inches of coat, a big gray eye patch and an Old English sheepdog smile.

I could tell he had had minimal leash training. But with a retired military "new father," I knew that would come soon, along with lots of love and pats, as evidenced by the ones he received before he got out of the vet's office.

The "new mother" was in the car. I'd love to say there was immediate recognition of the dog. But there wasn't. Alzheimer's Disease is a strange one, but, perhaps, with Churchill to bring her out some, the silent days would be over. As Brad told me, there were days she never spoke to him but would talk to her dog.

I knew there would be an adjustment time for them, but I hoped the walks on the beach would resume and that Churchill would soon be listening to words of love, whatever they be.

As I watched them drive off, I couldn't help the tears that welled up, for that old green station wagon, starting on the long trip home, was filled with more love than many people ever know.

For over twenty years, Jane Worthmann has been involved
in the welfare and rescue of Old English sheepdogs. She resides
in St. Mountain, Georgia.

*We give dogs love we can spare, time we can spare, and room
we can spare. In return, dogs give us their all. It's the best
deal man has ever made.*

—Margery Facklam, 1992

PART VI

Personality Profiles

Like snowflakes and fingerprints, no two dogs are alike.

No two dogs can ever equal the combined antics of Dave Barry's Zippy and Earnest. Experience Nancy W. Schoepperle's Sam, Barbara Flanagan Greenstein's Princess Poitin, dog of persuasion, Don Cherry's true Blue and Mildred Furman's faithful Sumi. Other dogs are labeled "favorite son" and "most beautiful girl."

In these readings, you may find reminders of dogs you know.

Taking the Zip Out of Zippy

Dave Barry

I regularly get letters from irate *MacNeil-Lehrer*–watching readers who ask: "With all the serious problems facing the world, how come you write about your dogs?" To which I answer: Because I don't know anything about *your* dogs. Also—you can call me an idealist if you want, but this is my opinion—by writing about my dogs, I believe that I can bring my readers—rich and poor, young and old, intelligent and "lite"-beer drinking—to a greater awareness of, and appreciation for, my dogs. I want my dogs to someday be at least as famous as Loni Anderson. I want them to receive lucrative offers for major motion pictures based on their True Life Adventures.

This week, for example, our adventure is entitled:

ZIPPY AND EARNEST GET OPERATED ON

This adventure began when Zippy went through puberty, a biological process that a small dog goes through in less time than it takes you to throw away your Third Class mail. One minute Zippy was a cute little-boy puppy, scampering about the house playfully causing permanent damage to furniture that is not yet fully paid for; and the next minute he was: A Man. When the new, mature version of Zippy sauntered into a room, you could almost hear the great blues musician Muddy Waters in the background, growling:

I'm a MAN
(harmonica part)
Yes, I AM
(harmonica part)
A FULL-GROWN man.

Of course in Zippy's case, "full-grown" means "the size of a Hostess Sno-Ball, yet somehow less impressive." But in his own mind, Zippy was a major stud muffin, a hunk of burnin' love, a small-caliber but high-velocity Projectile of Passion fired from the Saturday Night Special of Sex. And his target was: Earnest.

Earnest is a female dog, but she was not the ideal choice for Zippy because all of her remotely suspicious organs had been surgically removed several years ago. Since that time she has not appeared to be even dimly aware of sex, or much of anything else. Her lone hobby, besides eating, is barking violently at nothing. Also she is quite large; when she's standing up, Zippy can run directly under her with an easy six inches of clearance. So at first we were highly amused when he started putting The Moves on her. It was like watching Tommy Tadpole hit on the Queen Mary.

But shortly the novelty wore off and we started feeling sorry for Earnest, who spent the entire day staring glumly off into dog hyperspace while this tireless yarn-ball-sized Lust Machine kept leaping up on her, sometimes getting as high as mid-shin, and emitting these presumably seductive high-pitched yips ("What's your sign? What's your sign?"). So we decided it was time to have the veterinarian turn the volume knob of desire way down on the stereo system of Zippy's manhood. If you get my drift.

The next morning Earnest was limping, so we decided to take both dogs to the vet. They bounded enthusiastically into the car, of course; dogs feel very strongly that they should always go with you in the car, in case the need should arise for them to bark violently at nothing right in your ear. When we got to the veterinarian's office they realized they had been tricked and went into Full Reverse Thrust, but fortunately the floor material there is slippery enough to luge on. So when we last saw Zippy and Earnest that morning, they were being towed, all eight legs scrabbling in a wild, backward, futile blur, into: the Back Room.

When we picked them up that night, they were a pair of hurtin' cow-

For a quiet moment, Zippy watches TV with Dave Barry. Copyright © 1995 Brian Smith

pokes. Earnest, who had a growth removed, was limping badly, plus we had to put a plastic bag on her leg so she wouldn't lick her stitches off. And Zippy, to keep him from getting at *his* stitches, was wearing a large and very comical round plastic collar that looked like a satellite dish with Zippy's head sticking out the middle. He had a lot of trouble getting around, because his collar kept hitting things, such as the ground.

For the next week, if you came to our front door, here's what happened: you heard the loud barking of two dogs going into Red Alert mode, but you did not see any immediate dogs. Instead you heard a lot of bumping and clunking, which turned out to be the sound of a large dog limping frantically toward you but suffering a major traction loss on every fourth step because of a plastic bag, combined with the sound of a very small dog trying desperately to keep up but bonking his collar into furniture, doorways, etc. And then, finally, skidding around the corner, still barking, there appeared the dynamite duo: Bagfoot and Satellite Head.

During this week we were not the least bit worried about burglars, because if anyone had tried to break into our house, we would have found him the next morning, lying in a puddle of his own drool. Dead from laughter.

Dave Barry, a syndicated columnist for *The Miami Herald*, is the author of best-seller books, including *Dave Barry Does Japan*, *Dave Barry Talks Back*, and *Dave Barry Turns 40*. In 1988, he received the Pulitzer Prize for Commentary. The Barry family lives in Miami with their "large main dog, Earnest," and a "small auxiliary dog, Zippy."

I have found that when you are deeply troubled, there are things you get from the silent devoted companionship of a dog that you can get from no other source.

—Doris Day
American actress

The Most Beautiful Girl in the World

Stanley Bing

It was the last autumn of innocence, I think. Boston was green and gold and all kinds of bright orange, vermilion, and paisley, the air so crisp and fresh, and all things were possible. The Sox had just won the sixth game of the best World Series ever. Nixon had been gone for a year; drugs were still as American as scrapple; sex was safer than it would ever be again, at least physically. I was standing on the platform of the Red Line with my soon-to-be ex-fiancee, Doris, who was bothering me about something, as she did between 1972 and 1976. It was early evening. Down at the end of the station sat a midsize ersatz collie dog, just beyond puppy-hood, laughing. Her eyes glowed with a tremendous good nature and trust unencumbered by a surfeit of complicated insights. She was alone.

"Hi," I said. She came over, licked my hand discreetly, allowed herself to be scratched for a time, chased her tail in a dignified circle, lay down again. I remember thinking: "There are times God puts a choice in front of you." I often had such thoughts back then.

We took the dog.

She went totally nuts when she understood the news, bounding and leaping in a vertical parabola to kiss my face, and generally expressing an exuberance that made me want to laugh. As a world view, it was so inappropriate. Searching for the makings of a proto-leash, Doris found in her bottomless denim bag a hank of purple yarn, possibly the one she used for the three-year Sweater for Stan Project, the completion of which turned out to signify the end of our relationship. I wrapped several lengths around her neck—the dog's, that is—but it did not serve. To get her home in one piece, I had to pick her up and hold her like a baby. It is a silly position for a dog, and most fight it. Not her. She lay in my arms, feet poking skyward, head lolling back in a friendly grin, tongue draping out the corner of her mouth, eyes calmly investigating mine as if to say, "Hey, this is a nice idea. Why didn't you think of it before?"

At the time, I made $8,000 a year. My car was a pre-Nissan Datsun, basically a floorboard with wheels and perforated tin skin. My diet consisted of doughnuts, peanut butter, and Chef Boyardee ravioli straight from the can. Cold. My rent was $155 a month for six rooms. The sink was piled to eye level with every dish in the house, since Doris and I also couldn't get together on the politics of kitchen work.

I named the dog Elizabeth. Height: about thirty inches. Weight: thirty-five pounds. Eyes: brown. Tongue: red. Tail: rich and plumy. A coat of pure china white, so thick and lustrous and profuse that people would later suggest that I shear her and turn the output into a sarape. In the summer she shed badly. In the winter, worse. All my clothes and furniture were coated with a fine layer of white flax. When she was young, her tummy was as pink as a baby's bottom, and she had a marvelous, doggy smell, clean, pungent, yet sweet. Her personality? All I can say is that when the Lord made her, he forgot to add any malice, guile, or aggressiveness. Didn't chase squirrels, even. If another dog attacked her, she would roll over on her back immediately and expose her soft underbelly, clearly conveying the message: "Go ahead and kill me. I don't mind, but I think it would be a totally unnecessary waste of energy. But hey, just my opinion." Not once in her life was she hurt by any living creature.

Elizabeth was not smart, but she made the most of it. "She's the sweetest dog in the world," said a friend about her. "But she's got an IQ somewhere between a brick and a houseplant." When people asked what breed she was, we'd say, "Mexican Brainless." How we'd laugh! In retrospect, this seems kind of unfair. Could she defend her thoughts, assuming she had any? Not at all. For all intents and purposes, she was mute: Not a bark, yelp, nor whimper escaped her. In fourteen years, I heard her voice maybe three times. It was always a shock.

I broke up with Doris and rented a place that was nice before I got to it. I was not a master of business administration then, and it was not the living space of a responsible person. Many was the night Liz and I stayed up until dawn, eating biscuits and watching Charlie Chan. Her nose was big and black and wet and perfect for squeezing, and she liked nothing better than to sit at my side and lick my hand for hours on end. I think she got into a kind of trance when she did it, and I had to slap her around now and then to get her to stop.

No roommate could have suited me better. One afternoon, looking under my bed for a shoe to munch, she found a blue sphere covered with a gossamer pelt of fuzz. It had been an orange once, but now it was soft and alien to the touch. Any sensible person would have tossed it out immediately. I found her playing with it. Took a hell of a chase to get it away from her too.

Not long after, when the nation was spritzing its bicentennial all over itself, I met my soon-to-be future wife. Before long we were sort of living together. Dogs were not welcome in her building, so Elizabeth was forced to hold down the fort at my apartment. After a while, it became a dog's apartment, which I guess was only fair. Empty cans of her Alpo and my ravioli littered the rooms, and long skeins of toilet paper hung everywhere, for when Liz got bored, she loved to play with it, string it out, flip it over and under things. She tore into Hefty bags and distributed the contents. She kept herself occupied.

She also periodically ran away. If you opened a door or window, she was out it. One morning she tore through a screen and hurled herself to the street. I didn't blame her. The place was a pit. It was a good thing I lived on the ground floor.

She loved to run, that was it. I would take her to a nearby football field once every couple of days. It was fenced in. I'd let her off the leash, and she would sprint in an immense circle around the huge enclosure until I thought her heart would pop from exertion and joy. Then I'd pile her in the back of the car, where she'd sleep, heaving up and down as she dreamt, and shed. That was fine with me. It was a dog's car, too.

We got married, my wife and I, and for a while there Elizabeth was our only child. She got a lot of love. After a year, we moved to the city, and she, like us, learned to adjust to the demands of urban living. When we'd return home from a walk, I'd let her off the leash in the long hallway down to our three-room flat, and she'd tear down that corridor like a hound possessed, her tail tucked underneath her rear end for maximum aerodynamic lift and thrust, slam into the wall at the end, turn, and head back at even greater speed.

She was youth, and spirit, and dumb, careless vitality.

We were city people now, with city rituals. When we went to the mandatory summer community to visit friends, she was there, zipping freely down the beach in those days before the invention of deer ticks, chasing the waves until they crashed over her and I had to rescue her from the undertow. One night, we went back to eat sesame noodles and chicken, and our hostess put the salad on the floor since the table was full unto groaning. In the candlelight, as we talked, we heard a moist chomping sound, and a great smacking of lips. We looked beneath the table, and it was Liz, downing the last of the arugula and goat cheese and sun-dried tomatoes. She looked up at us, the vinaigrette glistening off her whiskers, as if to say, "Gosh, this is delicious, guys, but not that filling. How about some chicken bones to wash it down?"

To her, carcass of used poultry was the ultimate delicacy. One time, I left an entire oven-stuffer roaster wrapped in tinfoil on the kitchen counter. Two hours later, the only thing left in the room was a small piece of tinfoil and a grease spot on the floor. She had eaten not only the meat and bones, but the aluminum as well. I watched her for days, certain she had finally OD'd on her own sheer witlessness. But she hadn't.

She was indestructible.

She took the birth of our two kids with grace, even when they pulled her eyebrows or fell on her screaming and hugging and kissing her with the kind of passion adults usually reserve for the game-show hosts who award them cruises to Bimini. When my son was a year old, and particularly aggressive, he tried to ride her. She was thirteen by then, and growled at him. After some thought, it was determined that it was she who would be sent away to stay at my mother's house. The exile lasted six weeks. She went with the program after that.

One morning in 1988, she couldn't get up. I took her to the vet, who told me that her spleen was enlarged. Would I care to make a decision? After all, the dog was fourteen. We fixed her up. It was the best money I ever spent, and I spent a lot of it. While she was convalescing at the hospital, my son put together his first complete sentence: "I miss Wizbet," he said. And then he cried. How much is a dog's life worth?

Last winter we moved to a house with a backyard, a swing, and a piece of an acre. Elizabeth came, too.

So a month ago my wife and children went down to see my in-laws in Arizona. And the following Thursday, after breakfast, Liz fell down in the garden and just lay there, her eyes rolled up into her skull, heaving and panting and trembling. The episode lasted just a few minutes, but it scared me shitless. When she awoke, she was jolly and hungry, and spent the rest of the day in the backyard, staring off into space, always one of her favorite pastimes.

When she was falling down five times a day, the vet said to me, "You have to decide whether she is able to preserve her dignity leading this type of existence." I'd never considered it in those terms before. As she lay on her side, clearly not in the world as we know it, I held her paw and kissed her forehead, and all the fourteen years of my life with her swam before and I knew, yes I did. And it was not a good knowing. I made a call. I put her in the car. My brother came along. We were both crying.

The vet's office was clean and cool. He's a nice guy, my vet. I got the feeling that he'd never get used to that part of his job. "This shot will put her to sleep easily," he said. "Then the next shot will put her to rest." He gave her the first and suddenly she arched her back and from her throat came a horrible, gut-wrenching cry, a raking, moaning howl that conveyed an understanding nobody needs to have, and for which none of us is ever ready. And my brother and I held her, and we were sobbing, and the vet said, "She's not in pain, she's just had a neurological reaction to the sedative." Then a few minutes later: "She's at peace." He was weeping, too.

Her body was there, the coat still shiny, the nose still wet and warm. But *she* was gone. I noticed a small pulse in the tip of her tongue, which was hanging out of her mouth much as it had the very first night I saw her, in October of 1975, when Pete Rose was a hero and Boston was nine innings away from its first world championship in nearly six decades.

This is the last I will speak of her. I owe her this eulogy, dog to dog, for fourteen years of companionship, of laughs and devotion and cheek-by-jowl existence on this hard and incomprehensible planet.

You were the best. The kindest. The last who was wholly mine.

Bye, baby.

———————————

Stanley Bing is a contributing editor of *Esquire* magazine.

A man's best friend is his dog.

—Lord Byron (1788–1824)
English poet

Hagar the Horrible

Chris Browne

Chris Browne is the well-known cartoonist of "Hagar the Horrible." He resides in Florida.

Blue Cherry

Don Cherry

I first set my eyes on Blue in Long Island, New York. We had driven from Rochester to pick out a puppy, and when we got to the house, the lady said she was sorry, all the pups were sold.

I noticed a little white pup playing with her kids and asked, "What about that one?"

"You wouldn't want that pup—it's got two blue eyes." She continued, "I don't know what I'll do with it; that's a bad fault for shows. My husband had the pick of a litter. He picked this one at night and didn't notice the eyes. But the pup has character and the kids love her."

"That's the pup for us," I said.

Little did I know that this pup would be with us for the next fifteen years, through unemployment, firings, coaching, playing, TV and radio, heartache and joy.

On the way back home, my daughter Cindy said, "Well, she's got blue eyes. Let's call her Blue." And Blue it was.

We first noticed we had an exceptional pup when we built a ramp leading from our dining room window to our yard (we eventually put a door there). We put her on this shaky eight-inch-wide ramp, and down she trotted, no fear whatsoever, then up the ramp (in the dark, I may add), no fear here. For the rest of her life, she feared absolutely nothing and had the utmost confidence in herself.

Don Cherry and Blue Cherry
Photo Credit: Sports Select Proline

The first time I took Blue to the hockey arena, I was the coach of the Rochester Americans. The Richmond team was having their morning skate. Because they were teasing her, she went on the ice after them, a six-month-old pup taking on the whole team.

Blue was our mascot. When I brought players to sign, I showed them a puck Blue had chewed in half (yes, that is what I said, chewed in half) and I would say, "That's how tough I want my players. Are you ready?" And yes, we were the toughest team. We ended up first place overall.

We then moved on to coach the Bruins of Boston. People want to know how Blue got so famous for picking the goalies. Well, Fran Rosa of *The Boston Globe* asked me one day, "Who's playing goal tonight?" and I answered as a joke, "Blue says Gerry Cheevers will get a shutout." And by chance Gerry did get the shutout. Fran asked about the next game and I said, "Blue says Gilly Gilbert is ready." And sure enough Gilly won. So it was Blue picking the goalies.

Fortunately we had great goalies so she couldn't go wrong. But General Manager Harry Sinden was not too pleased that I talked things over with Blue and not him.

I remember one day I bought her into the Boston Garden and my captain, Wayne Cushman, thought he would have some fun with her, teasing her with his stick. "Let's see how tough you are, Blue, with this stick." When Blue bit the blade in half, he said, "That's tough enough for me."

I must add here Blue never started fights. In fact, the English bull terrier is called "The White Cavalier," meaning it will never hurt a smaller dog, even though the dog is attacking.

Blue taught me a great lesson in life. There were two huge dogs on Wolfe Island of the Thousand Islands in the St. Lawrence River. Each weighed at least 150 pounds. One was a spotted black and white, and the other was a smoke or grey with orange eyes. They were the terror of the Island, and once chased a Doberman till he had to escape going through a truck window. They attacked me and only the coming of their master saved my life. They were monsters.

The lesson began one morning just as the sun was breaking over the island. I opened the kitchen door to let Blue out, and at the bottom of the stairs were these dogs. Well, I said to myself, this is it. Blue's done. She's tough but even she can't handle these two.

Down she went. She seemed to be saying, "What's going on here? Who are you two big stiffs? Don't you know who I am? I'm Blue and this is my land and you two big jerks are in trouble." She walked around them, staring in their eyes, daring them to start something.

I had gone to get an axe, but even an axe couldn't stop these brutes.

Not growling, just as we say in hockey "wired" for trouble, down went the tails of the two dogs. And with her tail like a swagger stick, Blue seemed to be saying, "You got two seconds to get out of here." And lo and behold, they slunk off.

Blue looked up at me as if to say, "Piece of cake." Now I knew Blue was tough, but there was no way she could have withstood those two dogs.

This was the lesson she taught my family and me, that attitude is the most important thing. If Blue had gone down those stairs afraid, they would have sensed it and torn her to shreds. But Blue went with the attitude that "nothing beats me," and if you approach life like that, you will be successful.

When life knocks you down, get up and say, "Hey, temporary setback. Watch me go now." I know. I did this through unemployment and firings. You always bounce back with the attitude that "I'm the best," and "Nothing is too tough for me," and "I can tackle anything." Just like Blue. If you follow this pattern you will be successful in sports, in business and, most important, in life.

Blue's gone now. She passed away in 1987 at the age of fifteen. Like the lady said, she had character. And two blue eyes. But they weren't a bad fault.

———————————

Don Cherry is an internationally known hockey player, coach and media personality. He currently lives outside of Toronto and oversees Don Cherry's Restaurant, Inc.

Your dog is your only philosopher.

—Plato (c. 427–384)
Greek philosopher

Crunchy Versus Cranch

John E. Cranch

Sometimes my dog's intelligence is surprising. I remember one time when Crunchy and I were at our cabin, adjacent to which is a ten-acre pond. We decided to race, swimming the one hundred yards across the middle.

I'm not a slouch of a swimmer, but Crunchy's dog paddle beat me across. On the swim back, I lost again. Crunchy's face showed the gloating joy of a winner.

The next time across, I managed to beat Crunchy. That dog got out on shore and gave me the most withering look. This time as I swam back, Crunchy took off, running around the pond's perimeter. I won that time too.

With a tied score, Crunchy then decided, perhaps wisely, we'd had enough races for the day.

John E. Cranch is a colorant engineer living in Rochester, New York.

Lord . . . No one but you and I understands what faithfulness is . . .
do not let me die until, for them, all danger is driven away.

—Carmen Bernos de Gaesztold,
translated by Rumer Godden, *The Prayer of the Dog*

King of the Road

Gina D'Amico

His professional name was Hercules of Kenasayr, but we called him Herkie. We had driven to Weedsport to seek him out upon receipt of information from the then-practicing Dr. Basom. Our previous Herkie, also a show dog, had passed away a few months before. My father, who loved dogs, was extremely pleased and gratified that we were able to replace him so quickly.

Herkie was eight months old when we purchased him, and by the time he was one year old, he owned us all. He was a beautiful fawn boxer with white-stocking feet, a white diamond on his head and a black and white muzzle.

He became completely infatuated with my father who, being already retired, was able to spend endless play time and walk time with him.

My father loved to walk him. Our neighborhood streets were heavily populated with traffic because the airport was practically around the corner. Often on these walks with Herkie, people stopped their cars and got out to shake my father's hand and pet Herkie.

On one occasion during the early sixties, the then Senator John F. Kennedy planned an appearance in Rochester. He was expected to be driven from the airport, down Brooks Avenue and on to the downtown area. My father and Herkie made numerous trips to the Brooks Avenue corner to await the popular and charismatic VIP.

Finally the motorcade began winding its way toward my father, standing on the corner. The President-to-be Kennedy was in an open convertible. Upon seeing my father, he stopped the car and got out. He came over to my father, shook his hand and said, "What a beautiful dog you have. I've never seen a more beautiful boxer."

When I arrived home from work, my father was still euphoric. My mother said he had been laughing all day and refused to wash his hands.

Herkie was strictly a one-man dog. After supper, he lay across my father's lap and continued to hang on until his back legs were at half-mast. If my mother reprimanded him for any reason, he tried to argue, using a semi-growl.

Whenever our next door neighbor came over to reminisce with my father, Herkie confronted him after fifteen minutes had passed, giving the same reprimand my mother had received.

On Sunday mornings, my parents attended early Mass. After they closed the front door, our bedroom door would fly open. Ignoring my husband's commands to "go downstairs," Herkie confronted my side of the bed. Burying his face in mine, he urged me up in my father's absence. I felt like his second fiddle.

Car rides were Herkie's favorite pastime. The back passenger side belonged exclusively to him. There he reigned as back seat driver. If my mother stopped for a red light, he immediately nudged her shoulder to get moving again. He surveyed all surroundings and each pedestrian and driver for miles. I called him "King of the Road."

Even now I still remember wonderful days spent with Herkie and the love he gave all of us.

Dog enthusiast Gina D'Amico is especially fond of the boxer. She
actively supports the Wildlife Federation and the Lollypop Farm
Animal Shelter of Monroe County, New York.

*It is a strange thing, love. Nothing but love has made the dog
lose his wild freedom, to become the servant of man.*

—D. H. Lawrence (1885–1930)
English writer

Sumi

Mildred Furman

Many years ago my husband adopted a purebred poodle named Sumi. Faithful Sumi had always been a one-man dog—he took easily to my husband while I was always totally ignored.

We had acreage and a lovely camp outside of a small town near Letchworth State Park. One summer, we decided to plant a vegetable garden down the road a piece in a cleared area surrounded by beautifully wooded, hilly terrain.

After noting that the tender vegetable shoots were being eaten as soon as they popped through the ground, we put together a most attractive scarecrow, stuffed with straw. We dressed him in some of my husband's old clothes.

One evening, Sumi disappeared, which was most unusual. We called and called, walked the dirt roads and then got in the car to drive around, calling his name.

This went on for several hours. On the drive back to the cabin, we suddenly realized that there was one place we hadn't thought to look.

Sure enough, we found him. There he lay at the base of the scarecrow, protecting my husband's clothes. Faithful? You bet!

Mildred Furman resides in Rochester, New York.

Princess Poitin of Ireland, an Inn Dog

Barbara Flanagan Greenstein

Poitin (pronounced *Pah-tcheen*) is her name, meaning moonshine, that is illegally produced, 200-proof, potato-based hootch. The name is appropriate for our maxi-Benji bearded collie/Airedale mutt because everything she does is mildly illegal.

Since we gave her an Irish name, it seemed only fitting, just and proper that she spend three years with us as co-hostess at our country house hotel (country inn, in Americanese) on the magical west coast of Ireland.

To our dismay, we learned that Irish law requires a six-month quarantine period for all in-coming domestic animals. The reason for such seemingly Draconian policy is that this small island in the middle of the Atlantic Ocean and Irish Sea has never experienced rabies. Since it is an agricultural island, they are understandably dedicated to keeping the status quo. We sent proof of Poitin's rabies shots but to no avail.

Then we contacted American friends who had brought their twelve-year-old Irish (what else?) setter to live with them in County Cork. We saw their dog, who had sailed through quarantine with no ill effects, then or later.

Next we visited the Lissenhall Quarantine Kennels located outside of Dublin and found long outdoor runs, plentiful food and water, and spotless indoor and heated protection. We talked to the staff who told us they played daily with each dog. They encouraged us to send favorite toys and blankets or beds with Poitin to Ireland. Poitin would be watered and walked at the airport, then transferred to Lissenhall in a sterilized van, used only for animal quarantine purposes.

Outside the facility were twelve-foot, steel-fenced enclosures topped by razor-barbed wire and secured by many complicated combination locks and chains. Clearly, security would not be a problem!

We then considered giving our Irish Princess to a good home in Rochester. Our agony involved much tossing and turning of the conscience as well as the pocket book. Transatlantic dog-fares and six months of quarantine are not exactly in the budget category.

Before making a final decision, we consulted our veterinarian. He assured us that young dogs who are not overly attached to one person do very well. Poitin fit both categories. And we knew that canine confederate who had done beautifully. We then asked the crucial question, "If you were in our shoes, would you take your dog?"

"Yes." He answered without hesitation.

We rejoiced, thinking of Poitin running free around our ten acres of fields, salmon river and woodlands in Ireland . . . a much better bet than being a city dog in Rochester, New York.

We sent her on ahead of our move by three months so that she would miss the confusion of all our packing and be ready to move with us into our new home three months later. During the latter three-month period, we frequently visited Lissenhall. Always delighted to see each other, we were more delighted to note she had not lost weight, had retained her buoyant personality and seemed well-pleased with her new guardians pro tem.

When we finally came to pick her up, she raced around us barking happily, jumped into the back of our newly acquired nonquarantined van bearing Irish plates and driven by two newly certified drivers with spanking new Irish licenses, yawned and promptly went to sleep.

From our inn's former owners we inherited Coalie, a loving but not overly bright black Labrador retriever. At the last minute, by their design we suspect, we agreed to add him to our canine count with the proviso that Poitin and Coalie would suffer each other, if not gladly, then tolerantly.

Poitin took over immediately, as is her habit. She took over Coalie, the house, the staff, and the guests who began arriving a few weeks later. Both dogs were in dog heaven from the start—good food, good runs, good company.

Since it seemed de rigueur for all European country house hotels to maintain a proper menagerie of dogs, we held our own. Later we added three charming Irish donkeys: Joyce, Yeats and O'Casey. They kept the fields down by grazing, charmed the guests out of carrots from the kitchen and were great playmates for Poitin and Coalie.

Both our canine companions were trained under pain of death (well, at least a strong "No!") to keep off the guest room floors and out of the dining room. If guests liked (and, surprisingly, 80 percent did), the doggy duo was welcome in the drawing room after dinner for coffee and brandy (the guests, not the dogs, who were quite satisfied with a scratch behind the ears and a kind look . . . the dogs, not the guests!) Guests borrowed the dogs for long, rambling walks on the property.

Poitin, because she is a Corn Hill-Rochester terrier, was *oooo*-ed and *ahhhh*-ed more frequently than Coalie. Her beige-grey-white, soft-as-fog coat spilled over her body, nearly covering intelligent brown eyes. "*Oooooo!* She looks like a blonde Old English sheepdog!" "*Ahhhhh!* Now there's a smart, purebred dog if I ever saw one!" Coalie receive special attention from the occasional grouse hunter or guest who felt sorry for him because Ms. Moonshine was the target of most accolades.

The pinnacle of Poitin's social success was the evening all guests were paying more attention to Coalie than Her Worship. A houseful of grouse hunters was upon us, a rare and, to Poitin's mind, an undesirable state of affairs. She rolled on her back, nudged hands, offered her paw . . . but to no avail. After a clearly audible moan, she gave one short "I have to be let out for the usual reason" bark.

We rose from deep conversation, grousing, and followed her command. Out of the drawing room, into the hall, through the entry hall— Poitin the Flagship Queen, followed dutifully by Coalie the Consort. The heavy oak door opened to an Irish starry night. Cozy and animated voices rang from the drawing room. Poitin sashayed to the doorstep. She stepped aside. Coalie went past her without hesitation, out of the house and into the night. Poitin turned, pausing majestically, and high-tailed it back to her waiting audience, having ruthlessly rid herself of the competition.

It's for capers such as this that our Princess Poitin of Ireland is mentioned by name in no fewer than five guidebooks, including those of Egon Ronay, Karen Brown's *Guide to Irish Country Inns* and *The Connoisseur's Guide to Ireland*.

———————————

Barbara Flanagan Greenstein, a writer, actress and singer, lives in Rochester, New York, with her husband, Andrew. She is currently at work on a book about their Irish sojourn.

I am quite sure he thinks that I am God—
Since he is God on whom each one depends
For life and all things that His bounty sends—
My dear old dog, most constant of all friends.

—William Croswell Doane (1832–1913)

Airsoles and Airedales

Peter Hardwick

Being constantly on the road, so to speak, runners quickly learn to weave their way around the schedules of total strangers. I can remember how my own runs, along a canal tow-path near where I lived, were always a disaster during school vacation. Suddenly, the peaceful miles were obstructed by entire families strolling two or three abreast, showing no intention of stepping aside for a solitary runner.

Similarly, courses through industrial and public parks need rerouting during various times of the day and night. Just reaching a few blocks beyond a downtown "Y" at five o'clock can be as harrowing an ordeal as completing a first marathon.

But this interweaving of schedules has virtues as well as inconveniences. By choosing secluded routes, or running during the quieter hours, what would otherwise be a wave or a nod to a fellow runner often becomes a generous word of encouragement, maybe even a mile or two together through the early morning calm.

One typical morning several years ago, I was stretching it out in Thompson Park, on what has become one of my favorite runs. Taking a sharp right turn, I emerged from behind a group of forsythia bushes, only to be spotted by the worst type of running companion—a dog.

This huge, tousle-haired hunk of Airedale immediately took chase. "Don't worry, he doesn't bite," a distant voice recited the dog owner's anthem.

True enough, he didn't bite, just bounded, as Airedales tend to, and at a speed that made my 6:45-mile pace appear sedentary. Between avoiding his rushes, and feigning composure, I notice his owner unsuccessfully chasing both of us, demanding, "Clancy, return this minute." Clancy would have sooner passed up a T-bone steak than return to his master at this point. There was a game afoot, and I was very much part of it.

He rushed in front of me, forcing me to chop my stride, then turned and dashed behind me, brushing my heels en route. I soon realized that I wouldn't lose a chunk of calf or thigh flesh to my unneeded companion, but the chances of being sent sprawling increased with his every rush.

We ran down the Reservoir Road, Clancy gaining speed while my stride constantly faltered, until Clancy decided that either his owner's voice was becoming too distant, of perhaps I wasn't so much fun as he originally thought.

This was my first, or possibly second, time on this course, I'm not sure which, but the following morning I seriously considered altering my route. Eventually I decided that the overall pleasures of Thompson Park far outweighed Clancy's rushes. Besides, I mused, turning off Academy Street into the park. Clancy may not be there this morning.

He was. And he chased me just as far as the previous morning, with his owner still in pursuit.

As the weeks went by, a friendship slowly developed between Clancy's owner and me. Preliminary comments on the weather, his dog and my pace evolved into genuine inquiries on one another's well-being. We saw each other almost every morning, Monday through Friday, he wearing overalls and heavy work boots, and me in Gore-Tex running suit and Nike Airsoles.

From time to time, he was preoccupied training Clancy and merely offered a friendly wave. When I told my wife about Clancy's training sessions she laughed, saying that training an Airedale was a contradiction of terms. Watching the antics of these two some mornings, I tended to agree with her. The only order that would interest Clancy whenever I was around was, "Chase that runner." Why the owner stayed friendly, and why I responded, still baffles me.

Gradually, I noticed daybreak holding back a while longer. A slight chill crept into the air. Often a low mist hung over Thompson Park as I eased my way through the wooded trail on the northern slopes. I wondered whether I would see my early morning companions during the bitter New York winter, and would I really miss them if they didn't show.

Clancy's barraging certainly played havoc with my pace, but so far, he had never actually bowled me over. It was as if he enjoyed testing my nerve rather than my balance, cutting as close as possible without making contact, like a canine version of counting coup. My usual aversion to four-legged running companions had almost disappeared since this playful mutt had begun making sport of me.

Some mornings that winter, Clancy and his owner didn't make it. On some mornings, the sub-zero temperatures mastered me also. Clancy handled the ice better than I did, although with no more grace. His initial charge required a wider arc before he returned for a second lunge. His huge, squared-off head, that earmark of an Airedale, hung low to one side, while his front paws were always slipping away in the opposite direction, clawing in an ungainly fashion at the frozen ground. Yet, despite Clancy's inherent awkwardness, I was the one who left Thompson Park with a couple of skinned knees during the second week of January, proof that my nerve had finally lost our battle of wills.

Clancy, his owner and I continued our impromptu meetings season after season, and year after year. My wife often wondered why I never varied my training routes, but by now Clancy was as much part of my life that I would have missed his jostling. His enthusiasm never waned. In fact, I even became an easier target as my pace gradually slipped from 6:45 to around 7:00 minutes per mile. Clancy's obedience level showed a similar decline; occasionally his training sessions were resumed, but to no avail.

Early one morning, during one of my periodic attempts at returning to 6:45 pace, Clancy's owner stood beside the road, gripping Clancy's collar and waving me down.

"I won't be seeing you anymore, I'm retiring today," he called.

I immediately ground to a halt. After almost four years of anonymous friendship, we exchanged handshakes and formally introduced ourselves. I patted the back of Clancy's neck, and wished Lyle well. Then we continued with our morning schedules.

In the two years since, when my thoughts are preoccupied, I still find myself gazing across the park, expecting to see Lyle on the grassy hillside. And I still brace myself for the rushes of an Airedale that for some strange reason he believed trainable.

Peter Hardwick has been a runner for over seventeen years and a writer for over four. He lives in Watertown, New York.

A dog is a bond between strangers.

—John Steinbeck (1902–1968)
American novelist, *Travels With Charley*

Prince

Paul Humphrey

My puppy with little brown spots on
Is truly a pleasure and pride;
I worship the ground that he walks on,
But wish he would leave it outside.

Basket Case

Paul Humphrey

My neighbors got a puppy
As cute as any bug;
Its tail was brisk and uppy.
His nose was like a pug.

They put him in a cubby
Behind the cellar door,
A cranny dark and grubby
With crinkles in the floor.

I bought a wicker beddy
At Sears And Roebuck Inc.
And set it square and steady
Beside the kitchen sink

So then in bliss supernal
The rascal chose to snore
Through reveries nocturnal
BEHIND THE CELLAR DOOR!

Paul Humphrey is a commercial writer residing in Spencerport, New York.

Family Canines

Lloyd E. Klos

"A man's best friend is his dog." So has proclaimed a saying over the centuries. Certainly a dog is the superior to any other pet in its obedience to his master's wishes, if properly trained. There were a couple times, however, when I wasn't sure of this philosophy. You don't, for example, try to take a bone from a bulldog. At a very early age, I learned that potent lesson when my hand was ripped open by a cousin's dog. I've also sought friendship of dogs while out walking. A few have bared their teeth, causing me to "tip my hat and slowly walk away."

Our family, until recent years, always had a dog. Before the writer came onto the scene, his parents raised collies. A mother-daughter duo named "Daisy" and "Beauty" were pets of the household for years. One had a fondness for chewing gum. She'd chew and chew for some time, and then she'd gulp. She'd swallowed it!

The writer was about four when the folks purchased another collie. To me, the collie is the aristocrat of the canine kingdom. It has a regal air about it, moves with grace and beauty, and its colorful long hair, long tail, pointed nose and erect ears give the collie an aura which is approached by few of the other breeds.

Anyway, "Daisy" as the new canine was named, was quite a dog. She was sable, black and white and had a very docile personality. In fact, the animal was never a watchdog. Rarely did she bark. On one occasion, however, she showed an innate backbone to stand for her rights. One evening, she was outside the door, handling a bone with relish. A neighbor's dog came by and made a menacing gesture. In nothing flat, Daisy was on her feet with a bark and snarl which did her proud. Had the intruder elected to do battle, Daisy would have easily been the winner as her long, strong jaws would have made mincemeat of the intruder.

As a companion to the writer, Daisy was the living end, always near, offering protection which wasn't needed in those crime-free days. As a kid, however, I did have a sadistic tendency to pull her ears. It's probably why she didn't hold them in the accustomed erect position very often. Also, this fun-lover once tied a steel freight car to her tail in an effort to have a horse-and-wagon toy. When she felt that object tied to her, she dashed down the driveway, the toy beating against her legs. It's a wonder it didn't break one! Needless to say, a tanning was my reward for that episode of which I was reminded for many years!

There were two things Daisy detested. One was to ride in an automobile. She got so nervous that one would practically need a mop to handle the saliva treatment she'd give a car. When moving to Irondequoit in 1929, we brought Daisy to our new home in an open Hupmobile touring car. She was in such a state of agitation that on Norton Street near Red Wing Stadium, she jumped out. When Mother let out a yell and called her, she obeyed by instinct and returned to the car.

A second anathema was the sound of fire crackers or any loud report. Came Fourth of July, we'd fire a simulated gun which forced compressed air through paper with a loud bang. Daisy was in hysterics the whole day!

After moving to her new home, the next-door neighbor, who was an amateur horticulturist, made the remark upon seeing the dog: "She'd be good on a farm," to which Mother responded, "She's going to be good right here." And she was. Never put a foot into the neighbor's yard. A lady two doors over with an acute fondness for animals once called Daisy over. She wouldn't budge until Mother told her to go. But across the neighbor's yard? No sir! Down our yard walk, to the street sidewalk, and up the walk in the lady's yard. Incredible, you say? Well, Daisy was the ultra in canine intelligence. Her great-grandfather, Seedley Steely, was an international champion.

I could regale the reader with other stories of this animal. Suffice to say, she was the favorite of all the pets we owned. A few years before World War II, she became seriously ill and efforts to get her well failed. We had her put to sleep rather than allow her to suffer any longer.

Daisy's loss was felt very deeply, but it wasn't long before we had another dog. We were out riding on Sunday and noticed kennels on Paul Road in Chili, housing wire-haired terriers. Of course, we told the owners, Mr. and Mrs. George Warner, that we "merely wanted to see them." One looked particularly cute and . . . well, we came home with a new pet. We soon found out that this fellow we named "Terry" was not a docile animal. He took absolutely nothing for granted. He was a watchdog to a superior degree, make no mistake! No one could have gotten into the house without our knowledge. He loved to ride in automobiles, and he considered the family car his domain. No service station attendant could clean the windshield without Terry's show of teeth and a barking session which warned potential intruders.

The family's dogs were always trained to stay at home in observance of the dog ordinance. What good is a pet who is allowed to become a street bum? With Terry, the terror, things were a bit different. He had to be everywhere! One night he got out the front entrance when Dad opened the door and raced up the street to Clinton Avenue. A car came roaring along, hit him, sent him sprawling. The driver kept on going. Mother carried the knocked-out pet home and in the light of the kitchen, slowly revived him with warm milk. A little sore for a few days, Terry was undaunted, however.

Fortitude, tenacity, courage, a fiery personality. Terry had them all. One evening at the side of the house, he encountered a toad. Naturally, he attacked, picking up the hapless creature in his mouth. There must have been an ejection of fluid, similar to that of a skunk, for Terry dropped it quickly. It caused him to be ill for a day or so, but the next time he happened on that fateful spot, he searched for his enemy. Needless to say, he would have attacked again.

"Patton" or "Grant" would have been a more apropos name for this warlike creature. No table or chair was too high for him to leap onto. We once were in the backyard and looking out at us, seated atop the breakfast table, was Terry. It must have taken a Herculean leap to get up there, but he had to see what was going on!

When Terry died of old age, we said we didn't want another dog, but Mother always wanted one she could hold serenely on her lap. While out one day, Mom and Dad stopped at a place which advertised miniature fox terriers. Yes, you guessed it! Home they came with a cute little devil who was so small he could easily fit into a tea cup. He was promptly named "Jiggs" after the tiny dog in George McManus' famous cartoon strip "Bringing up Father."

Jiggs was not in the best of health when we acquired him as an enormous tapeworm was sapping his strength. Mother wormed him to good health and eventually he was to weigh 15 pounds at the peak of his life. He also had a second set of teeth which necessitated removing the older ones. An excellent watch dog and a real companion, he would let no one, not even members of the family, come near Mother while she was holding him. It's uncomfortable when animals act like that!

When Jiggs died, that was the end of dogs in our home. They are a lot of care, but if taken care of, not allowed to become street bums, given their three squares, plus a good bed in which to sleep, they are your friends for the duration. When one dies, it is as if a family member had gone.

But through it all, one has the remembrances of a lifetime, of companionship, fun and experiences. A person's life is considerably richer if a part of it has been shared with "Man's Best Friend."

Local historian Lloyd E. Klos is a free-lance author-writer-researcher.
He resides in Rochester, New York.

Gratitude: That quality which the Canine Mongrel seldom lacks; which the Human Mongrel seldom possesses!

—(Rev. Dr.) Lion P.S. Rees

Shelby's Big Day

Cynthia Kuhn

Sometimes, those big days in life turn out a little bit differently than they are supposed to. Our English springer spaniel, Shelby, learned this lesson the hard way.

Two-year-old Shelby comes from a distinguished line of hunting dogs. Springers, known for their stoic personalities, are able to endure extremely cold water and air temperatures. They will patiently hike through miles of field and forest happily accompanying their masters.

Shelby is a true lover of the great outdoors. She can outrun just about everything. (Our family affectionately calls her Zoom.) To keep up with her during a jaunt through the woods is impossible. As we trudge along like the slowpoke bipeds that we are, the only visible signs of Shelby are flashes of her liver-and-white coat through the trees. To her credit, she will occasionally circle back and wait until we almost catch up. And then she's off and running again. We like to think she is playing tour guide.

Her energy level is extraordinary. Her tail never even stops wagging. (We also call her Squiggle.) The sheer joy she feels in the fresh air is evident. Every fourth of fifth step, she leaps high into the air with the grace of a ballerina. Kicking up her heels, she truly soars, rejoicing in her freedom. Once when I was walking her to a nearby field, a young neighborhood boy pointed to Shelby and said excitedly to his mother, "Look, it's that *jumping dog!*"

While Shelby has mastered the fine art of skirting trees and other obstacles at top speed, she has not yet developed all of the requisite hunting dog skills. The instincts are there. She often puts her nose to the ground and "snuffles" along (a form of tracking that consists primarily of putting nose to the ground and sniffing with loud, snorting sounds—presumably this action processes the scents more effectively) in a crazy pattern, following the steps of something that once walked by.

She also races like the wind when birds fly overhead. The only problem is that she chases their shadows. Not once has she looked up into the sky to seek the actual bird. We don't think she's made the connection yet. At this point, though, the shadows alone seem to provide a completely satisfying chase.

My husband, Ken, is adamant that Shelby is going to be a hunting dog. (I use the word *hunting* lightly—I've never seen any game come home. I think it's just an excuse for the man and his dog to be outside together all day rather than indoors doing chores around the house or something.) Accordingly, we've spent many hours teaching Shelby to fetch. She is now one of those dogs who firmly believes that playing fetch at all times is the dog owner's most sacred responsibility.

Our penance for this is that we are constantly bombarded by her well-worn-by-chewing and drooled-upon bone. It is dropped in our laps whenever we happened to sit down. Actually, she has become quite good at fetching indoors.

Outside, however, is indeed a whole new ball game. If we throw a stick, she will fetch it and bring it back to us, but only to show off, quite proudly, what she has found. "I've got a stick and you don't," she says, parading before us. Regardless of the fact that to her it seems like a wonderful game, we (mostly Ken) were in fact attempting to prepare her for her big debut as an honest-to-goodness "hunting dog."

Finally, on one of these glorious autumn days, when the fiery reds and warm yellows created a glowing background for outdoor activities, we decided that the big day had arrived. Ken and Shelby set out enthusiastically for an afternoon of tracking through the leaf-laden grounds in a nearby forest. They walked for hours. Ken looked for game while Shelby raced and jumped through the trees. She wasn't paying much attention to her job as chief tracker, but she *was* enjoying herself tremendously. Ken concluded that perhaps she might need a little more training after all. It was not a fruitful day, game-wise, and eventually they headed back to the car.

En route, Shelby suddenly froze, growled for a moment, and POUNCED on something. She began to shake her head from side to side sharply. Then, just as abruptly, she stopped, dropping her prize. She half-heartedly lunged at it again before turning toward Ken with wide open eyes.

With horror, Ken realized that the black and white bristles covering the front half of her head were porcupine quills. The two of them stood staring at one another for a moment, too stunned to move. Her first real hunting experience had occurred and at such an inopportune moment. The only one moving was the liberated porcupine, and he was speeding away from them as quickly as his little feet could carry him.

The veterinarian's office was luckily very close by (bless him for having selected such a convenient location) and they made the trip in record time. After several long hours, the kind and diligent doctor had removed over five hundred deeply embedded quills from a heavily sedated Shelby. She napped for a bit, then was released.

Ken arrived home that night with a very groggy puppy who was carefully deposited onto her bed for what turned out to be a pretty long snooze.

Our little hunter needed a few restful days before returning to her supersonic energy level. She is now, however, once again up to her old tricks, zooming through the fields and forests.

In fact, later in the week, we noticed that her biscuit box was empty. As we watched television that night, every hour or so Shelby would rise, nonchalantly stroll behind a piece of furniture and triumphantly emerge with a biscuit in her mouth. Each time, she went to a new location and "found" another biscuit. She had apparently hidden them all over the house for her future snacking pleasure.

She must have felt that she deserved some sort of reward for having courageously conquered her big day.

We thought so, too.

Cynthia Kuhn is completing graduate studies in Rhetoric/Teaching of Writing at the University of Colorado-Denver where she also teaches composition. Cynthia, Ken and Shelby are natives of Rochester, New York.

Hogan

Deanne L. Lunn

My sister Laurie found Hogan, an abandoned puppy, alongside a road in Canandaigua. When she brought him home, my parents set down the "he's your dog, you take care of him" rules, and she did.

Since she worked for a golf course at the time, she was able to take Hogan with her to work everyday. As a puppy, he learned to stick close to her, but as he got older, he took off running as soon as they arrived at the golf course. He caught up with her periodically throughout the day, but, otherwise, he was busy doing his "dog" things while she was working.

Hogan got to know a lot of the golfers. They often told Laurie that if Hogan was running by, he stopped if they were teeing off, waited until they hit the ball and then continued on his way.

If Laurie and her friends stopped for a drink after work, Hogan was right there with her. When he was still very little, Laurie tells of sitting him on the bar so he could listen to the folks rehashing their day.

Later, when my sister could not keep him with her, my parents took Hogan into their home. They had him for almost thirteen years.

We never did know what kind of dog Hogan was. He was sort of a Hogan Heinz. His head resembled a retriever's. His shiny black hair was curly like a poodle's but with a somewhat relaxed perm, except for that tail of his. It remained long and curly and when he wagged it, the ringlets danced through the air. If he went to get gussied up, the groomers shaved him down so his coat shone like that of a wet seal's. But they'd leave his tail wild.

When my dad camped with the Boy Scouts, Hogan-Bogan (as we affectionately called him) usually went too. He chased squirrels and investigated every chipmunk hole he could find. Then, at night, he lay quietly by the campfire with the other campers and listened to the stories they told.

The times he couldn't go with Dad, he stayed home to protect Mom. One of those times, my mother was getting ready to go to bed. Bogey (another one of our pet names for him) persisted in following her, glued to her ankles, baring his teeth and growling. He broke into a spell of barking, then growled again, almost under his breath.

They found the ripped screens the next day. A prowler had attempted to break through a back window, and Hogan had alternately warned Mom and scared off the prowler.

Remarkably, he knew the perimeters of his yard and wouldn't cross them, unless one of us called to him or it was time for his walk. Oh, how he looked forward to those walks! Dad would stand by the door and jingle Hogan's collar not saying a word. Hogan came from wherever he was, galloping through the house. He knew it was time for his walk.

Even as he grew older, he ran like a pup on his walks, stopping every once in a while to look back to check if master were still there. Then, he continued, romping and sniffing and occasionally looking back as if to say, "Come on, hurry up!" When he reached the corner, he sat and waited for Dad to catch up, to walk him across the street, where again, he raced to the park to chase squirrels.

Hogan was used to being around older people, so his patience was tried when my little nieces came along. He sat tolerantly while they pulled at his ears and petted him a little too roughly. Eventually, he let them into his "family circle" and, wagging that wild tail of his in excitement, he ran to greet them with wet doggy kisses when they came to their Grandma and Grandpa's home.

We were never really sure where Hogan learned all the things he knew. He just seemed to know. I don't recall anyone ever consciously attempting to train him. He was quite remarkable in that respect, almost human. He seemed to understand and remember exactly what was being said to him.

Hogan died last December. It was very quick and he wasn't sick very long. He left a big hole in all our lives, especially my parents'. It was like they had lost a child and, more certainly, a friend. My nieces were very upset. They asked Grampa if Hogan would go to heaven. Grampa assured them that he was positive there was a place for Hogan in heaven.

We all still looked for Hogan when we came to visit. Eventually, the hurt lessened, and we stopped looking. But we came to find out that Hogan had not been forgotten.

His camping buddy, my father, died suddenly the following May. My brother and sister-in-law had the agonizing task of telling my nieces their Grampa had gone to heaven. Neither one quite grasped the fact at first. But when they came to visit Grandma, my younger niece seemed to have the whole situation resolved quite satisfactorily.

She approached Grandma and said quietly, "I know where Grandpa is."

My mother asked her where she thought he was.

She was poised and certain as she looked at Mom, patted her hand and said very knowingly, "He's up in heaven, walking Hogan."

Following her retirement, Deanne L. Lunn has returned to college in Rochester, New York.

The dog has no ambition, no self-interest, no desire for vengeance, no fear other than that of displeasing.

—Buffon (1707–1788)
French naturalist and biologist, *Portrait of the Dog*

Desolate Destination

Jennifer Maxwell

There was once a dog named Roger, who was not, by any means, extraordinary. He was of the mastiff breed and fell prone to not being overly intelligent or attractive. However, do not let appearances or actions deceive you, for underneath it all lay a dependable, strong and rugged dog whose disposition was similar to that of your own dog—chasing balls, fetching sticks, slobbering, acting very destructively toward your property and barking at every little rustle and whir.

Roger was deeply devoted to his owners, a family of four, and it was incomprehensible to question their actions or judgments because he felt that they were superior to him in both knowledge and logic. To fulfill his greatest desire you would merely have to place him in the midst of a compassionate and humane family.

His current owners were presently in the act of packing and marking heavy, bulky boxes in preparation for their move to a new and alien state that offered better wages and the opportunity for a promotion.

When the idea of taking a break from their tedious labor and driving through the countryside arose, it was pleasantly received. So, they (including Roger) all piled into the family station wagon and set out.

The individual minutes consolidated into an hour, and the hour lapsed into hours, until the monotony of it all lulled Roger into a deep and peaceful sleep.

How long he slept is one of those unanswerable questions of life that we mortals can only guess at, but when he awoke the car had come to a stop alongside a dusty, barren, back-country road. It was here the he was led out of the car and instructed to stay there until otherwise told. Roger sat there baffled yet nonetheless patient, wagging his tail as the very family he loved and adored drove away.

There Roger sat, abandoned on an unfamiliar road, with nothing but a broken heart.

Jennifer Maxwell wrote *Desolate Destination* while in eighth grade.
She attends Mercy High School in Rochester, New York.

Where are the dogs going? you people who pay so little
attention ask. They are going about their business.
And they are very punctilious, without wallets,
notes . . . and without brief-cases.

—Charles Baudelaire (1821–1867)
French poet

Dogs in My Life

Robert Goodyear Murray

Most people would never attempt to tally up and record all of the close friends and acquaintances they have had in their lives. When it comes to human friends, too many come and go to attempt to quantify. Yet, when it comes to dogs, most of us would be surprised at the number of memories we have of them.

My first memories of dogs go back to when I was a young boy. Feathers, Tar and Rusty resided with my aunt and uncle. Feathers was a friendly gentle collie, but he drooled quite a bit, which accounts for the stains on our wood floors at my parents' house. Tar was a large black dog who apparently did not like small children. I was scared of Tar, who was often kept in the dark office at my aunt and uncle's house. I really cannot recall ever seeing this dog. In fact, I only heard Tar bark and growl. I also remember Tar bit my brother once. Rusty was an exceptionally friendly Irish setter. My father always said Rusty was a great watchdog who would lick a thief to death. I realized that this wasn't exactly true the day somebody stole Rusty from my uncle's front yard.

Coco, Beethoven and Alexander were the dogs of my neighborhood when I was a young boy. Coco was a friendly black Lab. I remember crying the day my neighbors had to put Coco to sleep because she was getting too old. Beethoven was a large and sleek Weimaraner. I was scared of Beethoven. Seems like there is always at least one dog in everyone's neighborhood that kids are afraid of. Alexander was a very friendly dog who used to stand on his back legs and pump his front legs up and down in an attempt to coerce me into walking onto his yard and petting him.

My boyhood best friend's family brought home a puppy named Spot one day. Spotty somehow broke her leg while playing with her five human brothers. The vet put a cast on her leg. Spotty recovered.

Cinderella was the first dog to live with my family. She was only a puppy when she arrived at our house. Sadly, Cinderella developed heart worm and died only a few months after we got her. Cinderella was the first experience that my brother and I had with death. I remember crying most of that night while my parents walked back and forth between my bedroom and my brother's trying to console us.

Several dogs have also provided me with some funny memories. I remember my mother putting a frozen roast on an orange crate in our garage to thaw out. Someone's golden retriever came, uninvited, into our garage and left with the roast in its mouth.

As a college student, there were always many golden retrievers and black Labs on campus. Oftentimes these dogs would escape their owners and roam around in large friendly packs. It was not unusual to see eight to ten members within a raucous group, running about, chasing each other with frisbees, tennis balls, sneakers, sticks and some nonmentionable clothing items in their mouths. I am sure some of the more humorous nonmentionables, and I am not referring to homework assignments, were purposely given to the pack. Their carefree campus life-style was the envy of the students as they peered at them through library windows.

I worked on a cattle ranch in Wyoming along with Cheeky, Griz and Amos. Cheeky and Griz, on their own, were adept at herding cattle; however, they didn't get along and would spend most days stalking and fighting each other. I'm talking serious teeth-slashing, lip-snarling fights. Yet, no dog ever got hurt, and while the dog fighting was not funny, the ingenuity of the swearing and yelling that their owners would do when such a ruckus broke out in the middle of seven hundred head of cattle was usually quite humorous. In fact, Cheeky really only responded to his owner when his full name, Cheeky G*# D*%@#$, was improperly used.

Amos, a cattle-herding pup, seemed to have gotten shortchanged on cattle-herding genes. He would only attempt to herd horses, with or without a rider aboard. I will never forget his playful antics and facial smirks as his owner swore his best at Amos to stop horsing around.

I also have many fond memories of some of the best friends my family and I have ever had. Patches was my family's second dog. She was the one I grew up with. She slept in my room when I had pneumonia in the fifth grade. She used to play with plastic milk jugs and would tirelessly chase the light beam of a flashlight around our slippery kitchen floor. She also liked to get into the neighbor's garbage. The older she got, the more gentle and sweeter she became. She died in my parents' arms at the age of fourteen.

Scamp was taken in by my family after we noticed her walking around the neighborhood for several days immediately following my grandmother's death. A note on Scamp's collar asked anyone who found her to take her in because, as the handwritten note indicated, "our grandmother can no longer take care of her." Our four-year-old next door neighbor became immediately attached to Scamp, both with her heart and leash. Her love of animals developed while playing with the unbelievably patient Scamp, resulting in her fostering a menagerie of pets even to this day.

Kaycee currently resides with my parents. I have never known a dog who likes to play ball more than Kaycee. While playing, even frequent bouts of staggering and collapsing exhaustion do not daunt him. I am amazed by the sheer exhilaration that Kaycee finds in this simple game of retrieval with his family.

Nor do I think a more gentle dog has ever existed, one who only wants to please his family. When my grandfather was gravely ill and briefly lost consciousness, some undefined sixth sense nudged Kaycee out of his own dog nap and beckoned him to my grandfather's side. I saw him gently place his paw and muzzle on his lap, and even my grandfather said it was Kaycee who restored him to consciousness.

There are other fond memories, some deep and others as simple as a puppy's wiggle. For certain, dogs have provided me with an abundance of happy times in my life, and for certain, they will continue to do so.

Robert Goodyear Murray, a native of Rochester, New York, has a
Masters Degree in Environmental Science. He is a fish and wildlife
biologist for the United States Fish & Wildlife Service.

Dogs at Play

Laurence Pringle

Dogs are among the most playful of all mammals. The playfulness of a species seems to be related to the strength of its social bonds. Coyotes and foxes, for example, do not form the strong bonds seen among wolves, and they are less playful. As both young and adults, wolves are very playful, and so are their descendants, dogs.

Social play between two animals usually begins with a signal that means "This is play." Among members of the canine family, including dogs, the most familiar signal is the *play bow*.

A dog bows by crouching on its forelimbs, lowering its head and chest to the ground while still standing on its hind legs. This play signal was first described in a scientific way by Charles Darwin, who observed the play signals of his own pet dog. He also described his pet's relaxed open-mouth *play face*, which is another play signal shown by many mammals.

Since Darwin's time scientists have identified thirty-five different body positions, facial expressions and gestures used in canine play. One is the *leap-leap*, in which a dog or other canine makes two high leaps. Another is called the *play rush*, in which a canine approaches its playmate with a bouncy gait, often moving its shoulders from side to side and using such movements as tail-wagging, head-tossing, eye-rolling and face-pawing. Many other play signals, detected by careful study of films of dogs at play, are subtle and not easily noticed by people watching, but they have meaning to playing dogs.

Sometimes dogs play with other species. Happily for us, they often play with humans. Among wild canines, wolves have been observed playing with ravens. In Alaska a fox was seen biting the faces of mountain sheep rams playfully, and they in turn butted the fox gently with their horns. In Africa a young golden jackal was observed giving a play signal to a butterfly.

Besides playing socially, dogs and other canines play with objects. Pups play with all sorts of objects, and wild canines find toys, such as bones and feathers, in and around their dens.

Anyone who has owned dogs probably has seen a third kind of play that doesn't involve a partner or an object. This is called locomotor play. It can be as simple as a leap into the air, or as complex as running, spinning and making quick turns. Chasing one's own tail might be called locomotor play, though maybe to a playing dog its tail is no different than a shoe or other object.

Although we have no tails to chase, humans are among the most playful animals of all. That's one reason we have dogs as pets. Sometimes they are play partners. At other times, through their social, object and locomotor play, they give us delight.

Laurence Pringle studied wildlife conservation at Cornell University. He is the author of more than seventy books for children and teenagers on subjects that include nuclear war, microclimates, killer bees, biodiversity and animal play behavior.

Those sighs of a dog! They go to the heart so much more deeply than the sighs of our own kind because they are utterly unintended, regardless of effect, emerging from one who, heaving them, knows not that they have escaped him!

—John Galsworthy (1867–1933)
English writer

A Dog for All Reasons

Marilyn Riddick

If you ever find yourself considering a dog as a pet, you may want to think about a Cairn Terrier. Whether you live alone or with a large family, live in an apartment or a large home, a Cairn Terrier will fit very nicely into your life. Although Cairns are not as popular as other breeds in the United States, they have enjoyed great popularity in Scotland and England for centuries.

The Cairn's beginnings are said to have been on the Isle of Man off the coast of Scotland in the Atlantic Ocean. These determined, wee dogs emigrated to Scotland by swimming from the Island. The Scots noted that the Cairns were good hunters, and used them to hunt out the ferrets, whose mainstay was the Scot's crops. The Cairns became popular not only because they were very successful hunters, but because they had an indomitable spirit and fierce loyalty. Later, the Cairns became the darlings of King James' court. Somebody must have discovered the Cairn personality.

A foxy expression with bright, black eyes hint at a personality packed with intelligence and inquisitiveness. Ears are always at the alert—heaven forbid that they should be caught missing something. The tail could easily be called the busiest muscle in creation. There are three distinctive wags which I have discovered. First, there is the usual back and forth wag, which says, "I'm into it." Then there is the up and down wag which says, "I think this is pretty cool." Last, there is the round and round wag, which says,

"I'm feeling unbridled joy." These fun loving and affectionate little canines weigh in at between twelve to fifteen pounds and come in assorted colors.

Cairns can be all black, like Toto in *The Wizard of Oz*, or wheaten, a light beige, or brindle, a mixture of beige, copper and black. The brindle Cairn has the distinctive black ears and predominately black tail.

The Cairn sports three coats. The first coat is like down, the next is a bit more coarse and the top coat is very coarse. Because the top coat has an unruly appearance, the Cairns are called the dog in a work-a-day coat. That top coat is like a rain coat: it keeps the other two coats dry in wet weather. There is an added bonus about the Cairn's coat. No skin dander. That has been a real plus for people who suffer allergies to cats and dogs.

Knowing about Cairns from having one own me years ago, I was a perfect setup the day I walked into the pet shop. Peeking into the puppy cages with the little kids, I spotted him. His sign read, "Cairn Terrier, Male, Brindle, 3 Months." I wondered why the puppy was three months old and still not sold, and thought it might be because lots of people don't know about how delightful Cairns are. I looked in on a multicolored ball huddled in a corner. A little head perked up and I saw a foxy face with silky black ears and shiny black eyes. We just looked at each other.

Then, the very tip of his mostly black tail quivered. I smiled. He stood up, tail beating an enthusiastic, "Hi." I had to laugh at the quizzical expression on his face, and as I did, his little body left the floor of the cage in a straight up leap from a complete stand still. He just kept bouncing and watching, tail awag.

I couldn't resist. I named him Baggins, and we went home together.

Baggins and I have developed a comfortable relationship over the past four years. Although sometimes it's a struggle deciding who's really boss, he is a limitless source of fun. For instance, if I've been out, he wants to know where I've been and whom I've seen. So before any real greeting, he sniffs out all the information he can get. He's pretty limited though, since he can reach only my shoes and purse from the floor. When he has satisfied his curiosity, he gives me a proper, enthusiastic greeting, jumping up and down until I pick him up.

His inquisitiveness extends to everything in the house and around it.

If I so much as move a chair from one spot to another, and Baggins doesn't see me do it, he'll come prancing into the room and do a double take. He immediately checks out the empty spot, and gives me a "what's going on here," look. Then he goes in search of the chair. Upon finding it, he gives it a good talking to, every muscle in his body alive with indignation, and tail at flag (straight up). When he's satisfied, he gives a funny little "humpf" and continues on his way. This routine just breaks me up, and I confess to making the show happen pretty often. I do have to be careful not to laugh at him, because he sulks if he thinks I've put one over on him.

Baggins learned early and well that if he looks cute, chances are he'll get a dog treat. It's known as training your master. The routine starts first with finding me. With head down and rear end up in the air, he begins to talk to me with little "rmmps," beginning very softly and increasing the volume with each additional "rmmps," until he gets my attention. Next, he does a sit up with ramrod straight back, paws tucked into his chest. He waits. If I don't respond, he adds the full body twist, first in the direction of the kitchen (where the treats are) and then back to me. He waits. If that doesn't get it, he drops to the floor and does a roll over. He waits. Now we're coming pretty close to the limit, but I hold out for one more. He resumes the sitting up posture and goes into the speak-in-a-whisper routine. I love it. Sitting there, he thrusts his head forward with each silent bark. The only sound to be heard is his jaws chomping together. That does it. I get a lot of mileage out of one milk bone. Training is a different story. Teaching Baggins something new takes between fifteen and twenty minutes, however.

Both Baggins and I failed Obedience School. Part of the problem was short legs. Whenever dogs and owners had to do an exercise in single file, we couldn't be at the front or the middle of the line because longer legged dogs overtook us. We couldn't be at the end, because Baggins had to sniff out all there was to know about every dog and owner who went before us. The larger part of the problem was that I didn't know how to control Baggins. I kept trying to catch him doing something right so I could praise him with, "good dog," to reinforce his good behavior. But he went from one thing to another so quickly that the praise came out sounding like, "Good do . . . ah . . . bad . . . goo . . . no . . . BAD Dog." Because voice tones had to fluctuate between high for good and deep and commanding for bad, neither one of us knew what was going on. I left the class in chagrin. Baggins was happy to be through with it.

Later, through trial and error, I did learn that Baggins will respond to a command if I can sound like a Marine Corps drill sergeant. Also, he doesn't respond well to being spoken to in one or two word commands. I guess he feels it's beneath his dignity. If he's in the yard and I want him to come in, it does absolutely no good to follow the recommended, "Baggins, come." He just look at me, then looks away, as though to say, "Can't you get it right?" The almost command that works best is, "Baggins, come in the house." With that, he comes flying across the yard, sliding into home.

This tough as nails, hard to train wee dog, sometimes referred to as Mr. Baggins, is secretly heavy into mush. He loves to be petted and pays back the pleasure by licking my hand or arm to let me know he is really enjoying the attention he is getting. He follows me everywhere I go, and is often content to lie down on the rug next to where I am working. If I look down at him, he acknowledges me with a tail thump. He is my constant companion. I tell him all my woes and he listens intently and licks my face. If I cry, he comes and sits close to me. If I'm happy, he's happy to join in any fun going. With tail at full throttle, he chases around the house or yard with me.

He is the companion who is constant, who is funny and who takes his job of protector very seriously. I am the companion who loves the dog for all reasons, Baggins.

Marilyn Riddick is an administrative assistant. She enjoys music, gardening and writing in Rochester, New York.

The dog was cold and in pain. But being only a dog it did not occur to him to trot off home to the comfort of the library fire and leave his master to fend for himself.

—Albert Payson Terhune (1872–1942)
American writer

Dog-Tired

Susan F. Roman

One afternoon, I was in the backyard hanging the laundry when an old, tired-looking dog wandered into the yard. I could tell from his collar and well-fed belly that he had a home. But when I walked into the house, he followed me, sauntered down the hall and fell asleep in a corner. An hour later, he went to the door, and I let him out.

The next day he was back. He resumed his position in the hallway and slept for an hour.

This continued for several weeks. Curious, I pinned a note to his collar: "Every afternoon your dog comes to my house for a nap."

The next day he arrived with a different note pinned to his collar. "He lives in a home with ten children—he's trying to catch up on his sleep."

Susan F. Roman is senior editor of *Photo District News*, a magazine based in New York City.

Dogs laugh, but they laugh with their tails.

—Max Eastman (1883–1969)
American editor and writer

Shadrach and Sam

Nancy W. Schoepperle

It was time for Shadrach to have her kittens. She has investigated the linen closet, but I had caught her ronking the neatly stacked piles of wash cloths and towels, and had firmly turned her out. Next it appeared that my husband's lap might be her chosen place. But when her intentions became obvious, he had jumped to his feet and foreswore sitting down again in her presence.

And then Sam, our little red mutt, came in from his daily yard check. Months before, I had "rescued" these two waifs from a pet store window display. Sam had grown up to be a "normal" dog whose best buddy happened to be a beautiful, green-eyed, shining black cat.

Shadrach seemed more complicated. Okay, she was a cat. She had gone out and found herself a Tom. But she had also embraced some very doggy ways. When Sam ran down our long wooded drive to salute any family member's homecoming, Shadrach bounded along beside him. When Sam took a walk with us, Shadrach skulked along too, keeping to the edges, but keeping up.

Now it was birthing time. When Sam lay down on the bed he and Shadrach had shared since their kitty/puppyhood, she apparently found all the conditions just right. She lay down beside him and rapidly produced five healthy kittens. Sam acted as if this was perfectly ordinary—no big deal at all.

The kittens thrived. At first, Shadrach was a good mother, but well before they were weaned, her patience seemed to wear thin. And that's when Sam took up the slack.

He did everything but nurse them—he nuzzled them, licked them, let them climb his muzzle, his legs, even his ears. And he tantalized them into stalking his long feathered plume of a tail. He would lie down and twitch that tail until he had all five kittens in a happy tizzy, trying to capture and still it.

When neighbor children came to inspect our enlarged family, Shadrach seemed quite unconcerned that strangers were handling her babies. But Sam kept an eye on the visitors and remained alert and guardful until each kitten was returned to the pile.

And then the kittens were old enough to go to homes of their own. Shadrach showed no regret. Sam, though, we thought, really missed them.

This was our Odd Couple's only experience with parenthood. For the next fifteen years, the two continued being great buddies. Sam pretty much did his own doggy thing—barking, exploring, guarding us and his territory, observing our leavetaking and our homecoming, playing, sleeping in the sun. Wherever Sam was, whatever he was doing, Shadrach either joined his activity or stayed close to him and just watched. And purred.

And then, Sam died. The vet said it was simple old age. But, after his death, Shadrach seemed to lose all interest in everything and, in a matter of weeks, she wasted away and followed her buddy, wherever it was he went. The vet attributed her death to old age too.

But we knew otherwise.

Shadrach died of a broken heart.

Nancy W. Schoepperle cites her riches as being her family, friends, children, grandchildren and dogs. She lives in Buffalo, New York.

The old dog barks backwards without getting up.
I can remember when he was a pup.

—Robert Frost (1874–1963)
American poet

Gamin and Patches

Addison (Mort Walker)

Kansas native Mort Walker is an author and comic strip artist. His
many cartoons include "Gamin and Patches" (which he signed
Addison), "Beetle Bailey," and "Hi and Lois."

PART VII

Very Truly Yours

Robert Way, a dog enthusiast, believes "We are human only in so far as we are humane."

Writers in this section have rescued abandoned dogs, healed injured dogs, cared for handicapped dogs, fed hungry dogs and consoled lonely dogs—affirming we often are the Dog's Best Friend.

Walter and Ardelle Goulding's "Journey Home" is an account of despair, hardship and success. "Sirius" portrays Roger Caras's passion for dogs and justice. In "For the Love of Folly" and "A Gift from Githeion," compassion is expressed by action. In "Cool Character," mercy is exercised without fanfare.

Part VII, "Very Truly Yours," demonstrates how dear dogs and gentle people are mutually honorable friends, fit to serve and be served.

Steve's Dog

Mary Donahue Brown

We heard his heavy footsteps on the stairs. The long day of silence was ending. We gathered around the cellar door and watched my brother Steve climb toward us carrying the white bundle we knew to be his dog.

Early that morning, Star, short for Bart Starr, had crawled into the dark cellar to die. We guessed, too late, that he had been poisoned, maybe by rat poison left for him in a garbage can he had knocked over and pawed through.

Steve, then fourteen, followed his dog and stayed with him in the old cement cellar that we knew he feared.

A day-long vigil began. We six children crept through the house listening for some telling sound from below us. My mother moved about the kitchen all day, quietly closing cupboard doors, wiping away the traces of yesterday's Thanksgiving dinner.

In the evening, we heard the footsteps. His dark head bowed, my brother emerged from the cellar. The white form in his arms sharpened as he reached our group in the doorway, and I saw that it was my mother's Irish linen tablecloth that covered Star's body. It had belonged to my grandmother. Yesterday it had framed our Thanksgiving meal as it always did on special days.

I looked at my mother in horror. But she did not see the tablecloth.

She saw her son. She put her arm around him and we watched as they walked down the hill to bury Steve's dog.

Mary Donahue Brown is a fourth grade teacher. She lives with her husband and their two children in Webster, New York.

Until he extends the circle of his compassion to all living things, man will not himself find peace.

—Albert Schweitzer (1875–1965)
French philosopher

Sirius

Roger A. Caras

Although he was not yet three, Sirius was scheduled to die. A large, leggy brown-brindle and white greyhound—mostly white—he had made the terrible mistake of not winning several times in a row at a race track in New Hampshire and was packed off with a bunch of other "losers" to die.

That is the way it is for greyhounds, an incredible, a horrifying fifty thousand of them a year. Win or die. No mercy, no sentiment. In the money or put to sleep. That is a nice euphemism, put to sleep.

The greyhound rescue people try to take as many of the great hounds as they can find homes for, but only a small percentage of the cast off athletes can be saved from the needle. (The needle is an improvement. At some tracks they used to use an ice pick, thrust in between the ribs. Greyhounds have very large hearts that are easy to hit. It is not clear that that practice has been totally stopped.)

Sirius was one of twenty-five greyhounds that day and the rescue people had room for only two—twenty-three would have to be left behind to die. Sirius was not one of the chosen two and still wagging his tail, he was loaded up for his last ride to the veterinarian.

Sirius had a funny habit—he still does. Sirius smiles. He rolls his lips back and shows all his teeth, tilts his head and wags that nonstop tail of his. He smiles to greet you, he smiles when he thinks a biscuit is in the off-

Roger A. Caras, one of the leading spokesmen for the humane treatment of animals, being embraced by a blood-hound.

ing, he smiles just about all of the time. It is probably a leftover from a submission gesture used by his wolf ancestors.

The rescue people got a call from the vet. "I have put twenty-two down, but I am not going to do the last one—the big white dog. I can't kill anyone who is smiling at me. You'll have to come and get him."

They did. They went and got Sirius and loaded him up with another dozen they were taking down to Maryland where Betty Rosen, a member of the greyhound rescue network, had a dozen homes lined up. I was there when the van arrived and they let the hounds out in Betty's huge exercise yard. They ran like lightning, free after their long ride. Betty commented that she didn't have a home for the big white and brown male. I tried not to listen. We already had nine dogs, two of them greyhound rescues.

After half a dozen wild laps, the thirteen hounds began coming over to us to see what we might be all about. Sirius came toward me with a big smile on his face.

"You mean him?" I asked. "He doesn't have a home?"

Betty nodded.

"Well, he does now."

Sirius, still smiling at everyone he meets, is home on Thistle Hill Farm. It took less than a day to housebreak him, as it usually does with the ever-accommodating greyhounds. He lives with the nine other dogs, ten cats, four horses and two pet cows. He and the other animals have visits several times a week from at least two of our four grandchildren. He thinks everything is lovely and so he smiles much of the time.

Sirius loves it when we sing "There are smiles that make you happy . . ." to him. Even if he doesn't understand the words, he knows it is about him and that is exciting. So he smiles even more vigorously. Life is grand for Sirius. He has lots of room to do his laps in and he has a special friend, a border collie named Duncan.

When Sirius opens up, Duncan can't begin to keep up with him. To offset his comparative lack of speed, Duncan tries to use his instinctive skills as a sheep-herding dog. He tries to head Sirius off at the pass. He tries to ambush the fleet greyhound by popping out from behind trees and bushes. Sirius thinks that is neat and simply jumps over Duncan and keeps going. Duncan gets so frustrated he barks furiously and that brings Sirius up short. He stops, turns and barks back. The two of them stand there barking in each other's faces. When they have that out of their systems, they head for the house side-by-side, Sirius grinning, of course. We always reward our dogs with a dog biscuit for coming home. They eat their treats and then head off for a carpeted hallway where they curl up next to each other and nap.

Sirius will never know how close he came. He can't understand that he literally smiled his way back from the brink. His is a wonderful life and a wonderful story.

The story of track greyhounds is not. We will eventually take a fourth greyhound and I am sure one day a fifth. That will not make much a dent—five out of fifty thousand—yet if a lot more people took only one, or if greyhound racing could be outlawed . . .

There are so many ifs in the world or animals, so many ifs. Well, at least Sirius, Lilly and Reggie are safe. That is some comfort.

Roger A. Caras, author of over fifty books and former special correspondent for ABC Television, is the new president of the ASPCA. His family, currently including twelve dogs, lives in Maryland.

A dog will never forget the crumb thou givest him, though thou mayst afterwards throw a hundred stones at his head.

—SA'DI, Gulistan (1258) 8.99

tr. James Ross

The greatness of a nation and its moral progress can be measured by the way its animals are treated.

—Mohandas K. Ghandi (1869–1948)

Hindu nationalist

Home Is Where the Heart Is

Yvonne Cupolo

My late Grandmother Theresa Hennekey loved to tell the story of a mixed breed hound dog she knew in the 1920s.

Although he was owned by her neighbor, Mr. Schlegel, Sheppie was her constant visitor at the old house on the corner of Winton Road and Empire Boulevard. Grandmother always had a leftover treat for him, and he loved to play with her seven children.

Mr. Schlegel knew where to find his dog and, grumbling, would drag Sheppie back home.

When he moved to Sodus, well over fifty miles away, he took Shep with him. But right away the dog disappeared.

One week later, an exhausted Sheppie walked up the lane to Grandma's house and collapsed in the driveway. She gently pulled him into the garage and gave him food and water. He only drank a little and then fell asleep. He slept for twenty-four hours and everyone thought he was dying. When he woke, he stretched and shook himself—he was fine!

A few days later, Mr. Schlegel was back in town and he stopped at Grandma's, amazed to see Sheppie there. He gave the dog to her, and Sheppie lived with her many happy years until he died of old age.

Yvonne Cupolo of Rochester, New York, is an artist. From her grandmother she received a love of dogs.

All for the Love of the Breed

Madeline J. Erickson

large, matted Old English sheepdog was sniffing my flower bed. When I called this beastly looking creature, as I expected, he bounded to me, waggling his behind (Old English sheepdogs do not have a tail). He was friendly, rather healthy looking but in poor Old English sheepdog coat condition. Dog tag and ID tattoo were absent.

A friend with an extra dog run volunteered to keep him while I, in vain, looked for his owner and checked our newspaper's lost and found.

After ten days, I placed an ad in our local paper. Many wonderful people responded. I selected one family that fit my expectations.

Our new friend, bearing the new name of Muffin and a red bandanna around his neck, proudly left sitting in the front seat of a powder blue Mercedes. For seven years I received Christmas cards and photos of Muffin. His seventh-year photo was his last. That year Muffin passed away in his sleep.

Thus began my Old English sheepdog rescue efforts on a September morning twelve years ago. Where did Muffin come from? Who raised him as a puppy? I'll never know. But the joy of working with this wonderful dog and knowing that his last seven years were good ones prompted me to help the lost and abandoned of his breed.

And the rescue still goes on.

There was Alex. On a New Year's Eve day a few years ago, I received a desperate phone call.

"My dog is dying. Will you please take him?"

Crying, the caller could hardly speak. I managed to get an accurate history. Her three-year-old Old English sheepdog, Alex, had lived indoors with her family for his first eighteen months of life. The caller's father then came to live with them. He hated dogs.

Out went Alex. He was chained to an old car bumper. The car's underside provided his only shelter. Another eighteen months passed. Somehow Alex survived. He was fed "maybe every other day." His deterioration progressed. He no longer ate. That was what prompted her phone call.

The owner agreed to meet me along the thruway. When I saw Alex—frail, emaciated, badly matted and caked with his own excreta—I was overwhelmed with anger toward this woman. Yet when I reached out to touch Alex, I got the warmest licks any dog could give. Alex knew he would be helped.

I lifted him into my van. He could barely stand.

My vet waited on stand-by for him. Chili Animal Care has helped, day and night, with my rescued dogs. They deserve much more than "thank you," though they never expect more.

Dr. Wiseman greeted us. With rolled-up sleeves, she began to shave Alex to check for ulcerations, abrasions and any other abnormal condition. He was so thin—a mere forty-seven pounds—that the clippers went over his ribs like a roller coaster. Normally an Old English sheepdog weighs seventy-five pounds.

After several days of medical attention to get his diarrhea under control, Alex was moved to a nearby kennel. The following days, he blossomed into a happy-go-lucky clown, gratefully greeting his visitors.

Alex now lives with a wonderful Rochester family. He enjoys sleeping in a lovely, warm home—never to see a chain again.

Muffin and Alex are just two of eighty plus successful Old English sheepdog placements I have made over the past twelve years. I have recorded each rescued dog's unique story in a notebook.

The Old English sheepdog is a wonderful, lovable breed. The people who open their hearts and homes, and my husband, Wayne, and son, Travis, who answer calls to help, are also special. Without their support, these rescue efforts would never be successful.

Madeline J. Erickson of Churchville, New York, is a member of the Old English Sheepdog Club of America. She has rescued this breed for over twelve years.

Animals are such agreeable friends; they ask no questions, pass no criticisms.

—George Eliot (1819–1880)
English novelist

For the Love of Folly

Vicki W. Fowler, D.V.M.

She was born on March 8, 1974, in the surgery room of my hospital. Her mother was a champion yellow Labrador, Champion Groveton's January's Jill, owned by my friend and client, Eileen Ketcham.

There were seven pups in the litter, but only two yellow females. I had wanted to get a yellow female pup from Eileen for five years. This seemed to be an auspicious time to break down and buy one—two days before my birthday.

When the surgery was over and mom and pups were out of danger, I told Eileen that I would like one of the yellow females. Her name would be Folly because it was sheer folly to get a second dog when I already had a dog and three cats and lived in two rooms in the back of my veterinary hospital.

When Folly was seven weeks old, I went to pick her up. Eileen brought out both yellow female pups and asked me to select one. That in itself was special—Eileen usually made these decisions based on her knowledge of each pup and the perspective owner's personality.

I watched the two pups frolic and chose the bold and brassy one. I was learning from Eileen what to look for in conformation and this pup looked strikingly beautiful to me.

Completion of registration papers would make Folly mine. Eileen recorded her name as Groveton's Fun and Folly. She asked if I had considered showing the pup. My response was that she had promised years before to show my pup if I ever bought one that good. With a big smile Eileen confirmed that I had picked the pup she had wanted for herself, the most outstanding pup in the litter.

Folly's early years were filled with fun and excitement. There was my move to a real house and the birth of my first child. There were wading pools for Folly and Jack, my first Labrador. There were romps in fields and ponds, car trips and clients and friends for playmates.

Folly became the "movable furniture" used by my son in learning to walk. She was his bedtime companion. No house pet could beat her sunny disposition or her enthusiastic companionship.

She loved dog shows. She won her Championship in only sixteen shows, and Eileen was often complimented on how beautifully she moved.

One time I left Folly with Eileen so they could attend a series of dog shows. On this occasion Folly convinced me that dogs read our minds.

In Eileen's kitchen, Folly and Eileen were on one side of the counter and I on the other. Folly loved Eileen, always treating her like a long-lost mistress.

As I was thinking to myself that it was time for me to go, the dog suddenly shrieked across the counter into my arms. Her behavior seemed totally unprovoked by anything—except my thoughts of departure.

Folly's OFA certification of good hip joint conformation, her Champion title, her "birdiness," and her wonderful disposition made her the ideal breeding dog and confirmed the worth of her illustrious bloodline. I bred her three times, the first when my older son was eighteen months old. When he woke up in the morning, she had delivered two pups. He climbed into the whelping box, kissed the babies, then hugged and kissed her. She wagged her tail and went on delivering puppies.

Never did Folly object to people being present when she delivered pups. Never did she try to bite anyone for handling her pups. She was a devoted mother, and produced pups that she and I could both be proud of.

At age eight, Folly began to have abnormal heat cycles. I decided to spay her, expecting to find cystic ovaries. My heart sank when I opened her and found a baseball-size cancer on her ovary. I proceeded with the ovariohysterectomy, transfusing her as I closed the abdomen, because the cancer produced factors that interfered with blood clotting. It was a race between the capillary seepage and the transfused blood to see whether or not I'd lose her on the table. God was generous, and the transfusion stopped the hemorrhaging.

Consultation with a pathologist to determine cell type and with an oncologist to determine treatment led to two years of chemotherapy. Never did Folly act sick during that time. In fact, she convinced several of my clients to allow me to treat their dogs with various chemotherapy protocols for various cancers. I told them that Folly was on a cancer treatment program, then allowed her to enter the room to enthusiastically greet them. She looked as beautiful and energetic as ever, and certainly didn't match their concept of a poor dying cancer patient.

After two years she pronounced officially cured of her cyst-adenocarcinoma of the ovary and stopped taking her medicine. (Incidentally, of the dozen dogs that underwent chemotherapy during those years, half survived to be considered officially cured. The others all had significantly longer and less "sick" lives than they would have had without treatment, and their owners were glad that they had agreed to chemotherapy.)

Folly began to show her age the spring she was thirteen. Her legs began to bother her, and her lymph nodes began to enlarge. A good friend, Dr. N. Joel Edwards, a specialist in veterinary internal medicine, regretfully confirmed my diagnosis of lymphosarcoma (a form of leukemia).

Her oncologist, Dr. Richard Walshaw at Michigan State University's College of Veterinary Medicine, recommended chemotherapy. My first reaction was not to agree because of her age, but I found I couldn't stand by and watch her die without trying to help her. Under his direction, I again put her through chemotherapy, although using a different protocol and different drugs than before. It bough her a year of quality time before she no longer had enough function of her spinal cord (an area that the cancer had invaded early) to be able to walk.

We had helped her into the car, and had helped her with the stairs to the bedrooms, and had overlooked her decreasing control of her bowels. But when she could no longer walk I faced the inevitable. She was fourteen then, and had lived to see her great-granddaughter become part of our family. My younger son, who was six then, held her paw, petted her lovely head, and told her how much we loved her, while I administered the anesthetic that freed her ever-beautiful spirit from her worn-out body.

She died as she had been born and as she had lived, in my care, and surrounded by those who loved her.

Vicki W. Fowler, D.V.M., has a private veterinary practice
in Wynantskill, New York. Dr. Fowler grew up in
Rochester, New York. She is a native of Tennessee.

God give to me by your grace what you give to dogs by nature.

—Mechtilda of Magdeberg
Thirteenth-century hermitress

Journey Home

Walt and Ardelle Goulding

S he was a six-month-old miniature French poodle, bouncing around a predecessor's so-familiar arena. Chasing rubber toys and grandchildren, she was unaware that memories of the former occupant lingered in every corner for her adopted "parents."

This tiny furry object would never fill the paw prints of the old but intelligent standard, so we named her Misty.

On the morning that Misty's story began, we left her with our veterinarian for routine surgery. When the spay operation was complete, we would reclaim her and then attempt to learn to relax with little Miss Wildfire. Little did we realize that success, and a long struggle between reason and determination, would create Misty's own interesting legend.

Our doctor's call came shortly before noon. It was apologetic. "Your Misty's heart stopped twice during recovery but the operation was successful. Your puppy is one of the unusual cases where an animal is allergic to anesthetic. She may have some brain damage, but it may be less than we anticipate. She is breathing normal now, so let's give her a little time before we decide to terminate her life."

Suddenly the word "routine" took on the meaning of "unexpected helplessness." Before the ordeal would move behind us, we would discover the importance of time, teamwork, and simple animal tenacity.

We visited Misty that afternoon, bringing a favored toy from her bas-

We visited Misty, bringing a favored toy from her basket.

ket. We received no indication that she was aware of our presence. More important, she could not stand up on her rear legs.

While looking down upon a Misty we could not comprehend, she began to whine at that moment. The front legs moved slowly and the front quarters lifted. Meanwhile, both legs supporting the rear quarters remained together at the side. We watched as, still emitting the cry, she pulled her body in a circle, the rear quarters' weight riding throughout on the left-hand hip socket. We sensed confusion and fear.

She should be put to sleep, we knew, as we drove home. But if she is a family member, why not give her a little time for nature to assure the direction we should now take. The operation was not of her choosing. In fact it was not really nature's first choice in one of her creations. If the hospital staff is willing to give her a little time, we will do, we decided, as much. So the ordeal begins.

Days, finally a week passed. Misty still indicated no desire to stand up. Attendants kept her cage, behind the lobby door, clean. They began to treat her in the whirl bath. They even crushed her dog food because she could, or would not, chew.

This continued, and after thirty days, the letter arrived recommending euthanasia. There also would be "no charge." We later became aware of the "team work" part played by these concerned professionals.

Finally, equipped with a helpless puppy and her medical documentation, we headed one hundred miles south to Ithaca, New York, to obtain a final answer from Cornell University's small animal hospital.

Upon arrival, they lifted Misty from her blanket in the cardboard box and weighed her. She had dropped from seven to six pounds. They noted the severe, infected abrasions adjacent to her hips and a bronchial cough. Most disturbing however, to everyone, was her inability to lift her rear quarters. She failed to demonstrate the basic motor equilibrium. They suggested we leave her for further evaluation by the "absent" neurologist. The doctor in charge had a name not unlike Hornblower, so with a measure of confidence we drove home alone.

Three days later we received a call to pick up Misty. Her prognosis was not encouraging.

Severe cerebellum damage had been done to her brain—her muscle reaction was reverse to a normal response. Her cough, although weakening her physical condition, was clearing up. The ulcers on her flanks could be treated with medication. But her sight, or visual perception, could not be accurately determined.

"You're telling us, Doctor, Misty has really nothing going for her?" We asked, realizing this could be the end of the long ordeal.

"She has two big assets in her favor," he answered. "She can digest food and she can eliminate it. She also has youth, and we hope some get-well time. We are aware that strange things happen when an unwell animal returns to familiar landmarks. We hope you will give her that time."

We left with our tiny "responsibility," a large supply of medication and antibiotics and the good wishes of experienced professionals.

It was a quiet trip home to Rochester, wondering why we had been expecting a miracle. That was still ahead.

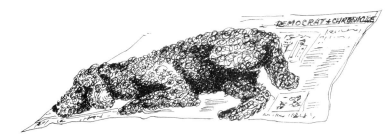

Misty was finally home again, stretched out on paper in her once-familiar living room.

Misty was finally home again, stretched out on paper in her once-familiar living room. The moment of truth, of our inabilities to do the physical impossibility, was overwhelming. Suddenly, it was Misty's turn to indicate our direction. It was the first of many tiny but important "miracles."

The familiar routine suddenly began, this time outside the confinement of a doctor's cage. She remembered her paper training! Somehow we realized that if she could remember this detail of her past, she could remember more. We decided to repay her little communication to us with what she needed above everything—time.

More weeks rolled by and Misty was still unable to stand up. During this time we devised a tubular frame, among other aids, by which to support her weight with rubber bands. It would facilitate bathing and bed arrangement, dry out the sore spots and, we hoped, remind her of the reason God gave her four legs. This was a big failure, but it supplied another "miracle." The first time she remained passive and limp as we strapped her in. The second and last time, she responded with a show of genuine belligerence. Her rear legs pushed away as she registered displeasure. She again displayed a reason to feel another measure of optimism!

We began to understand how partnership and time were intermixed

We devised a tubular frame to support her.

Finally Misty stood up on very shaky legs.

and that Misty had been supplied with the best. Success now rested within the determination range of our little patient.

Another concerned friend (and partner) suggested old-fashioned cod liver oil. So each morning, into the side of her mouth, went an eye dropper and from that a heavy spurt of its contents. She had graduated by that time to bottled baby foods and, still in her cardboard box, spent warm summer days toasting in the sun.

We left her in Webster with our daughter each day before work. After work, she began to indicate her pleasure in the drive home. One afternoon, rubbing her little teeth with my finger, I felt her attempt to bite down. She could remember to chew food; she gave us another reward.

Finally Misty stood up on very shaky legs and the entire family had its first celebration. We realized this was but a partial victory but it substantiated the medical experience of the doctor in Cornell.

The hip wounds healed over, unfortunately without hair roots. The bronchial condition no longer troubled her. She began to masticate her own puppy food. With assistance of someone ahead, clapping hands, she began to walk around the house and over wide boards and two-by-fours.

Misty's climb back to normalcy continued to gain momentum when we discovered she would detect movement across the street and, with her first barks, express her former fascination. Her love for the rubber toys came back slowly, and it was noticed that once again she could grip with her teeth while her rear feet left the floor.

She never did recapture her coordination to allow her muscles to spring her into chairs or up a flight of stairs, but she succeeded in her own way. She used her chin as her crutch. She could not balance on her hind legs but she rewarded us in ways never contemplated. She was a spectacular walker.

She never stopped sharpening her reaction skills.

Somehow, Misty, in her near-complete recovery, came back to us with a curious mannerism—she pranced in normal stride. All four paws lifted high in correct sequence. She generated comments such as "Is that a show dog?" or "Just out of the Marine Corps, Blackie?" The one we particularly recall was pronounced by an irate lady in Florida shouting, "Take the sand burrs out of your dog's pads, mister!" Talk about a conversation starter.

She traveled with us in our trailer home around the entire country, and often slowed down and sometimes stopped passing traffic as she paced herself proudly besides us in her daily walk.

Misty remained eight more years as a contributing family member. She never stopped sharpening her reaction skills by daily begging for and then playing her game of "dodge and return" soccer. She was as determined in this as in anything else. It was, we believe, the activity that finally removed her from us.

A Virginia camp was to be our home for a few days during a return from Florida. Unfortunately, we arrived on the heels of an earlier thunderstorm. After set-up chores, Misty indicated her desire for a soccer game and receiving her ball went down the camp road in her usual manner. She may have picked up live bacteria from a sewage overflow.

We can never forget her.

The following day her own system, with the assistance of a local veterinarian, attempted gallantly to clear her body of the poison.

We can never forget her.

Certainly, we believe we will see all of our beautiful pets again. We'll be especially attracted to a high-stepping black miniature poodle playing soccer.

———————————————

Since retiring, Walter Goulding volunteers his services in community organizations. When not in their Rochester, New York home, he and his wife Ardelle travel.

You become responsible forever, for what you have tamed.

—Antione de Saint-Exupery (1900–1944)
French author and aviator

A Gift From Githeion

Peter Heveron

Following several months of travel in Europe, Suzie and I settled down for a while in a Greek fishing village on the tip of the Peloponnese peninsula. We heard we could get work picking olives in October, so we got an apartment in town and went about looking for jobs.

We found work easily enough, but one day we found something we never expected. On the road that led out of town we encountered an injured dog. She was living in a little ravine by the side of the road, surviving on whatever scraps or bones some passersby might throw to her.

Suzie crossed the road to avoid her. Since she was such an animal lover, she was afraid she would take pity and there was no way we could help a dog in our situation. When Suzie crossed, the dog crossed too. She crawled on her belly and lay down at Suzie's feet. The dog apparently had been hit by a car or caught in a trap. Her back right leg was broken and swollen to three times its size.

That day we brought her some food and water. This starving dog paused to thank us before devouring her food. For the next few days we fed her, but she needed more than that to survive.

The village that we were living in, named Githeion (GEE-thee-on), is about the worst place in the world for dogs. Packs of them roam the streets and farms. At work in the olive groves we had to hang our lunch from trees or the dogs would get it. The people had little respect for dogs, and even less for injured dogs.

The local veterinarian, Christo, agreed to help us. Suzie carried the dog two miles to his office. On the way, local people told her, "Don't bother."

Christo was helpful. He gave her injections of antibiotics, cortisone and vitamins, and provided an apparatus so we could continue to give the injections daily until she became healthy. Unfortunately, her broken leg had fused at the joint and she would never regain its full use.

Fortunately he did not charge us for his services because his office was run by the government. Since he wanted to improve his English, we became good friends and visited often. He suggested that we name the dog Githeion after the village where we found her. We agreed.

With food and medicine Githeion soon was able to walk. We began to exercise her and walk her to the doctor's office. Sometimes we all sat in the office singing songs for hours. Githeion was just happy to be with us.

People in town marvelled that we had brought a poor dog back to health. Our landlady soon agreed to let us keep Githeion at our apartment, outside, making it much more convenient not to have to walk everyday to her roadside home to feed her.

There was one thing that we were not able to do, however. We could not find a home for Githeion. Nobody in the town was interested in taking the dog. And we had to leave the country after three months when our visas expired.

Githeion became our good friend in the months that we lived in Greece. In addition to being a beautiful dog, she proved to be very intelligent, and we realized that if there was any way possible to bring her home with us, we would.

We learned this could be done if we took care of all her shots, completed a small mountain of paper work and arranged for a commercial airline to ship her. This would require spending some time in Athens. We met a young couple from that city who invited us to stay with them while we made the arrangements.

Since public carriers to Athens would not allow a dog on board, Suzie and Githeion hitched a ride with a delivery truck bound for Athens. I hitched a ride with another truck.

Suzie's ride was a gruelling thirty-six-hour drive. The driver was slow, the truck was old and there were many deliveries to be made. During the journey Suzie and Githeion formed a bond that would last a lifetime. Githeion showed her gratefulness by the look in her eyes and her infinite patience.

Our time in Athens was both frustrating and rewarding. Most government agencies were closed as it was holiday season, so it took weeks to complete the paper work. During that time our hosts treated us to a most unusual holiday season of dining, dancing and playing cards. Many people met Githeion, heard her story, were somewhat amazed and supported our efforts.

After many weeks, Githeion finally had a passport complete with photograph and pawprint. We said a tearful goodbye to our dog at the Athens airport and sent her off to Rome, then New York, and eventually Los Angeles.

Suzie's dad took care of Githeion for the next four months while we traveled to Asia. He immediately fell in love with her. He took her to an American veterinarian to continue her care, and she soon gained weight and walked with only a slight limp.

Once reunited with Githeion, we moved to Rochester, New York, where we have lived with her for the last ten years. During that time we enjoyed the company of the best and probably the luckiest dog ever.

Githeion loved her life with us. She was extremely loyal and protective. She also never lost her survival instinct. One time when she was frightened by fireworks, she rain into the woods and was lost for almost two weeks. When finally found, it appeared that she easily survived and lacked only the human affection that she craved so much.

Recently Suzie took her on a long road trip to visit her aunt in Iowa. Githeion gladly served as her companion and protector. It was as if they intensified the bond that was formed ten years ago in Greece. During the hours on the road Suzie and Githeion communicated with eyes and voice. All her life Suzie had had dogs but never one where the friendship and love was so deep.

A couple of months later Githeion left us as suddenly as she had come. She collapsed one summer evening and died in Suzie's arms. Left with only the memories of this special dog, we are thankful for the unconditional love she gave to us and the life we were able to give her.

Peter Heveron owns a small business in Rochester, New York.

Every man is Napoleon to him, hence the dog's constant popularity.

—Aldous Huxley (1894–1963)

English novelist

Belle

Marjorie Holmes

We all knew our dog was doomed. After three long months in the hospital and three operations, she was getting no better. And it was all my fault. Nobody blamed me, yet I felt so guilty.

"If Belle's got to be put to sleep," I insisted that awful morning of our decision, "I'm the one who should give the order."

In vain they tried to spare me. "Mom, no, you don't have to. I will," a son volunteered, before plunging forlornly off to school. My husband said he'd do it from the office. But I was adamant. I should have tied her up before we took off in our boat to pull those water-skiers. I should have watched out for her. After all, I was driving the boat the day we hit her.

The family was finally out of the house. I paced the floor, struggling for composure. Get it over with. It should be a relief. We'd been debating this so long . . . I strode to the phone at last. "Doctor Mosseller? We've decided the most merciful thing would be to . . . let Belle go."

"Yes. Okay. I think you're right."

I hung up, drew a deep breath, turned the fire higher under the coffeepot. Don't cry any more; you've cried enough. She'll be so much better off. Drink your coffee, read the paper . . . but, Oh Belle, forgive me! New and more terrible tears suddenly blurred the page. I sprang up, appalled. Feeling like an executioner. As if I had just ordered that one of my own children be put to death—or at least a whole era in the life of our family. Even as I raced back to the phone I was crying out loud, "No, no! what have I done?"

This time the circuits were busy. I dialed again and again. Finally the doctor's aide was saying, "I'll see if I can catch him . . ." Then the doctor himself was on the line.

"Stop, wait, don't do it!" I gasped.

In the silence that followed, my heart almost stopped. "You caught me just in time," he said. "Are you sure?"

"Yes. No! . . . Yes, it's got to be done, but wait till tonight, please. At least we can come down and tell her good-by."

A bit sheepishly I called my husband then—and he agreed. "But let's not say anything more to the kids," he said. "They've accepted it; no use putting them through it all again."

As we drove the forty miles to the small Virginia town where we had our summer cabin, we reminisced about Belle.

This fat, polka-dotted Dalmatian had been an oddball from puppy-hood. Her eyes didn't match—by day, one was blue, one brown, and after dark they lit up like stop lights, red and green. She barked, she shed, she luxuriated on forbidden sofas, raided trash cans and ate everything that didn't eat her first.

And how she loved to swim. She was always first in the car when we headed for the lake, and the first one out, streaking for the water like a jubilant child. The skiers learned to swoop around her eagerly chugging head.

Then we got a new boat—secondhand boat, rather—but bigger and more powerful than our last. The teen-agers wanted to try it out that evening; I said I'd drive. I had a strange feeling I really ought to tie Belle up. But, sensing excitement, she was already dashing past us. We heard the usual big splash as she dived in.

I forgot all about her. It was enough just to concentrate on the controls, to watch and listen for the signals from my husband and the tensely waiting skiers.

"Hit it!" The traditional call from skiers ready to take off.

Marjorie Holmes breaks from typing while her daughter Melanie paddles, and their dog Belle dogpaddles at Lake Jackson, Virginia. Photo credit: Albert F. Rayl.

I pulled back the lever, we shot through the water . . . then that body-shattering jolt. That awful thud. Those wild, agonized yelps.

The details of that dreadful night came back to me so clearly. Our frantic calls to vets until we reached one who would see her if we'd bring her in. But we'd have to detour, we were told—there was a parade. Then the dash through the countryside, a daughter driving while the rest of us cradled and tried to comfort the blanket-wrapped bundle in the back of the station wagon. Despite the long bumpy detour, we ran into the parade.

Our daughter jumped out, dripping wet, and begged a policeman to let us through. He shook his head and turned his back. More desperate miles, only to encounter more parade.

The car stopped. "Here, Daddy, you drive." Again Melanie leaped from the car, and extending both arms, simply stopped the parade until we could pass.

Doctor Mosseller couldn't give us much hope. "I'll try to make her comfortable. If she makes it till morning we may be able to operate, but even then . . ."

Belle made it all through the summer, while that brilliant young vet put her mangled body back together. But one leg refused to heal. More operations loomed—a bone graft, perhaps, but even that would be arduous and doubtful. Amputation would probably be best. We winced at the prospect. Poor Belle—could she stand it? Could we? . . .

Then we were at the vet's office. We could hear Belle barking clear down the corridor, as if she sensed our presence. They wheeled her out on a little cart—and her tail was wagging! Wildly, eagerly, despite the cast and bandages, she greeted us, quivering, contorting in an ecstatic frenzy. People have words to express their love; dogs can only strain and wag and frantically lick your hands.

We knew we couldn't put her away. And the doctor read the message in the tears that ran down our faces. "Look, if you're willing to nurse her, why not take her home until you're sure?"

Rejoicing, we lifted her into the car.

The youngsters couldn't believe it. The dead restored. They were beside themselves. They helped with the nursing—and the spoiling. For she was queen of the family now, reigning from the once forbidden sofa, this former, often scolded renegade. But we knew we had only postponed the inevitable, and it haunted us. Especially the weekend we took her to the lake, and she lay whimpering, gazing toward the water.

It was at that point I remembered the words in the Bible, "Where two or three are gathered together . . ." (Matthew 18:20). Why not try prayer? My column "Love and Laughter" was appearing in *The Washington Star*. I would ask not only our church and our friends but my readers also to gather in a common spiritual purpose. And so I told the story of Belle, concluding: "The verdict is this. In another month, if the hip has not healed—amputation, or the end. There are no accounts in Scripture of the healing of animals. But I believe the Good Shepherd would have healed a pet had He been asked."

The newspaper was scarcely on the street when the telephone began to ring. Prayer circles. Animal shelters. Individuals. Then came the avalanche of mail. "The Lord is concerned about everything that is dear to us," one letter said. "He knows every sparrow that falls," another wrote. People shared their experiences, funny and sad. They advised, told of successful amputations. Above all, they told us they were praying.

As for Belle, had she any idea of the floods of love she had released? We can never know. We know only that as she stretched and scrambled around, she became less awkward with the cast, then surprisingly nimble. Two weeks later, when we went back to the doctor, he was amazed. "There's still a lot of damage. The pin has shifted . . . but the tissue is growing!" By the third week he was able to lessen the bindings, by the fourth to remove the cast altogether.

"It's remarkable," he said. "She'll have some arthritis, but she'll be swimming again next summer. This dog is well!"

Belle lived three more years. Still battle-scared, a little gimpy. And as she would stand, her hips in perfect alignment, I remembered what one reader urged. "Never offer God a picture of injury. Visualize perfection."

And with the living proof of that philosophy before me, I sometimes thought, *Maybe if we all visualized perfection and kept the image vivid, our lives and the whole world would be more perfect.* And if all of us would pray for each other with the selfless warmth and enthusiasm with which people prayed for Belle, miracles could occur every day.

———————————

Marjorie Holmes is the author of books of poetry, prayers,
and religious history. Her best sellers include *I've Got to Talk
to Somebody, God, Two From Galilee, Three From Galilee,*
and *The Messiah.* She lives in Manassas, Virginia.

*Marjorie Holmes with her husband
Dr. George Schmieler and their
golden Lab Ben and poodle Tanjy.*
Photo credit: Jim Judkis.

*If you have men who will exclude any of God's creatures
from the shelter of compassion and pity, you will have men
who will deal likewise with their fellow man.*

—Saint Francis of Assisi
Patron Saint of Animals

Caesar, Brutus, and St. Francis

Sue Monk Kidd

"I'm taking you guys to church, so please try to behave, okay?" Our two rambunctious young beagles, Caesar and Brutus, sat on the front seat of the car and ignored me, their floppy ears perked to attention as they watched the stream of traffic. At the stoplight, I braked as a woman walked her black poodle across the street. Caesar and Brutus let out a string of woo-woo-woofs.

"Now see? That's what I mean," I told them. "None of that."

It was a balmy October afternoon and we were on our way to a "Blessing of the Animals" service at Grace Episcopal church. I'd never attended one of these services, and frankly, I had no idea what to expect. I only knew it was held each year on St. Francis Day (since St. Francis had a special love for animals) and that folks were invited to bring their pets. From the moment I'd read about it, I'd had a nudging feeling I should go.

Now I wondered if I was out of my mind. What if Caesar and Brutus disrupted the service? It would be just like them. Beagles are bred to do three things: sniff, bark and charge at anything furry. Once my son found Caesar in our fenced backyard stranded up in a crepe myrtle tree where he'd *climbed* after a squirrel.

Earlier in the day I'd asked my children if they would like to come along to see the dogs blessed. "Let me get this straight," said Bob. "You're taking *our* dogs to church to get blessed with a lot of other animals?" He was biting the inside of his mouth to keep from laughing. Ann had simply gazed at me with her when-are-you-checking-into-the-asylum look.

I looked at the dogs, thumping their tails on the car seat, barking at everything that moved outside the car. "Will you be quiet?" I cried. The truth is, I'd never taken to these two hyperactive beagles the way I had to our beloved old, slow-moving spaniel, Captain. He'd presided quietly over the house for thirteen years before he died. These two were his so-called "replacements." Some replacements.

I turned into the church parking lot just as the service was about to begin. Beside the children's playground was a table draped in white with a St. Francis statue on it. A little crescent of children, adults, dogs (*quiet* dogs) and other animals had formed around it. I lashed Caesar's and Brutus's leashes to my wrists like a rodeo cowboy getting ready to ride into the ring.

The dogs came out of the car in a yapping frenzy, noses to the ground, dragging me behind them. I tugged and wrestled them over to the other animals. The priest was saying something about celebrating the presence of animals on earth, how they too were part of God's wonderful plan.

"Woo-woo-woof! Woo-woo-woof!" they barked and bayed at the other dogs, drowning out the voice of the priest. People looked at me and smiled sympathetically. Even the other dogs stared at me.

Caesar and Brutus then spotted a pet carrier on the ground to my left. Sitting regally behind the wire was a cat. "Woo-woo-woof!" They lunged toward the cat, nearly tipping me over. The priest was practically shouting now. I frantically tried to hush them as they strained on their leashes, which were cutting into my wrists to the point of pain. *Lord, what a disaster!* I thought. My children were right. This was a dumb idea. *Just wait till I get you two home.* I wanted to leave, but something—I don't know what— held me there.

The priest moved from one animal to the next, patting their heads, saying something to each one. Finally he stopped in front of my two disturbers of the peace and asked their names. "Caesar and Brutus," I replied in the most apologetic tone possible.

He touched their heads and smiled. "Bless you, Caesar and Brutus. We're thankful for your enthusiasm about life, for the joyful noise you make in response to it. May God watch over you and protect you."

Next we read in unison the famous prayer of St. Francis, our words filtering through the aria of my dogs' unending barking: "Lord, make me an instrument of Thy peace . . ."

Finally, mercifully, it was over. Back home I opened the gate, let Caesar and Brutus into the backyard, then trudged into the kitchen, muttering.

"What happened?" asked my husband, Sandy.

"Those fool dogs practically ruined the St. Francis Day service. They acted like animals."

"They *are* animals," he pointed out.

For days I refused to let them in the house, where they usually slept. I scolded them for the least thing: for the limbs they dragged onto the deck, for turning over my Boston fern, for scratching at the door, but mostly for barking. They responded by wagging their tails and dropping a ball in front of me, hoping I would toss it. I would not.

Five days after the St. Francis Day disaster I happened to glance out the window and see the neighbor's cat sashaying along the back fence. An eerie feeling came over me. Why weren't the dogs barking? I stepped into the yard, into an awful, empty silence. With a thudding heart I peered at the gate. It was hanging open. Caesar and Brutus were gone.

I ran down the driveway, remembering Sandy's caution to keep the gate closed. "If those two dogs ever get out, I'm afraid they'll be long gone," he'd said. Had the meter reader come through it and left it ajar? Had the wind blown it open?

I hurried along the street calling their names. After scouring the neighborhood for two hours, I came home. There had been no sign of them. They had probably seen a squirrel and tracked it clear to North Carolina by now.

Sandy came home during lunch and we drove all over town. "If we ever find them, I'll never fuss at them again," I told Sandy.

He smiled at me. "I know."

After school the children joined the search. Late into the afternoon I kept stopping people on the street. "Have you seen two little beagles?" They all shook their heads.

As the day softened into dusk, we gave up and went home. I passed their dog bowls sitting empty in the kitchen and walked on into my study. I sat alone in the shadows and traced my finger along the edge of my desk. Suddenly I remembered how the priest put his hands on their heads. What had he said? *"Bless you, Caesar and Brutus. We're thankful for your enthusiasm for life. . . . May God watch you and protect you."* I laid my head down and cried.

When I dried my eyes, it was dark out. I stood at the window and wondered if we would ever see them again. Just then a part of St. Francis's prayer came floating back into my head: ". . . *Where there is doubt, let me sow faith; where there is despair, hope . . .*" The words seemed full of urgency. I grabbed a flashlight and both dog leashes and headed out the door. "Where are you going?" Sandy asked.

"To sow faith and hope," I said.

I walked along the street, on and on, block after block.

"Woo-woo-woof!"

I froze. I would know that sound anywhere. I listened, following it until I came upon Caesar and Brutus sniffing through the garden in a stranger's yard. In the middle of the garden was a statute of St. Francis. Somehow I was not surprised.

As the dogs bounded into my arms and licked my face, I thanked God for St. Francis, who loved all creatures great and small, and was still teaching folks today to do the same. I thanked God for blessing my two beagles and for watching over them.

Back home I gave both dogs some milk and let them curl upon on the foot of my bed. I rubbed their ears, feeling that great and piercing awareness that breaks in upon us at certain times in life, the awareness of not realizing how much you love the people or things close to you until you almost lose them.

I was suddenly filled with the need to seize every day and sow it full of all those wonderful things St. Francis prayed about: love and pardon, faith and hope, light and joy.

Sandy and the children appeared at the bedroom door. I went and put my arms around them. "I don't tell you enough," I said, "but I love you." From the foot of the bed came a resounding "Woo-woo-woof."

Sue Monk Kidd is a *Guideposts* magazine author and contributing editor. She lives in South Carolina.

Perro Solo

Desmond Morris

Back in the 1950s, zoologist Desmond Morris, author of Dogwatching, *visited Spain for a holiday with his wife, Ramona. While there they encountered a local dog in need of a little help . . .*

Our round trip through Spain continued and eventually we came to rest at Ramona's personal goal—the beaches of the tiny fishing village of Calella de Palafrugell, where we rented a small apartment with a balcony overlooking the bay. I settled down to write a paper on the green acouchi, a curious South American rodent that looks like a guinea pig on gazelle legs, which I had been studying at the London Zoo, while Ramona demonstrated the art of relaxation which I had yet to learn.

Her luxuriating was rudely interrupted by the arrival of a haggard, almost skeletal dog, which established itself immediately beneath the balcony on which she was trying to encourage the second-degree burns she referred to as suntan. It gazed up at her with accusing eyes and I knew instantly that we were in for one of her protective campaigns. Abandoning her serried ranks of tanning oils, creams, foams and ointments, she plunged into the dark hole that had been described as a compact kitchen and emerged with the remains of a chicken we had eaten for lunch.

From my writing table I heard the thud as the chicken carcass hit the dirt track below. There was a short, silent pause and then a thunderous cracking and chomping sound, reminiscent of feeding time at the Lion

House. In the few seconds it took me to walk across the room and look down at the ground below, the entire carcass had disappeared. Every scrap of flesh and bone had vanished. The forlorn dog sat down heavily and unsteadily, it body jerking with noiseless hiccups, and licked its huge mouth. Then it subsided rapidly into a deep sleep.

"Whoever owns that dog ought to be . . ."

"Shot?"

"Well, it's disgusting. Go down and ask those fishermen whose it is. Perhaps it's lost." I abandoned the green acouchi's sex life and turned my attention to *Canis familiaris*. Plodding down the hot, dusty track (this was in the days before the Costa Brava was serving paella-and-chips and restaurants were hanging up signs reading "we warm the pot"), I approached an old man mending his nets. Pointing across to the large dog slumbering in the shade of our balcony I asked, in my primitive Spanish, where the owner was. The man turned down the corners of his mouth and shook his head.

"*Perro solo. Todo solo.*" He shrugged and went back to repairing his nets.

I climbed round the track and up to the apartment door, and explained to Ramona that it was a stray dog, completely alone.

"Then as long as we are here it will come under my personal protection," she announced, "and I will feed it up and make sure that by the time we leave, it is strong enough to fend for itself."

She threw on a dress and made for the local butcher's shop. The siesta period was nearly over and it would soon be open. She would buy the animal some meat. Biscuits were not good enough—it needed protein.

Half an hour later she returned visibly shaken, clutching a large lump of something wrapped in paper. It emerged that there had been a bit of trouble in the tiny whitewashed cell that served as the local butcher's. Before her in the line of women had been an immaculately attired nurse-maid, wearing a spotless uniform with a crisp, white apron. She also wore an air of acute superiority which had irritated the huge lady butcher. The trouble began when she described the chicken she was being sold as a pigeon that had been stretched through a mangle. The lady butcher angrily decapitated the scrawny bird with a large axe and deliberately flicked its blood across the pristine whiteness in front of her wooden chopping bench. The outraged nursemaid looked down at her blood-splashed apron and flew into a towering rage, fearlessly confronting the menacingly raised axe and screaming a torrent of abuse. She then rushed over to the freshly whitewashed wall of the shop and began to wipe herself along it, transferring to its surface a long smear of blood. When at last the blood stains remaining on her apron had been successfully concealed beneath a coating of whitewash, she turned on the butcher again and then, as Ramona put it, things began to get really nasty. Other women in the shop were screaming now and taking sides and at any moment it seemed that human blood must also flow.

"Not at all like shopping in Hampstead," muttered Ramona, as she started cooking the meat that she had eventually managed to purchase, after peace had, with some difficulty, and the intervention of several grinning men, been restored.

Serving up her dog's dish on a large plate, she set off to carry it down and round the track to the still sleeping Perro. It was dusk now and, in the half-light, I could hear her talking softly to him and encouraging him to eat. This was followed by much slurping and crunching, then silence.

She reappeared triumphant. Perro, as he was now called, had actually managed a brief tail-wag. Nothing fancy, just a few, slow, stiff beats of the air with his long, bony appendage, almost as if he had nearly forgotten how to do it. But it was a start.

In the days that followed, the stray returned regularly to his resting place beneath the balcony and Ramona continued her patient rehabilitation campaign. After about a week, his walk was more sprightly and he was beginning to look more like a dog than a skin-covered wicker basket. He was still a remarkably ugly dog, a fact which endeared him to Ramona. Where animals were concerned, she was never swayed by a pretty face—a trait of hers which I had always admired. It appealed to my zoological dictum of all animals being equal.

I took a closer look at her Perro. He appeared to be a cross between an anemic bloodhound and a mounted skeleton. His short, lifeless coat had the color of a nicotine-stained finger, and the harsh Spanish sun cast dark, vertical shadows between each of his ribs. His long drooping ears

Zoologist and best-selling author Desmond Morris. When asked if he could be any animal anywhere in the world, he replied, "My wife's dogs, because they have the cushiest time of any animal."

appeared to be weighted with lead, making his huge head sag down so low that his jaw nearly brushed the ground as he walked along. Behind his great rib cage, his body narrowed almost to a point, before it met his stiff hind legs and his long bony tail, which ended in a sharp, almost hairless spike. There was no denying that he was a pitiful sight, but somehow he managed to maintain a certain tragic dignity—a slow deliberation about all his actions, as if he had come to accept a permanent need to conserve energy at all costs. I had never seen a dog that moved so slowly.

The sprightliness and bounce that were slowly returning to his gait did nothing at first to speed it up. He still plodded along like a defeated prisoner, but there was less stiffness now. Toward the end of our stay he managed his first run, and to Ramona it was as satisfying a spectacle as if he had just won the Greyhound Derby at White City. On our last morning, he positively bounded up for his final meal and Ramona's happiness was complete. But short-lived, for there was a sting in the tail of his story.

With his last gulp of food, he looked around him and sniffed the air. With his new vigor, his sense of masculinity had suddenly returned. Spotting a diminutive, fat-bottomed bitch poodle in the distance, he took off in a lecherous gallop, leaped on the startled powder puff of a dog, and proceeded to rape her. The poodle's diminutive, fat-bottomed owner, a middle-aged French lady tourist with a poodle-style hairdo, ran screaming from her door and raised such a din that several grizzled fishermen dropped their nets, converged on the preoccupied Perro, and kicked him brutally all the way out of the village. He bounded off down the dirt road with stones hailing after him and that was the last view we had of him. There was a nasty irony about the fact that we had made him fit enough to warrant forcible expulsion from his home territory, but at least he had had his moment. And with any luck he was strong enough now to survive and perhaps make a new niche for himself in a less hostile environment.

Desmond Morris is an internationally known zoologist and best-selling author of over twenty-five books, including *The Naked Ape* and *Dogwatching*. He lives in England.

There is no nation which has not paid attention to these quadrupeds or given them a special role in its history.

—Alfred Barbou

A Cool Character

Margaret Poynter

Roscoe entered our lives courtesy of a workman who found him locked in an empty house. We knew nothing of his previous life except that his former owner may have cared for him at one time but had now abandoned him; that he appeared to be a basset/beagle mix; that he was on the shadowy side of middle age; and that he was blind.

It didn't take me long to realize that while Roscoe may be sightless, he is far from helpless. As soon as he entered my home, he began to explore, his nose snuffling along the floor, his head weaving rhythmically from side to side like a whiskery radar antenna. Creeping along, he examined first the length of a wall, then an upholstered chair, then the bottom hem of a drape. Cautiously extending each stubby front leg, he felt his way through the front room, then the dining room and the hallway. Although he seemed to sense each upcoming barrier, he occasionally misjudged the distance, but this cagey canine was prepared for that eventuality: He held his head at an angle, thus gently striking the side of his greying muzzle instead of his tender nose.

I watched, fascinated, as he committed the layout of the house to memory and his movements became more sure, more directed. After forty-five minutes, he began to display an urgency and made his careful way toward the open back door, down the two porch steps and into the yard. Here, he found a patch of bare dirt and promptly relieved himself. Roscoe, ever the civilized gentleman, was not going to use his handicap as an excuse for improper behavior.

After spending the next half-hour familiarizing himself with the yard, he cast about for landmarks that would lead him back to the house. In ever tightening circles, he weaved back and forth until he was honing in on the porch. Sniffing, probing and occasionally fumbling, he found his way back up the steps and into the kitchen. He then went directly to the bowl of water I'd placed on the far side of the room. Shortly thereafter, he happened upon the blanket that I'd put in a corner to serve as a bed. After rearranging it to suit his taste, he curled up, sighed contentedly and went to sleep.

Our foundling had evidently determined that our accommodations were satisfactory.

How satisfactory they really are remains a mystery, even after two years. Roscoe is not the type of canine who intertwines his life with that of his human family. Rather, he is a dignified, aloof sort of creature who seems to prefer a parallel, independent existence. He accepts his meals and his pats on the head with a noble sort of gratitude, never the fawning, servile expressions of appreciation that so many of his kind display.

While I sometimes miss those ecstatic bursts of doggy affection, I respect Roscoe's quiet stateliness and his apparent struggle to remain as self-sufficient as possible. Even when he's been inadvertently locked in a room or his passage has been blocked by an unfamiliar barrier, his only plea for assistance is in the form of a series of throaty, low-key, disgruntled-sounding woofs. Roscoe doesn't stoop to whimpering or frantic yelping. Such displays are beneath him, as are groveling, face-licking thank yous. After all, isn't it usually our fault that he had to ask for help in the first place?

I've often wondered whether or not Roscoe would act differently if he had his sight. Would he actively seek our caresses instead of simply accepting them when they are offered? Would he run to greet us at the door, demanding that we drop our packages and give him our undivided attention? Would he demand more from his world and from the humans who inhabit it?

It's possible that he would. Nevertheless, knowing Roscoe as I do, I'm convinced that he would be the same cool character he has been ever since he was discovered wandering unconcernedly in the bare rooms of that forsaken house.

Ten years ago Margaret Poynter helped establish Lifeline for Pets, a non-profit rescue service. She is an author, residing in California.

It is true that whenever a person loves a dog he derives great power from it.

—Old Seneca chief

Doghousesitting

Richard L. TenEyck

I had never thought of housesitting until one March when a friend asked me to care for her property while she went to California for three weeks. I agreed, knowing that, in addition to guarding ten rooms, a garage, a porch and a yard, I would be the slave of a blind Dachshund named Schrader.

I knew Schrader well and had been his "uncle" since he was the size of a hot dog roll. We always got along well; most of the time we were great friends. Some of the time he even let me have my way, but usually Schrader ruled his domain with a willful woof.

Our daily routine was established early. I arose at six, roused the dog from under the blankets and carried him downstairs to his shock of morning winter air. He usually did his business (wholesale and retail) and then scratched the aluminum storm door to be let in.

Breakfast was next: a blob of former beast in a Melmac dish. For being blind, Schrader had no trouble snatching his food as soon as the dish hit the floor. My hand miraculously survived the three weeks. Two treats followed: a charcoal biscuit as a halitosis inhibitor and a half a crunchbone in assorted colors and flavors. (I think "liver" was green, which could send you speeding to vegetarianism.)

After I readied myself and chowed down breakfast from my Melmac dish, Schrader was billeted in the kitchen with his bed and water bowl. I left for work and a neighbor stopped in at the right times for "walkies."

I returned around four. Supper for Schrader was nine or ten cardboard nuggets made malleable with warm water. Another bone followed (such as the pink-tinted fish-flavored variety). My supper was usually considered his second supper, accompanied by orchestrated supplications in the form of whines, smothered arfs, and downright hostile barks. Sometimes this scenario was successful.

Later, I stretched out on the sofa and watched the news. Schrader stretched out on me and dreamed, his lips and nose twitching as his mental marauder cornered some furious feline. Normally, between chases, he'd placidly nap for awhile, but one night, when the telephone rang, he leaped off my chest, sprang into the air, and with earflaps spread like a B-52, landed with a thud on the living room runway. He survived with only slight shock to the fuselage. He never did that again.

A blind dog knows his own home very well, which was one reason to sit the house and the dog rather than place the dog in a kennel. Schrader could trace his paths from chair to sofa to table to doorway to kitchen. He always remembered the most comfortable sleeping spots. His lack of vision was compensated by superior sniff and vigilant ear.

I am once again returning to Schrader and his house after several years of pleasant stays. That is, I will return if I survive my current stint. Some friends went abroad for five weeks, leaving me in control of a house and two cats. One is a Siamese. It's hard to get used to being awakened by the sound of an air raid siren in an oil drum. It's also rather disarming having a cat jump from the floor onto my shoulder as I'm watching *Masterpiece Theater*, crank its neck in front of my face, and stare at me through my bifocals.

If I can endure such oriental inscrutability, I'll be more than ready for Schrader's eccentricities.

Richard L. TenEyck teaches English in the Williamson, New York, School District. He shares his home with Katie, his family's springer spaniel.

Properly trained, a man can be dog's best friend.
—Corey Ford (1902–1969)
American writer

PART VIII

Dog Almighty

Our histories, language, fireside stories and souls are touched by this dear friend.

Gene Hill in "The XVth Day" postulates events leading to the creation of the Labrador retriever. With Argos, dog of Ancient Greece, as narrator, Richard Adams presents a slice of history. Magda Gonzales gives anew the Puerto Rican account of Jeronimo and his dog Felipe. Bill Tarrant's "Old Drum" is a powerful, behind-the-scenes chronicle of an historical law case.

For comic relief, Richard Lederer challenges the reader to a "Dog Search" word game. Truth, embellished with a tinge of imagination, is presented in the stories of "Soccer Dog" and "Taco and the Doughnut."

We conclude this section and our book with Josef Verba's "The Way of the Soul"—our only piece of science fiction. In it, there is a blending of both music and mystery—an appropriate close.

Argos

Richard Adams

Hullo, cat: come to lie on the dungheap with me, have you? Oh, rat-ting, eh? Well, there's plenty round here. Nowadays the whole place is full of rats: human ones, too. 'Might have caught 'em myself once; not any more; not now.

All right; if you're going to watch that hole I can keep as still as you. Keeping still—that's about all I'm good for now. I'm run down; but no more than the whole place is run down. Full of rats: and I'm full of fleas. 'Better mind you don't catch a few.

How old are you, cat? A year? Two years? Too young to remember much, anyway. Too young to remember the better days. I suppose you won't believe I'm more that twenty, eh? What's that you said? 'Don't hear well now, you know—"What's 'twenty'?" did you say? Well, it's a lot of years; very old for a dog. Very old indeed. I was a damned good dog once, though no one'd think so now. Not to look at me.

There's not an animal on the place now that remembers the master: only me. And even I wasn't much more than a puppy when he had to go away to the war. He'd begun training me, though. He told Diokles, the ken-nel-man, that he reckoned I was going to turn out such a fine hound that he'd train me himself; and so he did. I enjoyed every minute of it. We'd had some great times already and I was shaping up well. I could come when I was called, and wait where I was told, and walk to heel—yes, through a herd of goats, if you like. I could follow scent too: oh, couldn't I just? Everyone said I surely had the best nose in the world. The master used to say, give the two of us a year together and he'd take me anywhere; wolves, wild boar—the lot.

The way things turned out, though, it was precious little joy the master ever had of my marvelous nose. One summer morning—oh, that morning: I remember it as if it were yesterday!—we were just getting ready to go hunting, he and I. There was another, older hound with us, a dog called Kassos. Kassos—he's been dead for years now—I learned a lot from him. Diokles had just slipped our leads when suddenly the master stopped dead-still, looking down towards the harbour below us and the sea out beyond. There was a ship—not one of ours—still a goodish way out, but it was coming in towards the harbour all right. The master stood staring at it.

"I knew it!" he said at last to Diokles. "I knew it! It's them! And we know what *they've* come for, don't we?"

He began walking backwards and forwards across the grass, biting on his fingers. "I'm no coward," he said. "It's the oracle's prophecy that frightens me. The oracle said that if I went I wouldn't come back for years and years, and then it would be alone and destitute. Yes, it's them all right: see the lion on the sail?"

"I'm afraid so, sir," says Diokles. "We'd all heard tell of the war, of course; but I'd been hoping they might leave us out of it. After all, it's not as though the island's all that big or full of men—not compared to that lot over at Mycenae."

"They're scraping the barrel," answers the master. "That's what it is, Diokles: scraping the barrel; but they won't scrape me! Hurry, now! Go and get a plough and an ox and an ass, and bring them down to the beach: round the point, there, see? in the cove. I'll be down directly to tell you what to do." He stooped down and patted me. "I'm not called 'the angry one' for nothing," he says. "I'm angry now all right, but I'm not such a fool as to let them see it."

And with that he set off back to the house. He seemed to have forgotten about me, so I just trotted along behind him, waiting for orders. He went straight into the hall. The mistress was there, with the baby on her arm. She was talking to Eurycleia, but when she saw the look on the master's face she broke off and stared at him, sort of frightened.

"It's them, my love," he said, jerking his thumb over his shoulder. "I told you they'd be coming for me. But you do as I say, now, and we'll fool them yet. Give me that big salt-box by the fire, there. And remember, I've gone stark, raving mad. Tell all the servants. Tell everyone; and mind you act up to it yourself. Cry your eyes out! Everything depends on convincing them."

So then he kissed her and went out. Just at the door he met Eumaeus—that's the swineherd, you know: a decent fellow; he's almost the only one left that's still kind to me—coming in for orders. He didn't get any orders, though. The master just turned towards him, grabbed his cap off his head—a greasy old felt thing, it was, shaped like half an egg—and left him staring as the two of us headed for the shore.

When we got down to the beach, sure enough Diokles was waiting with the plough and the beasts.

"Yoke 'em up," says the master, "and then mind you stand back, because I'm not safe, understand?"

Then he started carrying on fit to terrify every man, bird and beast for miles. It even frightened me! He was frothing at the mouth and his eyes were rolling and staring—he didn't even blink; or not that I could see. Gods! he even *smelt* different, or that's how it seemed to me at the time, watching him.

"Harroo!" he shouted. "Harroo! Sow the snow! Sow the snow!" And he began throwing salt over his shoulder as he went, and the two poor beasts lurching along in front of him, looking just about as crazy as he did.

Then I saw the strangers coming. There were three of them, all dressed in armour, with purple plumes on their helmets, and soldiers behind them to carry their shields and weapons. You could see they were important men—kings, I reckon they must have been. The mistress was with them, still carrying the baby on her arm. She was crying her eyes out, just like the master had told her.

"He's been like this for five days," she was sobbing to the kings as they came up to us. "Five days! It's the madness of the goddess! He's cursed—

cursed! He'll die; I know he will! O Zeus, take pity on us! Take pity on a poor woman!" And she began tearing her hair.

Eumaeus was just behind her. "He's not safe, my lord," he says to the king next to him. "He killed the stableman yesterday: struck him down with an oar and said he was threshing the corn. Now you've seen for yourself, my lord, I'd come away before someone gets hurt. He doesn't even know his wife from his hound."

Then the mistress gave the baby over to Eumaeus and went and stood right in the master's way. She held up her arms and called out to him, but he simply drove the beasts straight at her and threw salt all over her hair and her robe, and she only just jumped clear in time. She flung herself into the arms of one of the kings, screaming.

"He'd have ploughed over me!" she cried. "His own wife! Oh, was there ever a house so afflicted! Pray, good sirs, only take pity on us and leave us to try to calm him! Strangers only make him worse!"

"What do you reckon, Palamedes?" says one of the kings. "I'm afraid we've had our journey for nothing. Poor fellow, he seems very bad."

"Just a moment," says the man called Palamedes. He went across to the mistress, who'd just taken the baby back from Eumaeus, and snatched him out of her arms. The master wasn't looking: he was just turning the beasts round to plough another stretch of the sand.

Palamedes laid the baby down straight in his way. "Let's see whether he knows *him*," he said: and he held the mistress back with his two hands on her shoulders. "If he ploughs on now, I'll believe it."

The master came straight on, still shouting and yelling, and for a moment I thought he was going to plough over the baby. But then he slowed down. He faltered and stopped. You could see he meant to: you could see he knew what he was doing. The baby was crying—all the noise and the big men had frightened him. The master went forward, picked him up in his arms and began soothing him.

"Not quite good enough, eh?" says Palamedes, going up to him quite friendly and putting a hand on his shoulder. "Can't say I altogether blame you, though. If you like I'll give you a hand getting your weapons and armour together."

Well, at that Diokles took hold of my collar, turned on his heel and led me away up the cliff. He put me back into the kennels, so I didn't see the master preparing to go away to the war with the kings. Kassos did, though: he was under the table in the hall when the master ate his last dinner and drank his last bowl of wine.

It was getting on for sunset when the master came round to the kennels himself. I heard him calling to Diokles.

"I want Argos!" he said. "Bring him out here."

They were all there in the yard—the mistress, the kings—everyone. The master had the baby in his arms. He went down on one knee beside me and held the baby up against my nose. I remember the smell of new flesh and women's milk: I remember it now.

"Argos," says the master, "I'm going away; for a long time, most likely. This is Telemachus. You're to guard him, do you understand? Night and day. You're never to let him out of your sight until he grows to be a man. You're to run with him and hunt with him and sleep beside him. You're to guard him; and you're to guard your mistress, too, because I shan't be able to."

He was crying. His tears were falling all over my muzzle.

"One day I shall come back, Argos," he said. "Don't you ever forget it! One day I'll come back and require it of you—this guardianship of yours. You always were the best dog of the lot, and you shall have your reward. The grey-eyed goddess will look after me; and she's the one who'll give you your reward, too."

So then he went away on his ship and I never saw him again. No one has, from that day to this. All my life the island's been left without a king—left to go to pieces. Well, who could take *his* place? That old man Mentor; I know he's always done his best, but he's never been much good, really. I guarded Telemachus, though, no danger. He grew up, and I grew up with him. I went with him when he began toddling along the shore, and I went with him when he got old enough to go out and play with the other children. Oh, they all learnt to know me. There was a hefty boy—Eumastas, he was called—who used to wait until there weren't any grown-up people about and then shout "Where's your Fa-ther?" One day Telemachus turned and went for him, and Eumastas knocked him down: he was so much bigger, you see. But after I'd finished with him he was limping for a month. He never said it again.

When Telemachus got old enough to go hunting with Diokles, he always used to take me with him as his personal hound. Diokles had finished my training, of course, and I can tell you, cat, there wasn't a hound in the whole kennels could keep up with me. "Podas Argos," they used to call me: the Bright-footed! I was like a thunderbolt in those days. There wasn't a wild beast could get away from me, even in the thickest woods: and I was the best hound on a scent in all the island. Everyone knew it.

All the time, of course, I was waiting for the master to come back; but he never did. Some said he was dead. I couldn't believe it. After all, he himself had said plain enough that he was coming back; and he'd said the goddess would reward me, so I went on believing him. But now—now I don't know what to think.

I remember, one cold winter's night in the kennels, Kassos called me over to him. He was very old by that time; white-muzzled, and getting on for blind.

"Have you heard the news?" he said. "That war thing—whatever it was—it's over, or so they're all saying."

"Who won?" I asked.

"Our lot won, apparently," he said. "So now I suppose the master'll be coming home."

Kassos died soon after that. But still the master didn't come back: and still I went on guarding Telemachus. He was eleven or twelve by that time—coming up for a youth. Often, in the evenings, he used to take me with him to the cliff-top, and we'd sit looking out over the dark sea.

"He *will* come back, Argos," he'd say. "The goddess has spoken in my heart and told me so. He will come back: just when we least expect it, I dare say."

But it was the suitors who started arriving; not the master. Well, that's what they called themselves—suitors. First just four or five, and then more and more of them. They gave out that the master was dead and the mistress had got to choose one of them for a new husband. But that was all just a lot of pretense and lies. They'd come to eat up our food—kill our beasts and live off our land, that's what. Yes, and they even helped themselves to the girls, too. That nasty little tart Melantho—I never did like her; bone-lazy and dirty with it—she fairly loved every minute. She's inside with one of them now, damn her.

Telemachus tried to send them packing; but what could *he* do; just a bit of a lad against all those bullies? When they weren't insulting him, they simply ignored him. And all the time they kept on telling the mistress she had to choose. She used to take me with her to her room at night, for fear one of them would break down the door and force her. A lot of the day she used to spend weaving at her loom; but then, when we were alone at night, she'd unpick it all again. I never did understand why.

Thing went from bad to worse; and at last I got too old to be any more good. 'Couldn't run; 'couldn't hear properly; teeth going, too, Diokles was dead and the new kennel-man didn't like me; he wanted younger dogs. All the same, I was all right as long as Telemachus was still around. *He* wouldn't stand by and see me ill-treated. He kept me with him even though I could hardly follow him about any more. That was one of the things the suitors used to jeer at him for. "You and your mangy old dog!" It was that bastard Antinous said that; and they all laughed. And then another one—Agelaus, it was—said he supposed by this time the master must look just like me, if he was still alive. Have you any idea, cat, what it's like to be despised and insulted by men you could once have chased over the cliff?

Ah, but that's not the worst of it, either; not by a long way. What's broken my heart happened about a month ago now. Telemachus went away—yes, secretly, in a ship; and he wouldn't take me with him. It's the only time we've been apart in all the years since the master left.

One evening, it was; just about this time of day. He'd been talking to old Eurycleia—her as used to be his nurse when he was a baby. They were up in the treasure-chamber. He'd left me outside, in the shade, while he went in to talk to her. When he came out he went across to the hall, where all the suitors were busy stuffing our grub and swilling our wine. It wasn't long before they were all as drunk as maenads, and soon after that they weren't even making a row any more; they'd either gone to sleep in the hall, or else staggered off to—well, to other beds. Telemachus bent down and patted me.

"Argos," he said—just like the master, long ago—"Argos, I'm going away. The ship's waiting for me now. I'd like to take you, Argos, believe me I would; but at your age you'd never stand the journey. But I'm coming back, d'you understand? I'm coming back *soon*."

I've heard that tale before, I thought; and I can tell you my heart fairly sank into the ground. He was all I had left, you see. If he went, there'd be no one at all to care a curse what happened to me. I felt so desperate that I even tried to follow him; but he went off very quickly—him and old Mentor together. At least, I thought it was old Mentor; only I couldn't be sure. It looked like old Mentor, but somehow it didn't smell like him. And the funny thing was, next day Telemachus was gone right enough, but Mentor was still about.

It was after that that the really bad time began. I've just been left to die by myself, that's what it comes to. I'm forced to hang about the kitchen door for scraps—me, Podas Argos as used to be!—and I'm lucky if I get any, at that. I'm full of vermin: 'can't exercise; 'can't get as far as the stream, even. That blasted Antinous wanted to put a spear through me the other day, only old Eurycleia begged him not to. All the same, she's forgotten about me now, just like everybody else.

Hullo, who's this coming? 'Can't see anything against this sunset. Why, it's Eumaeus, the swineherd. 'Haven't seen him around for a day or two. He'll remember me, though: I'm sure he will. With any luck he might even give me something to eat. But—but who on earth's that with him? Why, it's old beggar-man! He looks almost as thin and grey as I am! Whatever's *he* doing, limping along on a stick beside Eumaeus? And why's Eumaeus bringing him up here, for Zeus' sake? Now that a thing I'll be damned if I'm going to put up with—beggars round the house! I may be old and done for, but I can still see a beggar off. Out of the way, cat, while I get on my feet.

Now, then, you! On your way! Oh! What—what is it? What's happened? That smell—that smell—it—it can't be! It—it's the master! It's the master! He's come back! And there's someone standing behind them! It's the goddess—it's the grey-eyed goddess! She's smiling—she's beckoning to me!

Gods, what a food I am! I've been asleep. I've been dreaming! I dreamt—why, I dreamt the master had gone away, and the house was full of villains, and Zeus knows what else besides! And it was all just a stupid dream! Just a dream! I'm young! I'm strong! Podas Argos, that's me! We're going hunting, and the goddess—the goddess is coming with us! O master, dear master, here I am!

Here I-

———————————

Following a career in Civil Service, Richard Adams served as President of the Royal Society for Prevention of Cruelty to Animals. He is a poet and author of many books, including the best-seller *Watership Down*. Mr. Adams resides in England.

The bond with a true dog is as lasting as the ties of this earth can ever be.

—Konrad Z. Lorenz (1903–1989)

Austrian naturalist *Man Meets Dog*

Taco and the Doughnut

Serena M. Aman

I woke up early one bright spring morning, yawned, stretched and nudged Duke. Duke had been my adopted son for five years at the time, a miniature schnauzer the People had named Duke Eric von Schnauzer. What a name!

"Yeah, Dad" He woofed softly.

"I'm gonna go out for something to eat. Cover for me."

"You got it. Bring me back something?"

"Sure, kid. See ya later." I trotted out the door made special for us and down the street.

Halfway down the street, there was an empty glass bottle, and I stopped to look at my reflection. I was six inches high and twelve long; all black except for the white on my paws, at my throat, on my nose and on the tip of my tail. I am a pedigree miniature Chihuahua, and naturally vain.

I set off again, heading in the direction of my favorite park. There the grass was green and perfect for rolling in, and there were plenty of trees. It was Doggie Heaven.

Sitting on a bench was a little old lady. In her lap was a box from which a delicious odor came . . . doughnuts! I couldn't help myself. I did all sorts of leaps and bounds and other tricks to get her attention. She smiled, set the box down and opened a bag. She pulled out a dog biscuit and set it on the ground.

A dog biscuit? I snatched it up and waited a little distance off, watching the lady and rethinking what I should do. After a while, little children began to come up to her, and she opened the box.

I saw my chance, and I naturally took it. Lightning fast . . . well, okay. Super-fast . . . all right! With surprising speed for a dog of my age and size, I leaped to her lap, grabbed a doughnut from her hand and ran off.

When crossing the street to get to my house, I looked both ways. I was in the middle of the street when I heard a voice shriek, "Taco!"

I looked up and saw a little sports car coming my way. In my hurry to get out of the road, I dropped the doughnut. Strawberry jelly squirted out as the wheels ran it over. A girl from my house picked me up, but my gaze was locked on the red mess that had once been a jelly doughnut with powdered sugar.

When I was inside, Duke asked, "What'd you get?"

"Shut up," I growled.

———————————

Serena M. Aman, a high school student in Phelps, New York, hopes to attend law school. She enjoys writing. "Taco and the Doughnut" was fabricated after her miniature Chihuahua, Taco, was seen crossing the town's main street bearing a jelly doughnut.

I am joy in a woolly coat, come to dance into your life, to make you laugh!

—Julie Church
Joy in a Woolly Coat

The Legend of the Fisherman and His Dog

Magda A. Gonzalez

Sometime around the eighteenth century, the Spaniards were in full possession of the enchanted island of Puerto Rico, making it like a little chunk of Spain, thrown in the midst of the Caribbean Sea. The Spanish aristocrats spared no effort to provide social events that would bring them closer to the life they were accustomed to, and thereby mitigate, somehow, the homesickness for the motherland they had left behind.

It was Jeronimo's duty to supply fresh fish for the banquets of the Spanish aristocracy. And so he ventured every day into the sea, sailing his old fishing boat but leaving ashore the most faithful and loved companion of many years, his dog Felipe. Felipe, a mixture of Labrador and retriever, patiently awaited for his master's daily return, usually lying down by the huge rocks that framed the bay of San Juan. Day after day, year after year, the pattern continued.

Even though Jeronimo felt lonesome without Felipe, he did not worry about the long waiting hours the dog had to endure while he was at sea. For Felipe was the favorite friend of all the children that came to enjoy the beach, and he would play with them, and eat with them and even swim with them.

But one tragic day, the sun had set in the horizon, the waves had receded, the beach-children had disappeared and a cool silent breeze had moved in. Soon it would be dark and Felipe's searching eyes had yet to see the old boat bringing his master home.

The next day came, and so the next, and many more till Felipe's broken heart began to realize that the merciless sea had kept his master, perhaps forever . . . "If I could only cross the ocean and rescue him, if I could only hear his voice calling me, if I could only see him once more and lick his hand and jump with joy and then lie at his feet, the way it used to be."

One unforgettable morning, the legend goes, the children of the beach arrived as usual. It was a splendorous day. The sun was in full control of his majestic island, the endless ocean wrapped all in a celestial blue, the restless wind combed the leaves of the exotic palm trees, and the intoxicating fragrances from the tropical flowers combined with all to make a dreamy day on the beach.

Then, suddenly, one of the children asked if anyone had seen their friend Felipe. Immediately they began to look. But Felipe was nowhere.

"He probably is at his favorite spot, by the huge rock on the shore," hoped a precocious little boy. And as they ran together in a labyrinth of voices and laughter, they could only find the rock, which to their immense astonishment had taken the shape of a dog, just like Felipe, staring at the endless sea!

Today, the rock, which visibly resembles the figure of a dog, still remains in the Bay of San Juan.

Magda A. Gonzalez was born and grew up in South America.
She enjoys traveling, painting and writing poetry. Mrs. Gonzalez
resides in Fairport, New York.

It has been 20,000 years since man and dog formed their partnership.

—Donald McCaig

The XVth Day

Gene Hill

On the fifteenth day, or thereabouts, God and the Recording Angel were just taking it easy. Spread out beneath them was *The Creation*, and despite last-minute changes, they were feeling rather smug with the way it had all gone; so many miracles sound easier than they really are.

God was especially interested in Adam and Eve. He considered them the centerpiece of the whole scheme, and as he watched them, he got the feeling something was a bit off.

Eve had taken to spending more and more time sitting and staring at herself in one of the pools, fussing with her hair and trying to decide which was her best side. Adam was throwing sticks in the brook and watching them sail away. As God and the Recording Angel watched, Adam threw another stick, walked over to where Eve was working on a braid, and shouted, "Back!" pointing at the stick with his finger. Eve barely gave him a glance as she stuck a large red flower in her hair, and continued to stare into the pool.

The Recording Angel finally broke the silence. "Lord," he said, "something's missing."

"I know," God said, "but I can't quite put my finger on it."

Adam was still standing close to Eve and watching another stick he'd thrown. This time they heard him say, "Back Eve!" As they watched, Eve slowly got up, waded out into the water, and brought back the stick. Just as God was about to smile, Eve swung the stick and broke it against Adam's shin.

"I think he needs a creature that will play with him" God said. He made a quick motion with his forefinger, and the stick that was lying across Adam's foot suddenly became a snake. Adam looked at if for a moment and then got another stick, waved it in front of the snake, threw it a few feet into the water, and shouted, "Back!" The snake looked at Adam in a curious way, then slithered over to where Eve sat and whispered something in her ear. Eve looked up at Adam and made a small circular motion with her finger at her temple. The snake seemed to nod in agreement, and the two of them went off together, leaving Adam standing alone by the edge of the water.

"It's not the right size or something," the Recording Angel said. "It ought to be bigger."

"I've got just the thing," God answered. The rock that Eve had been sitting on suddenly stood up and yawned, showing great shining ivory teeth. God smiled.

"What's that?" the Recording Angel asked.

"Hippo," He said, obviously pleased with Himself.

Adam could see that the hippo enjoyed being in the water. He got another stick, larger than the one he'd thrown for the snake. The stick made a great splash and Adam watched expectantly as the giant beast slid into the water and disappeared. After almost an hour and no sign of the hippo, except an occasional water spout, Adam sat down on the bank and cradled his head in his arms. He was still sitting there in the fading light when Eve returned with the snake at her side. She was carrying a handful of leaves, which she tried on, looking for Adam's approval. He finally pointed at one she'd discarded and she angrily tore it in half and tossed it in the pool.

"Eve's acting a little cross, Lord," the Angel remarked.

"Well, nobody's perfect," God answered, somewhat annoyed.

It was getting dark when God turned to the Recording Angel and said, "I'm going to hold up the night for awhile until we get this thing solved. What's left on inventory for delivery?"

The Recording Angel hauled out a thick scroll and began reading out loud, starting with *aardvark*. God listened attentively but did nothing more than occasionally shake His head, now and then making an outline of something in the earth with the quill-end of a long white feather. At the end of the list, the Recording Angel waited fretfully for God to ask him what a *zygote* was, but He didn't. The Angel was quite relieved; so much of the small stuff tended to look alike.

Suddenly God smiled. "I think I've got it," He said, waving His hand at a small passing cloud, which stopped and rained on the ground where He had been sketching. God began taking handfuls of mud and shaped them this way and that. As He worked, He spoke aloud, as if to give the Recording Angel a lesson in creating.

"It's got to be just the right size; strong, but not so big it's always knocking things over," He said. "It ought to like the water about as much as the land, so we'll give it a nice thick coat and a powerful tail—and even webbed feet!"

"You're not making another duck, are you?" the Recording Angel asked, somewhat anxiously. He knew God loved ducks, but He'd made so many already that it was difficult to tell them apart.

"No, nothing like that at all. This creature has four legs and can't fly. The really important thing is the disposition. I don't want it to ever get cross with Adam. I want it to follow him around and be good company, to please Adam more than anything else. If Adam wants to run, it will run with him; if Adam wants to play, it will play with him."

God paused for a moment and then said, "I thought Eve would be like that, but maybe I used a little too much rib."

He continued to work with the clay, broadening the head and chest, shaping the leg and tail until they were just so. He looked it over with great care, and then said in a deep and warm voice that more than hinted at His pleasure, "That's good."

The Recording Angel walked around behind Him. "I really like the looks of it, Lord," he said. "What are you going to call it?"

The Lord smiled and said, "A Labrador retriever."

"Won't that be a little hard for Adam to spell?"

"No," He said, "all he has to remember is *i* before *e*."

Then He reached out and touched the clay and said, "Sit." The glossy black hair rippled over the heavy muscles as the Labrador sat, brown eyes sparkling merrily. He seemed to be begging to be asked to do something. God reached for the Recording Angel's staff, broke off a foot or so, and threw it. Then the Lord said, "Back!"

Instantly, the Labrador broke into a full-speed run, tumbled head-over-heels as he grabbed the stick, and brought it back. God threw it again, and the Labrador bounded off even more joyously. When he came back, God and the Recording Angel were grinning like schoolboys.

"Let me try it!" the Recording Angel asked, and threw the stick far across a distant stream. The Labrador leaped into the water, and almost before they could believe it, was back in front of them, quivering with happiness.

The next day, the Recording Angel and God watched for most of the morning as Adam threw stick after stick and his retriever, seemingly tireless, ran and swam and brought them back with an almost palpable joy. Eve stood off to one side watching them. Finally, she walked over, picked up a stock and threw it. The Labrador sat, watching. When she cried, "Back," he leaped into the air and almost flew into the water. Eve laughed as the droplets wet her. When he returned and gave her the stick, she took it and playfully tugged his ear. The Labrador raised his head and licked her hand. God and the Recording Angel watched her smile; it was radiant in its loveliness.

"I think I'll make one for Eve," God said.

"Exactly the same?" asked the Recording Angel.

"Yes and no," God replied.

The Recording Angel had made his staff whole again and stood leaning on it for the longest while. Then in a very quiet voice, he said, "Lord, would it be too much to ask you to make one more? Then we could keep it here just to make sure it's perfect."

The Lord smiled and said, "I was thinking the very same thing."

Author Gene Hill is the department editor of "Hill Country,"
Field & Stream magazine.

Dog Search

Richard Lederer

The American love of dogs pervades our language, and expressions involving these household pets abound in our speech and our writing. In this dog-eat-dog world of ours we meet top dogs who are dog-gone rich, underdogs in the doghouse, hot dogs who put on the dog, and dirty dogs who dog us with shaggy-dog stories. "Dog my cats!" we might say when it starts to rain cats and dogs. Then we may go inside and fight like you-know-whats.

Now that I've let the cat out of the bag, here are some statements about the canines hiding in our language. In some cases the dog in a word or phrase barks clearly. The compound *dog days*, for example, which des-

Richard Lederer. Photo credit: Tim Savard.

ignates summer periods of hazy, hot and humid weather, has a time-hallowed history. The Romans, who also experienced summer discomfiture, employed the expression *caniclares dies*, or "days of the dog," to describe the six to eight hottest weeks of the year. The ancient theory was that the dog star Sirius, rising with the sun during July and the first half of August, added to the solar heat and made a hot time even hotter.

In still other cases a word or phrase bears no relationship to the word *dog* beyond a mere coincidence of sound. But each word or word grouping in the game you are about to play does begin with the letters *d-o-g*, and these letters are pronounced exactly like the name of the animal.

1. This dog is an established set of beliefs.
2. This dog is another word for "darn."
3. This dog is a stretch of land that bends.
4. This dog swims underwater.
5. This dog is an elementary form of swimming.
6. L'il Abner lived in this dog.
7. This dog is clumsy verse.
8. This dog is shabby and worn.
9. This dog is exhausted.
10. This dog is a poisonous plant.
11. This dog is used for identification.
12. This dog is up a tree.
13. This dog is also up a tree.
14. This dog is a quick, easy gait.
15. This dog is a fiercely disputed contest.

ANSWERS

1. dogma	6. Dogpatch	11. dog tag
2. doggone	7. doggerel	12. dogberry
3. dogleg	8. dog-eared	13. dogwood
4. dogfish	9. dog tired	14. dogtrot
5. dog paddle	10. dogbane	15. dogfight

Richard Lederer is the author of national best-seller books, including *Anguished English, Crazy English,* and *The Miracle of English.*
He is a language commentator on National Public Radio.
Lederer resides in New Hampshire.

It Happened in Heaven

Jean Quercy, translated by Marion Koenen Perri

Once upon a time there was a saint named Roch. He was a great saint who traveled over the world curing the madness of men and animals. He had a dog called Roquet, which he loved very much because it had saved his life. The dog was also a saint in his own way; he licked the sores that his master took care of, and the sores went away never to return. St. Roch and Roquet never left each other. A person could no more conceive one without the other than a steeple without a bell or a woman without a gossipy tongue.

One day St. Roch died—everybody dies, including the saints. And when he had died, his dog began a death howl, and he too died. The dog had only a small, light soul, so that accordingly it arrived at the same time as Saint Roch before the door of Paradise.

St. Roch knocked with his pilgrim's staff and called out his name with assurance. He had cured so many miserable people that he was certain of entering Paradise by the great door. St. Peter hastened to open the gate at the knocking . . . but presently, his eyes behind his glasses showed astonishment. He saw the spirit of a dog following the spirit of the saint.

"Halt, my friend! There isn't any place for dogs in the Paradise of the good God."

"It will be quite necessary to *find* a place for Roquet," replied St. Roch. "We are inseparable. He saved my life, and he is a saint also in his way."

"Ha, ha, ha—that *is* a story. I also have a cock who saved my soul by reminding me to repent. And yet, did I bring my cock when I came here? Did I bring him even to this spot by the door, far from the angels of God? No, my friend, the cock remained outside, and I came in. Your dog will have to join my cock, and you will join the saints, who are waiting for you. Let us go—I have my orders, I have told you what they are."

"So much the worse," said stubborn St. Roch. "If Roquet does not enter, I do not enter. I prefer my dog whom I know to your Paradise which I am not yet acquainted with."

"Ah well, clown," cried furious St. Peter, "depart then, both you and your dog!" And he slammed the door.

What became of Roch and Roquet? I believe they took up their travels again, and their spirits performed miracles, and they always cured madness. The whole world talked about them. The Pope, who was just, wished to recompense them; he made Roch a true saint by official pronouncement, and he ordered that a tablet be displayed in his church on which the new saint would be represented with his dog. You understand, this was a way of canonizing Roquet without actually saying it.

When this news arrived at Paradise, the Eternal Father had St. John the Baptist, who is the first of all the saints, summoned to Him, and He said to him, "Well now! there is a good man who is called Roch—the Pope made him a saint. You must look for him and bring him to me. I wish to see him, and to celebrate a little. You will tell St. Cecile to play some music for us."

John the Baptist ran three days and six nights, but he didn't find any more of St. Roch than one finds of young swallows in winter. In his perplexity he thought of going to consult Saint Peter.

The good doorkeeper had not forgotten the man and the dog. When he learned that his man was a saint because of all his good qualities, and that the Eternal Father wished to see him, he was disconcerted for a moment. You realize that he was afraid of being punished for having acted without consulting anybody. St. John, who loved St. Peter, consoled him, and promised to take care of everything. Thereupon St. John returned to the Eternal Father and said to Him, "Lord, have pity on my unskillfulness: for three days and six nights I have looked in vain for our new saint. He is not here. One evening thirty years ago he presented himself at the door of Paradise; but he had a dog, and as St. Peter did not wish to permit the dog to enter, St. Roch went away again and I do not know where he is."

The Eternal Father began to meditate upon it, and in order to listen to him reflect, all Paradise fell silent. Then He said, "It is very good that St. Peter has performed his duty as usual. But St. Roch will return because I wish it. He shall have his dog. Permit both man and dog to enter—I am making an exception."

When he was told this news, St. Peter changed color. "An exception! Yes," he said, "the dog of Roch is to be permitted to enter! You will see; the door is open, and all the animals of creation will follow him. Soon Paradise will no longer be habitable." And he angrily opened the door; but in order not to see the dog, he took refuge in his lodge, and he requested Zaccheus, his junior, to discharge the duty. Zaccheus, who loved animals because he was small, stepped across the threshold and called with all him strength, "Here, Roquet, my little Roquet, come here—the good God wishes to see you!"

And thereupon Roch and Roquet came forward. The kind saint smiled with pride; he put the heels of his walking shoes down hard, and turned back ten steps to caress Roquet, who licked his hands and waged his tail like a feather duster.

All Paradise was there, angels, cherubs, archangels, saints. Everybody hastened to see the fine dog pass by, sniffing the odors of Paradise, and seeming to laugh knowingly. Ah, that was a nice holiday! They totally forgot Roch; caresses, dainties, everything, even the music, was for Roquet. And one who was quite content to be forgotten was St. Roch, who loved his dog so much.

The first gladness passed, there was a movement in the crowd, and St. Peter was seen advancing, with bristling hair and a not-too-pleasant look, holding his keys in his hand.

"Lord," he said, addressing the Eternal Father, who was smiling at Roquet lying right against his feet, "Lord, I am returning the keys. I am no doorkeeper for dogs."

God smiled without replying. St. Peter continued: "Lord—and besides, this is not just. Why should the dog of St. Roch be here alone? Since the door is open, I say that the other animals ought to enter. That will be my revenge—now, I have spoken."

The Eternal Father smiled just the same. St. Peter continued, "Lord, if you wish me to retain the keys, permit my cock to enter: he is on all the church steeples, and he calls sinners to penitence. He is a kind of saint."

And God, without ceasing to smile, said, "Let us permit the cock to enter; he will be another exception."

Then there was a fine uproar! All the saints who loved animals began to protest and to plead . . .

"And my dove," said Noah, "my dove who brought me the olive branch."

"And the crow who nourished me in the desert," said Elias.

"And my dog, that wagged his tail!" wailed Tobias.

"And my donkey that prophesied," said Balaam.

"And the whale that kept me for three days in his stomach," said Jonah.

"And the pig that saved me from boredom," said Antoine.

"And the deer," said Hubert, "the deer that had a cross on his head."

"And my brother the wolf, and my brothers the birds, and by brothers the fish," said St. Francis.

"And the mule that knelt down before the Host that I carried," said another St. Antoine.

Ah, my friends, it was a fine uproar!

But the Heavenly Father, who had not ceased smiling, restored silence with a signal, and said:

"This dog which is lying at my feet made the warmth of its goodness ascend to my heart like a prayer. Peace to the animals! The animals that the saints have loved have something more than the others, a kind of soul. Have them enter. Each of you usher in the animal which was your friend."

A strange procession was seen then: four-footed and two-footed beasts, beasts with fur and beasts with feathers, birds and fish, slowly advanced toward the throne of God. And there was much goodness in all these animals, which made the light of Paradise clearer. A young saint who was very spirited said laughingly, "It should be called Noah's Ark!"

And St. Augustine replied, "Exactly! Noah's Ark was the image of Paradise."

Jesus, bending His all-seeing gaze on that assembled crowd which adored Him in silence, said, "All are not here. The donkey and the ox that warmed me with their breath when I was small, are missing."

Both the donkey and the ox arrived quickly, for they were at the door waiting their turn. And Jesus caressed them, smiling.

That is why there are animals in heaven; all the animals who are loved by good people go to Paradise. It is necessary, my friends, to love dogs, cats, oxen, and all other beasts.

———————

Marion Koenen Perri is active in her church and community in Schenectady, New York.

Talking to dogs is one of the few acts of faith still made nowadays.

—Paul Jennings
Next to Oddliness

Five Brave Dog Fables

Susan Beth Pfeffer

1

Mildred, a brave Scottie, was standing on the six or less items line at the supermarket when she noticed that the large burly man in front of her had seven items in his cart.

"Excuse me," she said, bravely and politely, "but you have too many items to be on this line."

The man looked at his cart. "You're right," he said. "Thank you. I'll go to the twelve and under line immediately."

And he did.

2

Otto, a Saint Bernard internationally renowned for his virtuoso violin performances, finished his concert and was met with resounding applause and the shouts of Bravo!

Although such approval was gratifying to the dog, he knew it was undeserved.

"Please stop" he said, raising his paws up high over his head. "I was off tonight. I had other things on my mind. Come back to the concert hall tomorrow, and I will perform another concert for you for free, that will prove, I hope, more worthy of your time."

3

The Chicago Bears had just scored a game-tying touchdown in the last few seconds of play. With only ten seconds left on the time clock, they kicked the ball to the rookie Jets specialty teams returner, Spike, a mixed-breed terrier.

Spike knew he could call for a fair catch and let the Jets take their chances during overtime. But as the ball came spiraling down, he decided what he had to do. He caught the ball on the eighteen yard line, and dodging the brutally talented Bears players, ran down the line, staying in bounds at all times to win the football game for the New York Jets on the very last second.

4

Chi Chi, a dachshund, was attending a party where she knew very few of the other guests. They all seemed much smarter than she, and more socially skilled.

She wandered over to a group of people who were talking about the latest nonfiction best-seller, a book about the coming economic crisis and how it would affect wheat prices in Mongolia.

Everyone agreed it was the most brilliant book they'd read in a long time.

"Excuse me," Chi Chi said, "but I thought it was terribly boring, and couldn't get past the second chapter."

"Neither could I," all the other guests said in unison, and they laughed at their own pretentiousness.

5

It was a scene out of a movie for Buttons, the Pomeranian. He alone on the jury believed in the innocence of the accused man.

The votes had been taken anonymously, and no one knew that Buttons was the one holdout. He sensed the wrath his fellow jurors must feel for the one member who was keeping them from completing their task.

"Is there any chance the single Not Guilty vote will change his or her mind?" the foreperson of the jury asked.

Buttons knew this was his moment of truth. "No," he said. "And if you just give me a chance to explain, maybe I can convince you of the accused's innocence as well."

By the time he finished, his logic swayed the other jurors and they voted to acquit.

———————

Susan Beth Pfeffer is the author of forty books for children and young adults. Some of her popular works are *What Do You Do When Your Mouth Won't Open?*, *Just Between Us* and *Twice Taken*.
She lives in Middletown, New York.

I have sometimes thought of the final cause of dogs having such short lives and I am quite satisfied it is in compassion to the human race; for if we suffer so much in losing a dog after an acquaintance of ten or twelve years, what would it be if they were to live double that time?

—Sir Walter Scott (1771–1832)
Scottish writer

Soccer Dog

Howard D. Randall

Mandy's adoring owners rate her the greatest export China ever made, outranking green tea and bamboo fans. She is a white, with a little black, Shih Tzu dog, fourteen inches long and weighing fourteen pounds—after she has had breakfast and lunch. A dog expert suggested that she be groomed for a show dog, but grandmaster said he did not want a dog named Champion Lily Pad IV prancing around with nose held high. So Mandy is jut a happy dog who welcomes everybody with an ingratiating wiggle.

Mandy has a fenced backyard to play in. One day, looking under a bush, she saw a rabbit. With a friendly yip of greeting she left him there undisturbed. Besides, she didn't like to crawl under bushes.

Another time a wandering woodchuck entered her yard. When he saw Mandy he sat up and clicked his long sharp teeth. To the little dog he looked big and fierce, so she made a strategic withdrawal (that is modern military for a retreat). She gained the house before the chuck turned away.

One time she tried to hide behind a soccer ball that rolled when she touched it. She pushed it harder so it rolled farther and she discovered that the round sides fit her concave face. Soon she was rolling it around the yard as fast as she could run. Sometimes it got caught under a bush and she had to bark for help.

Her master, between baseball and hockey practices and high school studies, taught her a game. He would throw the soccer ball out and she would roll it back. He waved his hand to one side and she learned to roll it by him and, finally, a right and left feint that was most fun. But nothing was said of this accomplishment.

Laura, her mistress, played soccer on a high school team but Mandy was not taken to practices and games. One day the grandmistress was going to get Laura after a game and decided to take Mandy along as she thought the game would be over.

The game had been late starting so was still in play. Putting a short leash on Mandy, the grandmistress joined friends half way down one side of the field. It was 0–0 score. The play was on the other side of the field, so Mandy quietly watched the people around her.

Then a bee buzzed around grandmistress's head and she dropped the leash. At the same moment play swept up that side of the field and the ball stopped just inside the line in front of Mandy. What an opportunity!

Mandy darted onto the field, headed the ball to the center and then to the right toward the opponent's goal. Players of both teams watched with amazement and amusement, with no attempt to stop her. The goalie shifted on her feet awaiting a goal try that she didn't believe could come.

Then Mandy was in front of her and with a right-left took the ball around her and over the goal line and sat down. Cheers and laughter sounded from both sides.

What should the referee do? Any ruling would be unpopular with some. He called the captains and managers for a conference. Mandy solved it. With the goalie looking up the field, she nosed the ball out and headed up the field—the long, long soccer field.

Again no one tried to stop her as they couldn't believe that she could reach the other end. The wind behind her helped and now as she got closer to the home goal, a guard dived for the leash. But too late. The goalie had seen the right-left at the other end and resolved that she wouldn't be fooled.

Mandy didn't shift. She went wider to her right and with a final push, the tying goal rolled in. The referee ruled that both goals would stand as they canceled each other.

Her grandmistress came around the end of the field and called. Mandy walked slowly to her and a very tired dog was picked up, hugged lovingly and carried to the car.

The game went on and after two overtimes ended 1–1. Neither team had won, but they had played in a game they would talk about the rest of their lives. Soccer fans would read of this game, but only those who saw it would believe.

———————————

Howard D. Randall is in his ninth decade. With the exception
of the game, the characters and events of his story are true.
Mr. Randall lives in Rochester, New York.

*When the dog was created, it licked the hand of God and God
stroked its head, saying, "What do you want, dog?" It replied,
"My Lord, I want to stay with you, in heaven, on a mat in
front of the gate. . . ."*

—Marie Noel

A Time Piece

Nancy W. Schoepperle

Of course, Dooli, our miniature poodle, loved us all, but her clear favorite was Dan, the husband, father, and only male in the family. She regretted his leave-taking, and she worried him home. In fact, she refused her supper every evening until he was safely back in the fold, thoroughly welcomed, quite frankly appreciated.

She sat with him while he read or watched TV. How many football, basketball, baseball games, even boxing matches, did they watch together?

And the games they played!—all variations of Fetch, which she would play only with him.

Dan was big and burly. Dooli was petite and fragile. Together, they looked . . . well . . . ridiculous. The Master/Faithful Dog image would have been much better served had she been a mastiff, or an Irish wolfhound.

Every day, when it was about time for Dan to be getting home, Dooli positioned herself on a bench under the picture window in the living room. From here, she could see down the driveway and be primed to herald his return. Just by watching her, we could tell when Dan was in sight, by the way her ears perked, and every single hair on her head seemed to stretch upwards in joy when she spotted him. And then, the greeting! It never became old hat.

When Dooli was seven, Dan died. She seemed to have no comprehension of the fact. Every evening, she sat on that bench, looking down the driveway as if intent on willing him home. After an hour's fruitless vigil, she would jump down from her view spot, respond to our overtures, accept her supper and again take the role of the family pet.

For one whole year, Dooli maintained this pattern. And then she gave it up. Had she forgotten Dan, or had she finally accepted that he was not coming home, not ever? Perhaps the tradition of the "year of mourning" is a concept we have borrowed from the animals.

Nancy W. Schoepperle cites her riches as being her family, friends, children, grandchildren and dogs. She lives in Buffalo, New York.

At one time a synod of the Catholic Church was held in which the question of whether or not animals had a soul was discussed very seriously: would good dogs go to paradise and bad ones, who stole slices of leg of lamb, burn in hell eternally. The denial of the soul was voted: it is enough for the honor of the species that the question was posed.

—Alfred Barbou

The Legend
of the Littlest Basenji

Sally Ann Smith

Human history did not record the pawprints made by a faithful little Basenji that followed the Three Wise Men out of Egypt on their quest for the Christ Child. But Basenjis have not forgotten, and the story has passed from mother to pup for two thousand years. Here is the story they tell.

Long ago, as humans reckon time, a new star appeared in the sky. Looking up, we were curious and listened intently in the council chambers of the mighty, for we were an ancient breed even then, companions to the great lords of Egypt. The philosophers and priests told of a prophecy they believed had come to pass: A glorious soul had come to teach love and peace to all living beings. It was decided that three wise and learned men would seek out this beautiful soul and bring him gifts of precious ointments and gold.

Now at this time in Egypt, there lived in the royal household a young Basenji girl who had always sought out the company of learned men. She was gentle, refined and small, and her name was Candle because she brought a glow into everyone's hearts.

The bond between Candle and the man she called master went deep, and when she learned he was to be a member of the expedition, she would not be denied her place at his side. Faithfully she traveled, and the journey was not always easy. They went to a far country, where they finally found the child.

The Wise Men knelt down to give their gifts, but little Candle was suddenly very shy. She could see the glory around the child and the angels about him that the humans seemed not to notice.

But the angels saw Candle and one gently asked, "What is it you want, little one?"

"I, too, would like to bring a gift to the young king," she said, "but I have nothing to offer but love."

"Love is the greatest gift one being can give another," said the angel. "In honor of your devotion, we declare your breed shall always wear white to commemorate the pure light in your heart. Through the ages, Basenjis will remember this moment when you bowed down before the child and will be quick to bow, both in work and play.

"Basenji eyes will be far-seeing and will never lose sight of the stars, just as you never lost sight of the great star in the sky this night. Basenjis will go quietly through the world, just as you came quietly to this place.

"And, little Candle, Basenjis will have a flame of love in their hearts that will never go out, and they will watch over their humans and become guardians of their spirits."

So saying, the angel bent down to pet the littlest Basenji, but Candle was suddenly overwhelmed by the majesty of the angel, and she covered her eyes with her paws. So that is where the angel's touch fell, and that is why all true Basenjis have white on their feet.

Sally Ann Smith is the author of Candle, A Story of Love and Faith, *an expanded version of* The Legend of the Littlest Basenji. *In addition to writing and teaching, Sally breeds the Basenji dog. She lives in Jasper, Georgia.*

Some of our greatest historical and artistic treasures we place with curators in museums: others we take for walks.

—Roger A. Caras,
A Dog Is Listening

The Dog at Night

Cassie L. Smyth, as translated by her person, Sally Ann Smith

Under a starlit sky I stand.
Master of the darkened land.

Out the door, with tail held high
Moving under a blackened sky
Confronting mysteries. My humans know
Nothing of places where I go.

We are not pets outside at night.
Alone, we turn to early might
Of pack rule. Running with the wind
My blood leaps with demanding din
Of ancient hunt, forgotten foe
As onward toward the past I go.

My mistress settles in her chair, wild
Chorus of my heart unheard. Primeval child
Within her stirs, but's quickly drowned
In depths of blank discarded sound.

Truth can lurk just out of sight.
And only the nose can see at night.

Cassie L.(ab) Smith is Sally Ann Smith's beloved dog.

Old Drum

Bill Tarrant

Turn the clock back 122 years, bare your senses, and attend to this scene. The Civil War has been over four years. Nowhere has it left deeper scars and a more granite temperament than in western Missouri (they said, "Show me!"), where two armies and assorted renegade irregulars had pillaged the countryside and terrified the people. Every Missourian knew of death and destruction so his response had become quick to fight, to be self-sufficient, to forever hold a grudge, to be inflexible in his opinions and demanding of justice.

Now, narrow your focus. It is rolling country, heavily treed, with intersecting streams that teem with varmints. We're five miles south of Kingsville, Johnson County, Missouri (some fifty miles southeast of Kansas City) down in the second bottom of Big Creek. Log cabins nestle in the clearings with packed dirt yards, a corn crib, root cellar and spring house. This night in October 1869, a faint kerosene lamp glows from the store-bought window of the two-room log cabin occupied by Charles Burden and his family. The members are busy washing dishes after supper, or shucking corn to make lye hominy.

Charles Burden stands (he is strikingly handsome, a tall, thin man with an athlete's physique) and says he's going to check the stock before turning in. He walks out the front door where Old Drum, a five-year-old black-and-tan hound, rises from sleep on the front porch and ambles close behind. They walk in the sodden leaves of a wet autumn; frost will sugar the land white by morning. Suddenly, Old Drum casts to the left and heads down into Big Creek. Immediately he strikes game, and the yip of his find pierces the air. The race is on. And Charles Burden stands to listen to the mellow bawls of his prized hound as the dog puzzles trail.

Later, Burden sits in a rocker on his front stoop, smoking homespun tobacco in his corn cob pipe. Suddenly, a gun shot claims the still night. Burden lurches forward, straining to listen. There is no other noise. But in his gut there's a wrenching hunch. He leaps to reach inside the doorway and grabs his hunting horn. He blows until all hounds appear at his feet but one—Old Drum. And somehow Burden knows. His brother-in-law, Leonidas "Lon" Hornsby, has killed his dog. Hornsby has been losing sheep to wild dogs, and he has vowed he would kill the next one caught on his property.

Next morning Burden approaches Hornsby, who is pressing cider, and asked, "Lon, have you seen anything of Old Drum around here?" Lon replied he hadn't seen anything of him. Then came the question, "What about the dog you shot last night?" Hornsby said he hadn't shot any dog, but his hired hand, Dick, had. He added he thought the dog belonged to Davenport. Dick took Burden across the yard and showed him where he had shot the stray dog. Burden looked for traces of blood and found none. Then he returned to Hornsby and said, "I'll go hunt. It may not be my dog. If it ain't, it's all right. If it is, it's all wrong, and I'll have satisfaction at the cost of my life."

On the morning of October 29, Old Drum was found just a few feet above the ford in the creek below Haymaker's mill. He was dead, lying on his left side, with his head in the water and his feet toward the dam, his body filled with shot of different sizes. Burden concluded Old Drum had been carried or dragged to this place: there was blood on his underside, his hair was bent backwards, and there were sorrel hairs on his coat. Lon Hornsby owned a sorrel mule.

Burden headed for an attorney. Later he would tell another attorney (the case went to court four times), "When I found that Old Drum had been killed I wanted to kill the man who did it. But I've seen too much of killings in the border warfare. And so I said, 'I'm going to go by law. I'm going to clear Old Drum's name . . . he was no sheep killer . . . and I'll prove to the world that Lon Hornsby killed him unrightfully if it's the last thing I do.' "

So came to pass the most noted dog trial in history on September 23, 1870. It concluded on a rainy night at the county courthouse in Warrensburg, Missouri, with the top legal talent of Western Missouri arguing what was, by now, the celebrated dog case. One of the defendant's attorneys told the jury, "Such a lawsuit about a mere hound dog is of little value if not a neighborhood nuisance."

George Vest, principal attorney for Charles Burden, sat detached from the day-long proceedings. He was short, a bull of a man with thick neck, broad shoulders, fiery red hair, and a voice that would fire ice or melt steel as he would wish. All of Warrensburg turned out for the trial: it was like circus day. The restaurants were packed, the hitchracks taken, the livery stable filled. People who could not find accommodations intended to sleep in their rigs. And those who couldn't get into the courtroom peered in multiples through the courthouse windows, enduring a lightning storm and downpour. The sheriff had made sure no man entered the court with a gun. All inside sweltered in the high humidity. Only Vest never wiped his brow. As he was no part of these proceedings, neither was he part of the suffocation of the place.

For a moment let's examine the legal talent assembled for this hound's trial. Charles Burden had retained the partnership of Sedalia, Missouri's John F. Phillips and George Graham Vest. The former would become a federal judge, the latter a United States Senator.

Lon Hornsby countered with Thomas T. Crittenden, who later became governor of Missouri, and Francis Marion Cockrell, who ended up in the United States Senate along with his adversary, George Vest. These were not mediocre men, nor had they met for a mediocre moment. Old Drum had pulled them together for the most celebrated case in dogdom, as surely as he once rounded up every varmint that tried to take up residence on his beloved master's farm. And as these litigants made Old Drum immortal, the hound dog went a far way toward making each of them a legend in his own time. None of them could eventually discount Old Drum's part in making their legal lives a success.

There was no court reporter for any of the four Old Drum trials. What is known about what happened there has come down to us from word of mouth. Men assembled later and reasoned together to put the court's testimony into writing. And this becomes important, as you will see.

George Vest stood. He rose scowling, mute, his eyes burning from under the slash of brow tangled as a grape vine. Then he stepped sideways, hooked his thumbs in his vest pockets, his gold watch fob hanging motionless. It was that heavy.

And he said, "May it please the court," and began his oratory. Gerald Carson, writing in *Natural History*, December 1969, relates: "Vest began to speak quietly and earnestly. He ignored the day's testimony. For about an hour he ranged through history, poetry, legend, and classical literature, calling attention to sagacious and faithful dogs whom men have loved. . . .

"After pointing out the weaknesses in the arguments of opposing counsel and drawing attention to the law applicable to the case, Vest appeared ready to conclude. But then he moved closer to the jury box. He looked (someone remembered afterward) taller than his actual 5 feet 6 inches, and began in a quiet voice to deliver an extemporaneous oration. It was quite brief, less than four hundred words."

These are the immortal words Vest spoke: "Gentlemen of the jury, the best friend a man has in the world may turn against him and become his worst enemy. His son or daughter that he has reared with loving care may prove ungrateful. Those who are nearest and dearest to us, those whom we trust with our happiness and our good name, may become traitors to their faith. The money that man has, he may lose. It flies away from him, perhaps when he needs it the most. A man's reputation may be sacrificed in a moment of ill-considered action. The people who are prone to fall on their knees to do us honor when success is with us may be the first to throw the stone of malice when failure settles its cloud upon our heads. The one absolutely unselfish friend that a man can have in this selfish world, the one that never deserts him and the one that never proves ungrateful or treacherous is his dog.

"Gentlemen of the jury, a man's dog stands by him in prosperity and in poverty, in health and in sickness. He will sleep on the cold ground, where the wintry winds blow and the snow drives fiercely, if only he may be near his master's side. He will kiss the hand that has no food to offer, he

Bill Tarrant with his mongrel terrier, Pooder.

will lick the wounds and sores that come in encounters with the roughness of the world. He guards the sleep of his pauper master as if he were a prince. When all other friends desert he remains. When riches take wings and reputation falls to pieces, he is as constant in his love as the sun in its journey through the heavens. If fortune drives the master forth an outcast in the world, friendless and homeless, the faithful dog asks no higher privilege than that of accompanying him to guard against danger, to fight against his enemies, and when the last scene of all comes, and death takes the master in its embrace and his body is laid away in the cold ground, no matter if all other friends pursue their way, there by his graveside will the noble dog be found, his head between his paws, his eyes sad but open in alert watchfulness, faithful and true even to death."

The jury erupted in joint pathos and triumph. The record becomes sketchy here, but some say the plaintiff, who was asking for $150, was awarded $500 by the jury. Little does that matter. The case was appealed to the Missouri Supreme Court, which refused to hear it.

Both litigants were bankrupted by the proceedings. They returned to their homes, living one mile apart, and time eventually healed their differences. At the place where Old Drum was found lying in the creek with the sorrel hairs embedded in his coat, a monument has been erected which once contained stones from every state in the union and practically every nation on earth. Before the new county courthouse in Warrensburg now stands a life-size bronze statue of Old Drum.

And if you journey five miles south of Kingsville, Johnson County, Missouri, tonight, you'll likely hear the plaintive call of some hound dog coursing the stream's woods, giving voice of his find, the night air ringing like an empty oil drum struck with a sledge at the music of his going. There will always be an Old Drum. And a man to defend his honor.

Bill Tarrant is the veteran gun dog editor of *Field & Stream* magazine, author of ten dog books, and the only person twice-named Dog Writer of the Year by the Dog Writers of America.

The dog is the most faithful of animals and would be much esteemed were it not so common. Our Lord God has made his greatest gifts the commonest.

—Martin Luther (1483–1546)
founder of Protestantism

The Way of the Soul

Josef Verba

She awoke from the smell of fire.

The crackling of the smoking wiring and the flying blue spark filled the capsule's compartment. Warning alerts echoed in the back of her dazed mind.

Shaking slumber from her body, she tried to rise, but deep-freeze contacts entangled her, and some that were still active were promising easy peace and hollow darkness. It was tempting to close her eyes, to fall into the comfort of not hearing the noise, not smelling the burning insulation of the agonizing ship.

Ship . . .

A trans-space message went out from the last remaining antenna of the quickly deteriorating space probe, XT-5.

It said, "I want reactivation . . . source found . . . I LIVE."

The message was received by a somewhat puzzled communications technician as he was about to have lunch. It was duly logged in as soon as he finished his last sandwich.

Unfortunately, it did not remain in NASA files for long, since an idea came to the man that perhaps the message was another in a string of many practical jokes his friends played on him. The incident was soon forgotten, as the technician rewarded himself with a smug smile, and marked

"Number One" in the air with his index finger, indicating another percep-
tive victory.

The sun-sail, a micro-thin layer of super-reflective material that powered the first craft out of Earth's solar system at a never-before suspected
speed, was an experiment much debated.

Some scientists believed that the sun's radiation would incinerate the
sail, as it would come frighteningly close to the "father of furnaces" in its
gravitational slingshot effect. It would hurdle the man-made artifact of
curiosity out of our solar system at an incalculable breakaway speed, leaving the vessel powerless to continue the voyage.

Based on this argument, the traditionalists argued for the conventional fuel approach. The ship would be powered by four giant thrusters
that would be sequentially exhausted, leaving the continued flight to iner-
tia after the fuel was consumed.

The argument was won by those who felt the ship would sustain the
stresses of acceleration while energies collected on the giant sail—as long
as the structure of the ship held together.

The general consensus was that a dog would be most suitable as an
experimental organism to "go up."

In a not-too-distant galaxy, emerald mists bathed a small planet's
surface. They swirled in a cacophony of crystalline sounds and movement.
Distant lightning played ever-changing flashes of color on the reflective
atmosphere, echoing and outlining the hidden forms of the planet's surface. Seaweedlike creatures floated vertically on the gentle breezes of the
temperate climate, and their schools of shadows followed them in the mists
below.

A strange wailing sound of an alien origin pierced the stasis of the
planet's dream.

Carmen struggled to shake off the wire contacts. Regaining some of her
powers, she felt the cold metal of the first robotic arm clamped to her. With
vocal chords remaining half-frozen, she responded with a half-whimper.

As the last of the ship fell into deep space, a capsule detached itself from the main body. Consisting of the latest man-made thinking apparatus and a living, breathing organism, the capsule was encased in the remains of the mothership and powered by the remnants of the solar sail. The form sped toward the closest planet in the system.

Thoughts raced through Carmen's altered mind. Thoughts of identity and analysis of self.

"Ship . . .? We are one . . . I feel fear . . . fear? Sensation? Thought?"

The dog, perhaps for the first time since creation, comprehended its feelings while the computer struggled to understand new emotions of a fragile dog. Incorporated into a new lifeforce, the Candroid crash-landed on an unsuspecting ancient world.

The crimson dust cloud floated downward, sparkling with a life of its own. Frightened seaweed creatures scattered, but some lay in unidentifiable pieces beneath the smoking remains of an alien artifact.

Peace returned. Routine returned. The last sparkles of surface dust covered the resting metal shape. A servo motor whined plaintively.

With a small explosion, a hatch flew open. A creature emerged, tentatively stepping with gleaming insectlike limbs, precariously finding footing amid the swirling mists. Suspended atop the creature, a plexibubble held a breathing organism in a life-sustaining fluid.

The side of the creature, to anyone human, read "XT-5." Inside the bubble, the dog was coming out of shock aided by its newly juxtaposed computer rationality.

Pain . . . Must shake off the water . . . Play? . . . Run! . . . Hide . . . Bite . . . Smell . . . Puzzled—cannot smell, cannot hear!

Correction . . . Error . . . Feelings? . . . Sensors functioning at 98 percent efficiency. Repeat request.

Where am I? . . . Want to go home . . . Cannot move? . . . I feel? . . . I think . . . THINK? . . . WHO AM I?

XT-5, artificial intelligence prototype deep-space explorer now merged with Canis Familiaris of undetermined breeding.

Wag tail?

That appendage is affixed to my defense/navigational/communica-

tions systems as are all your body language systems. WE HAVE INTER-
FACED.

I feel . . . ALONE!

I feel . . . ERROR! . . . You are not alone, I am here.

I think . . . can I howl?

Your voice has interfaced with my input/output circuits. Speakers on?
/AOOUUUUUUUU!/

The Candroid regained its mechanical precision and footing as the
dog's jumbled emotions were sorted by its new-found logic and subsiding
panic. An antenna emerged from the frontal section, and an array of signals was sent out in the standard—and not-so-standard—interspecies
greeting.

No answer was heard.

On the southern-most pole of the planet, changes were taking place.
Mists that were most vivid congealed and moved in one direction skim-
ming the planet surface. The bare crimson of uncovered planet followed
the retreating concentrated mists. Changing color, the mists approached
the fallen ship, assumed an almost solid, shifting form and pulsated with
a sapphire glow.

Although the XT-5's sensors failed to pick up anything, the intuitive
half—the dog—felt a presence around her. She shuddered, momentarily
interrupting connections. The Candroid stumbled.

Error. No complex lifeforms detected.

I feel them.

I understand.

Growl. Bare my teeth.

The XT-5 speakers conveyed a canine growl, scattering seaweed creatures in all directions. Laser cannons moved back and forth. Only the
thickening mist remained.

Cannot triangulate coordinates of lifeform. Sensors ineffective.

All around us.

Initiate Communication Procedure C42?

Assume submissive posture.

The Candroid's cannons retracted. It settled down to the soft sand. Leaning to its side, it froze. The amorphous being surrounding it parted, and with a soft chiming sound, a tentacle of vapor reached for the still Candroid. It moved slowly, almost hesitantly stopping its advance as soon as the strange creature stirred uneasily.

The steady, reassuring chiming continued hypnotically, calming the Candroid into inaction. It reached and penetrated the plexibubble with such surreptitious tactful movement, that this time, neither the computer nor the dog reacted with aggression.

The Candroid, sensing contact, transmitted greetings in all modes and frequencies. The chiming coming from the vapor fluctuated and resumed in a questioning, agogic manner.

Cannot establish communication. Alien transmission does not correlate.

Do not understand, but feel . . . /WHINE/ . . . tilt front section to side.

The Candroid assumed a questioning position any self-respecting dog would understand. As soon as the chiming sounds around it were replaced with an echoing whine, the role of communication switched to Carmen's consciousness within the Candroid.

The answering whining coming from the surrounding form, however, was now sliding down in pitch in a reassuring way that Carmen, and thus the Candroid, could understand.

Feeling sympathy, the Candroid sounded another series of whines, yelps, and even a few sharp, demanding barks before the computer's processors kicked in.

Must transmit coordinates of alien life contact.

A short burst of static was all that penetrated the reflective atmosphere of the planet, as a tight beam of radio signals was directed to Earth, carrying out the last pre-programmed command. Thus, all directives fulfilled, the Candroid was now a fully independent being—an independent being devoid of all responsibilities.

It felt very alone.

A howl of chilling loneliness and passion pierced the amorphous form. The arm of vapor recoiled momentarily as if hit by an empathic shock. Then, more trails of the being separated from the mass, and like gentle arms, comforted the Candroid. A soft song of bells, intermixed with howl or whine, caressed the newborn being.

The Candroid felt the strong contact, but more so, it felt the warmth of alien emotions trying to penetrate the barriers of understanding.

Communications established!

The soft music flowed like a stream of mother's milk/input data—calming, reassuring and questioning. Sounds interweaved, shifting with colors and contours of the now enveloping, friendly cloud. A dance of emotions initiated, into which the Candroid was invited, and a true exchange began to take place.

A totality . . . oneness . . . a being covering the surface of the planet. Once tangible, trapped . . . now free, feeling. Are you trapped? Can I help?

Lonely . . . puzzled . . . cannot sense but feel. Grateful . . .

Life . . . precious . . . source? . . . sustenance? . . . purpose here?

Life . . . curious . . . love . . . contact . . . friend!

Acceptance . . . love . . . friendship . . . understand! . . . Can I help?

/HOME/ . . . Master . . . source . . . beginning . . . happiness . . . purpose.

Sorrow . . . Shifting reality . . . Place . . . Home? . . . Release your self????

Travel as we do . . . HOME . . . dream—is reality . . . YOU ARE FREE . . .

Quite a starry night hung over the NASA airstrip. The kind of night that made you sigh and breathe and think of things you don't usually think about. A kind of quietness and peace, the young engineer thought, that makes you wonder if you're doing what's right in life.

He saw a falling star and closed his eyes in momentary contentment. Five minutes remained before his shift was over. He breathed the freshness of the night air, and thought he wouldn't mind doing some overtime out here. This was great. What could possibly happen tonight? Might as well get a quick snack before going home.

With shuffling steps, he walked to the building. The soft, dewy grass felt good as it gave in to his boots. He watched his shadow shrink and double on the ground behind him as he neared the spotlights.

He stopped. "Not so giant now, are we?" Musing, he shook his head and smiled.

A movement caught his eye, and turning, he did a double-take, for this was impossible. He thought he saw a familiar dog's silhouette, bathed in starlight, drift across the runway and fade into the night. He swore under his breath. "Must be a coyote," he mumbled. After all, he put that dog on the XT-5 himself.

"Poor Carmen. Where is she now?" A tinge of regret tickled the back of his mind.

"Well, what's done is done. It's for science," he said to himself, quieting the unwelcome emotion.

He entered the control center and sat into the security of his chair. Biting his sandwich, he tried to savor it, but the uneasiness wouldn't go away.

It was then that he almost fell out of his chair, as the final straw hit home. The engineer realized that all maincore computer programs were inexplicably and irreversibly displaced. Almost as if the computer had somehow unimaginably evolved. Who would have thought his friends would take their jokes this far?

———————

Juilliard graduate Josef Verba is a concert pianist, composer and
faculty member of the Hochstein Music School of Rochester, New York.
Mr. Verba was born in Russia and is now a citizen of the United States.
His family's dog is named Carmen.

All knowledge, the totality of all questions and answers,
is contained in the dog.

—Franz Kafka (1883–1924)
Austrian novelist, *Investigations of a Dog*

Louise Goodyear Murray

For as long as she can remember, Louise Goodyear Murray has been dog-struck. Dogs are a major part of her life, and they hold long-time membership in her family tree. Currently, she and her husband, Jim, share their Fairport, New York home with their wonderful dog Kaycee, a former street dog and animal shelter resident.

Aside from her enthusiasm for dogs, this Kingston, New York native and English teacher, values family and friends, books and writing, teaching and swimming. She holds degrees from the University of Rochester and Nazareth College and is a year-round, All American Masters swimmer. *The Dogs of Our Lives* is her first book compilation.

Grown sons, Bill and Bob, also quite naturally share their family's love for dogs. As dog enthusiasts, they encouraged the making of *The Dogs of Our Lives.*

To further humane activities, Louise's profits from *The Dogs of Our Lives* are being donated to Lollypop Farm Animal Shelter of the Humane Society of Rochester and Monroe County.

Anne Branagan, Illustrator

Anne Branagan, a life-long animal enthusiast, has been a professional artist in Rochester, New York, for many years.

Working mainly in pen-and-ink and watercolor, she is best known for her wildlife illustrations. Her art work has won numerous awards and is in collections both in the United States and abroad.

Anne currently works on consignment from her home studio in Payson, Arizona, where her three dogs and two kittens provide inspiration and companionship.

Illustrations by Anne that appear in *The Dogs of Our Lives* are donated in remembrance of the many four-legged furry children that have filled her life with joy and friendship.

A Tailpiece

Jimmy Kieffer

Jimmy Kieffer attends school in Fairport, New York. At age ten, he drew his dog
Pierre, chasing his tail.